Hothouse Kids

ow the Pressure to Succeed is Threatening Childhood

Ali Quart is the author of the acclaimed book *Branded*. She writes opi pieces and book reviews for *The New York Times* and features for *Lin Franca, Elle, The Nation* and *Salon*. A former child prodigy, she started wri novels at the age of seven and won numerous national writing cor itions. She is a graduate of the Columbia School of Journalism.

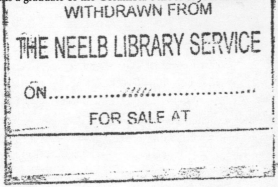

Also available by Alissa Quart

Branded

Hothouse Kids

HOW THE PRESSURE TO SUCCEED IS THREATENING CHILDHOOD

Alissa Quart

arrow books

Published in the United Kingdom by Arrow Books in 2006

1 3 5 7 9 10 8 6 4 2

First published in the United Kingdom in 2006 by Arrow
First published in the United States in 2006 by The Penguin Press

Arrow Books
The Random House Group Limited
20 Vauxhall Bridge Road, London SW1V 2SA

Random House Australia (Pty) Limited
20 Alfred Street, Milsons Point, Sydney,
New South Wales 2061, Australia

Random House New Zealand Limited
18 Poland Road, Glenfield
Auckland 10, New Zealand

Random House (Pty) Limited
Isle of Houghton, Corner of Boundary Road & Carse O'Gowrie,
Houghton 2198, South Africa

Random House Publishers India Private Limited
301 World Trade Tower, Hotel Intercontinental Grand Complex,
Barakhamba Lane, New Delhi 110 001, India

The Random House Group Limited Reg. No. 954009

www.randomhouse.co.uk

A CIP catalogue record for this book is available from the British Library

Papers used by Random House are natural, recyclable products made from wood grown in sustainable forests. The manufacturing processes conform to the environmental regulations of the country of origin

ISBN 9780099509271 (from Jan 2007)
ISBN 0 09 950927 X

Designed by Amanda Dewey
Printed and bound in Great Britain by
Bookmarque Ltd, Croydon, Surrey

For Peter Maass

Contents

ONE The Icarus Effect · 1

TWO The Baby Genius Edutainment Complex: The New Smart Baby Products · 22

THREE The Educated Infant: Classes for an Improved Childhood · 46

FOUR Child's Play or Child Labor? Preprofessional Kids · 64

FIVE Gifted and Left Behind: Enrichment in the Public Schools · 86

SIX Gurus of Giftedness: Intelligence Testing and Talent by Other Measures · *109*

SEVEN Extreme Parenting: Mothers and Fathers as the Ultimate Instructors · *131*

EIGHT Young Competitors: Youth Contests for Good and for Ill · *151*

NINE Children of God: The Teen Preaching Tournaments · *169*

TEN The Prodigy Hunters: Math Whiz Kids Become Wall Street Recruits · *185*

CONCLUSION Rethinking Giftedness: Against Perfection · *204*

Acknowledgments · *211*

Notes · *213*

Bibliography · *235*

Index · *249*

Hothouse
Kids

ONE

The Icarus Effect

And time shall force a gift on each.

JOHN ASHBERY

I used to be smart, and now I'm stupid.

EX–WHIZ KID DONNIE SMITH, in the film *Magnolia*

Larisa Stephan became an adult without having experienced childhood. She now has all the markers of conventional sanity and, indeed, plenitude: a family of her own, and a flourishing career as an engineer. But the thirty-seven-year-old's travels there started too early. Her father began the educational enrichment when she was two. That was when she took her first IQ test, and began an activity-rife childhood west of Beverly Hills.

"My IQ was outlandishly high, 180 to 190, so my father believed I was a genius and that I was never up to my potential," says Stephan, her pale, unadorned face framed by light brown hair in a short bob. "The IQ test was taken when I was two–which means it was so high because I had the skills normal for a four-year-old when I was two," she says. "That doesn't mean I was a genius."

Her father held up other prodigies as examples, including child musician Dylana Jensen. Stephan remembers her father taking her to see Jensen play a concert; Jensen was then on the brink of adolescence. Larisa's father remarked forbiddingly that Dylana was experiencing a tough time in her young life–passing from a time when she was a prodigy to a time when she would be just like everyone else, competing with adult violinists who were as talented as she was–or more so. Stephan felt the chill of comparison in her father's words.

"I totally try to repress my childhood," she says. "The 'enrichment' bled the joy out of me. Today I don't do horse riding, or play the violin or do ballet," she says, her voice rising. "I do nothing that was part of that enrichment."

She shows me the pictures of her own childhood–indeed, she is doing something in all of them. Playing a violin, reading a book, accompanied by her blond hair and a big smile. The smile seems intended to reassure the onlooker that she is enjoying these pastimes.

Stephan lives in the Westchester section of Los Angeles. It is near the LAX airport, a part of town where, in homage to the flight industry, roads are named Boeing and Aviation. Stephan has worked in some capacity or other for the defense industry since she was seventeen. Today she is an electrical engineer for the defense company Raytheon, in El Segundo. Her one-story home, of a piece with its neighbors in an area of modest middle-class houses from the 1940s, houses her husband and their three children–Dylan, Tara, and Maya. It's just after Christmas, and her children's names have been painstakingly lettered with sparkle glue on stockings that hang near the tree.

"My father believed that there were these external success indicators of your value," Stephan says. "If you got those indicators, you were good and you were smart. If you could say that you learned to ride a horse at a gallop, you were a good equestrian, check. If you could say you took the Golden State Math Exam and scored in the top two percent, check. One built up a roster of indicators that made you feel all right. True achievement and true accomplishment, I believe now, is a process you enjoy. Adults who are good at playing violin are good at it because they enjoy playing the violin. I disliked it, even when I was three. I was angry at having to go to lessons all of the time. It was all a blur. I never had less than two or three things going on at one time: flute, violin, and chess, art lessons and guitar." If she ever showed interest in an activity, she says, her father "converted this interest into an education."

While she did achieve mightily–she attended Harvard at fifteen, and earned a master's degree in math from Berkeley when she was twenty-one–it all stemmed from her father's insistence that she *had* to achieve. To Stephan's mind, that demand emptied her achievements of value.

"My father was like, 'My child is a genius,'" says Stephan. "He tried to enrich me, enrich me like flour."

Stephan's experience was a precursor to the movement toward more intense parenting of recent years. The characteristics of that movement include a growth in enrichment activities; an increase in children's structured time as opposed to free play hours; an explosion of new classes, specialized camps, and competitions; and the enrollment of ever-younger kids in these competitions. One side effect of this is a tendency to professionalize play–to turn what children do for amusement into their vocation–as soon as possible.

Add to that the IQ testing of toddlers, and it's clear that child enrichment has filtered down into infancy, with such keystones as the baby sign language vogue and the fad for infant edutainment videos like the Baby Einstein series. I call it the Baby Genius Edutainment Complex.

And child enrichment has become even more precocious prenatal. BabyPlus Womb Songs, a product that we will encounter in the next chapter, promises maternal consumers that their infants will "have longer attention spans and reach developmental milestones more quickly" and "demonstrate expanded cognitive abilities–testing has shown higher than average IQs."

But the process of encouraging and developing children's talents is not always as extreme as tutoring one's "prenate." While many extravagant products claim to encourage brightness in the womb and shortly after, encouraging an already visible cultural fixation on the most flagrantly gifted, many children remain on the more prosaic end of the gifted spectrum. Such children attend gifted and talented programs at their local schools or perhaps take an honors class. They may be cast as intelligent in their schools and families, but not extraordinary: while the very gifted are defined by IQs of 145 and above, and the profoundly gifted check in at 160 and above (on the few intelligence tests with the possibility of such high scores), the children who attend public school gifted programs tend to score 120 and above on intelligence tests. The adjective *gifted* dates back to 1644, according to *Webster's Ninth New Collegiate Dictionary*. It means "having great natural ability: talented" and "revealing a special gift." But the muddled nature of being "gifted," which can mean everything from scholastic competence and the ability to ice skate at a young age to being something closer to a prodigy, comes out more clearly in the *Webster's* definition of the noun *gift.* Synonyms for *gift,* according to *Webster's,* include such related but varied nouns as *faculty, aptitude, bent, talent, genius,* and *knack.* The dictionary's second definition for *gift* also gives some insight into why those with the range of qualities that commonly earn the term *gifted* are subject to resentment from those who feel they have not been deemed gifted, as well into public debate on whether "gifted" children should have special accommodation and funding in the schools: a *gift,* according to *Webster's,* is "something voluntarily transferred by one person to another without compensation." In other words, a "gift" may not be reciprocated and may even be undeserved.

The causes for the growth of the gifted complex–from baby videos to promote infant reading, to sports and physical enrichment programs (for example, soccer classes for kids as young as a year and a half), to a rising "prodigy industry" of experts who locate and encourage the profoundly gifted–are many. Most important, parents perceive an increasing competitiveness in the world, and feel they must do everything they can to enhance their children's abilities–as early as possible–according to David Anderegg, a psychology professor at Bennington College and author of *Worried All the Time: Rediscovering the Joy in Parenthood in an Age of Anxiety.*

Nor are parents mistaken to focus on early learning. Anders Ericsson, a psychology professor at Florida State University who has long studied the relationship between talented adults and their youthful "deliberative practice" (i.e., hard work), argues that it is practice and enrichment rather than natural gifts that create talent and "gifted" children. Ericsson writes that each individual in a group of elite musicians were estimated to have spent over ten thousand hours practicing alone by the time they turned twenty. The same is true in other "performance domains," such as ballet, gymnastics, and figure skating–"a similar progression through increasingly difficult tasks, in which the guidance of a teacher is critical for success." Ericsson's research bears out the old saw that practice makes perfect. When parents send their children to early music lessons and push them to achieve mightily and publicly, they believe they are preparing the children for an adulthood of ever-greater achievement–and sometimes they are.

A classic longitudinal study of gifted children begun by Stanford University psychologist Lewis Terman supports Ericsson's findings about deliberative practice, and the value of discovering and developing the intellectual talents of strong learners not only in private lessons but also in public schools. Terman's study, begun in 1921, followed 1,500 children with IQs of 135 culled from California's urban areas. Published as *Genetic Studies of Genius,* the study generated many articles and findings. One of the many positive outcomes was that by 1951, the 1,528 Terman subjects had already published 46 nonfiction books, 21 novels, 1,411 scientific papers, 313 short stories and plays, and 55 essays and works of poetry and criticism.

The Terman study may have launched the idea of championing the early discovery and enrichment of talented children, but a host of similar scholarship followed. The Study of Mathematically Precocious Youth (SMPY), started by the late Julian Stanley (who as the founder of Johns Hopkins University's Center for Talented Youth was in a sense Terman's intellectual heir), has so far examined 5,000 people who scored very well on their SATs in junior high school. Like the Terman study, SMPY has tended to affirm the benefits of locating and developing intellectually precocious children. A supergifted clan of 320 students, skimmed off the top of the larger SMPY sample, was found to have pursued doctorates at fifty times the normal rate. Members of the clan had also made noteworthy literary, scientific, or technical accomplishments by their early twenties. The study's authors felt safe in concluding that "precocious manifestations of abilities foreshadow the emergence of exceptional achievement and creativity."

Despite these repeated demonstrations of the benefits of early learning and the location and enrichment of gifted children, however, the outcome of such intervention is not always positive. For instance, there's little long-term evidence to support a lot of the so-called enrichment to which parents subscribe. A study of early music lessons found that they had little effect on children's harmonic or tonal abilities; an immense improvement of implied harmony at age nine seems to be due to normal neural development rather than instruction.

What began as a focus on mainstream educational enrichment–high-level math at early ages, for instance–has morphed into a generalized approach to enriching kids that gives some kids top-heavy schedules. Encouraging children who have shown great aptitude in science to let their interests develop, no matter how peculiar they are, is one thing. But putting them through a jittery regimen of memorization, urging them to perform in front of audiences, teaching them baby sign language with excessive vigilance, and taking them to early music classes is quite another. The line between genuine educational enrichment and bogus enrichment has increasingly blurred. Meanwhile, the idea that kids have to be doing something "productive" at all times has only grown in influence, although there's little evidence that the better-baby products have the felicitous effects on infant brain development that they claim.

In fact, the psychological literature demonstrates that designating children as gifted, especially extremely gifted, and cultivating that giftedness may be not only a waste of money, but positively harmful. The overcultivated can develop self-esteem problems and performance anxiety. Psychologists have long known about the transmission of parental anxiety to children, but particular later-life problems can await adults who once expected to have infinite capabilities. As the poet David Shapiro writes, "The child says infinity is a small word."

Psychology professor Anderegg tells me that gifted children can grow up to expect their wives, husbands, and lovers to devote themselves to developing their brilliance. They can also develop a dread of the mundane. Felice Kaufman, the author of a longitudinal study of Presidential Scholars–high school seniors who yearly win a governmental scholastic and talent competition–from 1964 to 1968, was quick to tell me that highly gifted students have their share of unhappiness. In a 1992 article, Kaufman wrote that one "unexpected demographic finding was that 73% of the respondents had no children," and "a few poignantly stated that since their own childhood had been so troubled they had serious reservations about bringing a child of their own into the world."

Even the cheery SMPY study has produced a cache of gloomy data. One article found that a "modestly gifted group" was considered more athletic and popular and had better social standing than an extremely gifted group, a group that at thirteen got great math or verbal SAT scores. The conclusion: "extremely precocious adolescents, especially the verbally precocious, may be at greater risk for developing problems in peer relations than modestly gifted youth."

That pressure to achieve can have such adverse effects on some kids that it can incur the Icarus effect. Icarus, as you may remember from reading Greek mythology, was an inventor's son. His father, Daedalus, supplied Icarus with artificial wings made of wax and feathers, and he warned his son not to fly too high or too low. Icarus ignored the advice. He flew too high, the sun melted the wax, his wings fell apart, and he plunged into the sea.

A boy undone by a failure to accept human limits, Icarus is a useful metaphor for the hothouse kid.

Building these champions does create a generation of high achievers. But they do not necessarily stay aloft. They may grow up resentful of their parents' inculcations. They may forever romanticize the childhood they never experienced. They may spend their adulthood aspiring to be children. They also share a feeling that normality is banal, even terrifyingly so. They may feel as though they have fallen from glory. And in fact they have; the attention they once received has never returned.

The Icarus effect is not a formal psychological diagnosis. It is simply a name I'm giving to a tendency I've observed. The Icarus effect includes negative self-assessment of adult achievements, as well as at times bleak memories of childhood. In adults who were defined as gifted, especially those whose gifts were deemed extraordinary, one can see a range of these characteristics.

Yet despite the potential for dreary outcomes, today's gifted complex continues apace. The impetus to raise and push gifted children can have many causes, ranging from genuinely good intentions to a desire for reflected glory to simple parental narcissism. But the mania has built in recent years, as an increasing number of parents find themselves economically anxious. Navigating the middle class without a safety net, they see "gifted" children as a sort of insurance.

In a sense, the expansion of the culture of gifted children primed for accomplishment is yet another side effect of the growth of the middle class, and an attendant merit-based ethos. With so much competition for everything from preschool, to summer camp, to colleges, to impermanent jobs, children must work harder and train more extensively than ever. They do this not only to achieve class mobility but even just to maintain their family's place in the social strata, as they are confronted by avid, equally trained young rivals. Parents sometimes construct giftedness to lift their children and themselves above the fray.

Fervid parenting can shape champions at the expense of childhood. For all of their parents' best intentions, adult former "gifted" kids can illustrate the perils of being raised with high expectations and high competitive drives–the Icarus effect. Some of them do become high achievers, but some end up underachievers, and significantly unhappy with themselves. The way things will turn out for any given kid is somewhat alchemical. There is no formula. It has to do with a set of X factors.

George Spaeth is one variation. A Steinway grand piano hangs from the ceiling of his apartment, suspended over him like the sword of Damocles–a fitting symbol for this onetime piano prodigy's home. After all, Spaeth has lived "under the piano," in a sense, ever since he gave up his musical training and public performances at the age of seven. Spaeth was raised to be a piano prodigy, but he never hit full prodigyhood.

Spaeth began playing as an infant, on his family's grand piano in the old-money town of Chestnut Hill, Pennsylvania. "I was not prompted by anyone to start playing so early," he says. At a café near his apartment, Spaeth drinks his coffee while lowering and raising his head almost coquettishly. He's very thin, with pale skin, high cheekbones, and brown hair that radiates an oily sheen. He smokes Marlboros and wears tight black jeans. Predictably, perhaps, given his ethereal, glam-rock beauty, acting has been one of his numerous avocations: Spaeth describes himself as an actor long before he mentions his work as an amateur pianist.

"I remember all the different stages of my early playing–when my fingers could reach three notes and how exciting it was," he says. "I remember when I could reach four or five notes with my thumb and forefinger. When I was a toddler, I was inspired to make up my own things. I played a lot."

It started going wrong, says Spaeth, when he was five and his father began taking his training too seriously.

George's piano teacher was married to a modern composer and taught a number of advanced pianists. George was by far her youngest student. She invited him to practice in her home, and he liked her.

His father, however, was constantly testing and judging him. "My father pushed me too hard," Spaeth remembers. His father even gave Spaeth an intelligence test for children, which he devised himself.

The story has the ring of a parlor drama–a child who figured out how to please his father and shaped himself accordingly, and a father who set himself up to be the ultimate arbiter, guide, and even guarantor of his son's brightness and talent. But according to Spaeth, the intelligence test was just the beginning. Spaeth's father was a music-obsessed eye doctor who, as if to underline his excessive influence over his son, had named his son after himself. George Spaeth Sr. was the great-nephew of one of the great child music pedagogues of the twentieth century, Sigmund Spaeth. Sigmund taught music appreciation to America's youth via a radio show during the 1930s and '40s, making recordings and writing books such as *Teacher's Manual for Use with the Common Sense of Music in Classroom and Assembly* and *Great Symphonies: How to Recognize and Remember Them.* When George was a child, George Spaeth Sr. quizzed him continuously on music history and trivia. "My father had a lot of harsh ideas of his own as to how I should be practicing," says Spaeth. "I wasn't supposed to look at my hands because I wouldn't be able to read notes then. He called playing without reading 'diddling.'"

Spaeth and his family went to see the Philadelphia Orchestra almost every week. His father spent a fair amount of energy and time educating him about the history of music–what composer, what period, from Renaissance to modern. (Spaeth says he has since "lost that information" from his memory, one of those "blocks.") From the ages of five to seven, he lived out his hothouse-kid life as a pianist in so accelerated a fashion that it seemed to play out on sped-up film.

"The things I played when I was a child sounded like I had skill. 'They' liked what I played," Spaeth says. It wasn't the advanced nature of his study, he says, that made him so disconsolate. In fact, he remembers it as "a thrilling experience" to read notes at the age of five. "My piano teacher was the first person telling me to let go, to stop worrying, to stop worrying about playing correctly, and I did and I was able to play. I had an out-of-body experience."

It was, Spaeth says, his father's perfectionism and lack of approval that undid him. "It all ended when I played my teacher's composition once perfectly at my parents' Christmas party," he recalls. "My father didn't come to hear it; I played it again. He still didn't come into the room to listen to me. I decided I had been learning to play for him." By the age of seven, he remembers playing a "difficult composition and not believing I would get much better." Immediately thereafter, George gave up the instrument. "It was punishment for my father, so that he would see he had pushed me too hard."

It would seem that Spaeth, at some level, is still punishing his father. His story is a parable, the story of the complex knot of emotion at the root of the efforts of many a hothouse kid. That knot contains the desires both to be loved and to live out parents' ideals–to be nurtured as the emotional children they still are, while being praised as the professional adults they haven't quite become. As the barfly says to an ex-prodigy in the film *Magnolia,* "It's a dangerous thing to confuse children and angels."

"My father was repentant when I gave it up," recounts Spaeth. But the renunciation of music at any early age didn't produce happiness either. "I never really felt like a child," he says.

He tends to deliver sentences like this with a certain romantic appreciation, seemingly aware that his narrative could seem as fabulous as it is sad, the story of the foiled wunderkind. Spaeth sabotaged his own youthful career–but because he was only seven when he did so, his making and unmaking might seem to have been out of his hands. He remembers his family friends in the lush, wealthy suburbs garlanding Philadelphia asking his parents, "Is George still playing? Will he play something for us?" The answer was always no.

Today, Spaeth will play only pieces that are entirely improvised. He plays "moods," he says–not just hippie love moods, but moods like "indecision" or "the moon reflecting itself on the water."

"Some friends at some point were classical musicians who could only play written music," remembers Spaeth. "If you sat them down, they couldn't develop anything of their own. I found that appalling.

"The way I played as a child is not at all how I play now. I make mistakes. I make things up. I record my improvisations on the reel-to-reel. My father thinks I am an undisciplined person. Then, I just wanted to be perfect. I was old when I was young. I am young now that I am old."

He plays his pieces only for friends now, says Spaeth, who seems in his forties still to be recovering from the hothouse-kid experience. He has "been searching, not entirely successfully, for something to build as a base for my life." He dropped out of college more than two decades ago, and has spent his adulthood earning a living by building cabinets, and failing to earn a living by acting. He likes jobs that don't feel like work unless you do them all day long–jobs that are, in a sense, self-directed play. The jobs are like the piano playing one does at five: playing that does not have to be perfect, but is done out of love. Spaeth's professional choices can be marked by magical thinking: walking along the street one day, he saw a man with a big gray beard carving a stone angel in front of a church, and decided he wanted to do the same thing right away. Something about the man and the stone called out to Spaeth. Now he spends his days carving stone and working with wood. Since he could have been a concert pianist, his father thinks what he plays now leads nowhere, and lacks discipline.

I know what Spaeth means. I learned to read at three, and my father counted on me to offer presentations on modernist art by the time I was five. "It was nice," I replied about a particular exhibit.

"Nice?" my father thundered. "*Nice* is such a boring word!"

For me, nothing would be nice again. Soon I was teaching my friends how to read. By ten, I was judged on the quality of my responses to avant-garde film, and lecturing on everything from film stock to astrology. I made sure to read a book a day. I identified with the Brontës–their youth of intertwined literary suffering. The stickers and pink sneakers of my peers seemed bizarre.

I was insufferable. I skipped a grade. As a thirteen-year-old high school freshman, I was editing my father's writing.

Did my father, who dreamed that I sat up in my crib and talked to him about Proust and Kant when I was six months old, understand his aims? Did he know that his peculiar drills of the names of B-movie actresses, vocabulary words, and revolutionary political movements would stunt my fourth-grade social life?

My father would have bristled at the notion that he was an overbearing puppet master. If I sat absolutely quietly and wrote lyrical verse about tree-tops, I was peachy. My father was hell-bent on bettering my lot–and by extension our family's lot. He was also hell-bent on keeping me from languishing in what he considered the Blank Generation. He sought to ensure that I would be as different from my peers as he was from my immigrant grandparents. The kids I brought over after drinking wine coolers and smoking a pipe in the park in ninth grade were not to be called my friends. No, my father told me–those were acquaintances.

"There are soul mates, and there are acquaintances," he informed me, after I had called one of them my friend. "The vast quantity of people in our lives are acquaintances. Don't forget it!"

This was bitter, if profound, advice. I was far too young for it. I was also far too young for the Czech films and the difficult novels I was coerced to digest. My father's plan succeeded on one level, of course. I became a hothouse kid. I wrote my first novel at seven, and won a dozen creative-writing competitions before I turned seventeen.

I began to need those award ceremonies, where women in late middle age with amazing moles and octagonal glasses clapped for the child winner of their yearly poetry prize. I became a master of SASEs (self-addressed stamped envelopes, which I had first heard of on the public television show *Zoom*). I weighed my competition entries at the post office week after week. I photocopied my collected writings monthly. I sold out early. I tailored a play to suit a playwriting competition, plying religious themes to appeal to a batch of moralistic judges. I inserted a clarion-call ending in each of my poems, knowing it would give the grandiose verse extra resonance. At sixteen I was flown to Florida to compete with a number of other hothouse kids. We performed onstage for an audience of tanned benefactors. We were taken on a cruise ship to celebrate our precocity. A maternal white-haired author there told me I would be the next great American poet. She seemed like a saint and a seer. I had no idea, of course, how that idle remark would deform the rest of my life, giving me great expectations that I wouldn't begin to fulfill, suffusing all of my actual accomplishments with the scent of failure.

Still, ever the self-loving dupe, at the end of the year I entered and won another writing competition. I stood at the Smithsonian in an ill-fitting vintage dress, flushed with possibility, reading my poems about teen lust and juvenile morbidity.

(The "dupe" part of this, of course, is the hothouse-kid trap. I was, as are all children, self-loving until someone convinced me otherwise. It isn't wrong for a child to want to be glorious or to believe she is—every child is sort of glorious, after all.)

When I turned seventeen, I became childlike, as it was the year I left home. I ran around campus. I listened to bad sentimental music my father disdained. I mistook all sorts of friends for soul mates.

Having been built in the fashion I was as a child—created and then deflated—has left me with a distinct feeling of failure. Although I grew into the life of a culture producer, depth of knowledge sometimes caused pain, and I tried to learn less than I could have. Although it has not told me all that I need to know, my experience has given me discernment about precocity. Stories like mine and those of Larisa Stephan and George Spaeth are just pieces of a larger story, of early expertise, childhood advantage, loss, and our favorite of all—precocity.

Of course, some gifted kids don't wind up resentful or lost. Thirty-four-year-old cellist Matt Haimovitz, a former classical music prodigy, now has éclat on his own terms.

When Haimovitz was four and a half, he started playing cello with his mother. She had trained at the conservatories of Bucharest and Tel Aviv. The family—Haimovitz, his father, an Israeli engineer, his mother, and his sister—immigrated to Palo Alto, California, in the mid-1970s, in the usual search for increased prosperity. In Matt's case, prosperity was at hand. When he was ten, the great Itzhak Perlman found him. A year later, the family relocated to New York City so that Matt could go to Juilliard.

"My mom never expected me to be playing Jimi Hendrix," Haimovitz tells me as we walk around New York City in 2004, a week after his performance at the nightclub CBGB. "When I started touring, she started asking questions. She thought I was diminishing the brand."

In adolescence, Haimovitz says, he was the boy with "the bird's-eye view." He describes himself as "frustrated and remote," comfortable only when playing music. He was performing thirty concerts a year; he had grown up to applause. The plaudits were addictive.

"Imagine being a kid, getting a phone call that Zubin Mehta wants you to play with the New York Philharmonic," he says. "So Sony had Midori. Deutsche Grammophon wanted me. We were the young musicians. We were asked to be on television for a few years."

On microfiche, you can find Haimovitz at the center of the most conventional classical-music glory. See him at age thirteen, a round-faced boy wonder, playing a cello that was nearly his own height at Carnegie Hall alongside living legends Isaac Stern and Pinchas Zuckerman. In the 1980s he hung out with Midori, his fellow child star performer. They attended the Aspen Music Festival together, an aesthete's answer to Hollywood's Brat Pack. (Midori is living proof that at least a few former prodigies have long and solid careers.)

"The critics loved it," says Haimovitz. "The industry loved it. As a child performer, you are more malleable. Meanwhile, prodigies book up shows. Then it's over after a few years. And nobody cares."

He was protected as intensely as he was exposed, sheltered by his mother. Haimovitz says that it was not until his twenties that he took over his career. By 1995, he was a product of Juilliard and Harvard, but his elite credentials didn't keep him from receding from public view. One day, the Boston Philharmonic called him to play, and he turned them down. He didn't play again for five years.

His career, as he puts it with dark poetry, took on the shape of a parabola–rising fast, and falling at the same pace. He was able to unfold into an all-out adult talent only by diverting his career away from playing perfect renditions of Bach. Music scholar Jeanne Bamberger calls this and the far worse angst prodigies experience in their teens and twenties the prodigy midlife crisis. As Haimovitz puts it, he had come into contact with the greatest musicians of his time–but still, he "questioned about the way the whole system was set up–the music subscription mentality, the playing at large concert halls when the music was meant for small spaces, and the formality. Why do we all have to wear tails? Why are we distancing ourselves, rather than connecting with an audience? I opened myself up to different musical experiences than what I was brought up for." The turning point, he says, came when he felt he had been "manipulated by a manager" and made into a "product that's easy to market. It was easier for the big management firms to sell fresh new talent by putting me on a path that only a couple of years later could lead to a dead end."

In April 2004, Haimovitz performed his radical take on classical music onstage at the legendary New York punk-rock club CBGB. His rendition of Bach's Solo Suite in D Minor on a cello made in 1710 competed with the club's noisy air conditioner as well as with the even louder punk band playing next door. CBGB was one of the many unlikely venues in the musician's fifty-state U.S. tour. He also played a pizza parlor, and a honky-tonk where tractor parts hang from the ceiling.

Haimovitz has become an illustrious crossover, receiving the ultimate in millennial media exposure–political censorship. Haimovitz tends to make pacific, anti–George W. Bush remarks before performing. His outspoken left leanings helped turn him into a veritable high-art Dixie Chick–boycotted by radio programmers in Denver and booed by an audience in Wolfeboro, New Hampshire. When Haimovitz shifts from Bach to his version of Jimi Hendrix's sublime take on "The Star-Spangled Banner," his cello squalls and keens like an electric guitar. As Haimovitz wishes, his instrument expresses his anger at the distortions and wrongheaded acts of aggression that he feels the American flag has come to represent. Think of his sound as Patti Smith crossed with Yo-Yo Ma. You can't dance to it, but you might want to raise your fist. Tonight's audience applauds wildly.

After the show, four pretty boys and one plainer but as eager girl, all in high school, all with curly hair, the boys clad in vintage men's shirts, smoke cigarettes together. "I have a bootleg of Haimovitz when he was sixteen, and he really kicked it," one is saying to the other. "Because he was so good, because he trained with the best, he could just . . . he could just throw it away."

The boy sounded wistful, as if it were the coolest thing in the world to be talented enough to waste your talent.

Haimovitz's reputation is built, in part, on his biography. As a former prodigy, he knows how to draw a crowd's attention. The music prodigy has a perennial, almost carny lure in a business that offers few cheap hooks.

Haimovitz was at first stumped by the end of his prodigyhood and ultimately reinvented himself to some extent. "All I can say is that I wasn't ready for this as a human being back when I was fourteen," Haimovitz told me after he evoked cheers at one of his shows. In performance, Haimovitz seems almost shamanistic. He beats the cello. Thumps it. The score lies before him, splayed out, looking like abstract art. He is reclaiming a spark, stealing back the expressiveness: Haimovitz seems to have exploded his former self only to paste himself back together. He is doing what many of us do in our day-to-day lives, rearranging the details of his biography to form a new pattern. The difference is that he does it onstage and on his CDs. Like other adults who tend to successfully survive childhoods of being named externally–either praised or disdained–Haimovitz has remade himself, forging a new persona and a new art. In other words, he followed the route scholar of gifted children Ellen Winner has limned: those who make notable contribution in the arts or the sciences, she believes, need a rebellious aspect, and prodigies tend to be imitative. Sometimes they must lose their prodigyness in order to become fully realized artists.

Haimovitz isn't the only prodigy to have altered his former self. Another who continues to shape-shift is Vezen Wu, an ex science whiz kid, winner of the Westinghouse (now Intel) Science Talent Search and antibiotic inventor by the time he was eleven. At twenty-six, Wu is now a vice president at Morgan Stanley. His firm calls him a "technical Mozart," and his intelligence and range of knowledge remain staggering.

Wu, an equity portfolio analyst, is a distillate of the American Dream. His Taiwanese parents immigrated to Florida. Like many parents of gifted children, Wu's mother encouraged him, providing financial support for his deeply independent mental preoccupations. His father taught Wu computer programming at the age of three. His mother, a nurse, placed her medical textbooks on the lower shelf so that Wu could reach them at around the same time. Indeed, the first book Wu remembers reading was a textbook on the medical care of surgical patients. But Wu has also been self-propelled from the start. At age five, Wu saw a PBS *Nova* program on carnivorous plants and formed a wish to buy some and do experiments. His mother indulged him, going out to buy a pitcher plant from the local grocery store. She helped him buy plants from around the world, as well as look for them in the Florida swamps. Wu soon amassed a collection of 3,000 carnivorous plants, all paid for by his mom, and built climate-controlled greenhouses in his family's backyard. In order to trade with collectors all over the world, Wu obtained a fish and wildlife license, giving him access to plants from Borneo, New Guinea, and New Zealand. At home he would create lasers and experiment with data transmission and holography. He also started a chemistry club in the third grade.

By age twelve, Wu was working in a professor's laboratory ten hours a week, learning microbiology, growing bacteria that he collected from his own body (really) and testing that bacteria's vulnerability to antibiotics. He then started to test the carnivorous plants he had been collecting since he was a young child. He fed the plants birds and other small animals, and when the plants' acidic enzymes broke the animals down, Wu ground them up and analyzed them. By high school, he had succeeded in extracting a new antibacterial chemical compound to treat a drug-resistant strain of *Staphylococcus aureus.* He won the Westinghouse for it when he was eighteen.

"I am not with the plants anymore, but they were once my best friends," he tells me now, during one of our many visits to a carnivorous plant garden. "The *Nepenthes,* that is from Borneo, and beside it, the American pitcher plant and then the sundew and the *Drosera.* That's a plant with fangs. And look at that plant's bulbous cup. It is used to treat smallpox. See, over there? That's the Armenian pitcher plant. Full of enzymes." He points out the sticky, silvery sundew plant, which resembles a fruit roll-up. Its leaves actually roll over its fly prey, swallowing the bugs whole. "That plant is used in Germany as an antibiotic," he says.

Wu wishes that no glass separated the plants from their visitors. He wants to feel them move, and wants me to feel them, too. "And with the glass," he says, "you cannot see the insects become drowsy and fall into the plants." Wu is floridly eccentric. He thinks out loud and to himself in four languages: Latin, Mandarin, German, and English. He refers to things in all four languages, not just to impress but also to stimulate his mind, which seems to be constantly in search of a new object of knowledge, as if knowledge itself were a plaything. He also has a penchant for frank self-analysis: "I am a person who is unable to let go," he says. "I am one of the most repressed people out there."

Wu remains the decisively quirky person he was as a young child. Still, he has easily changed his professional identity, from medical botany to finance, "to stay competitive," as he puts it. He credits his mother with providing the support that allowed him to shift from biology to financial services at twenty. Wu created and is now recruiting for the Intel Science Talent Search internship program at Morgan Stanley. He has become a prodigy hunter. He seeks out the three hundred semifinalists identified by the Science Service and tries to lure them to investment banking.

Wu has not lost the belief that he is one of the lucky ones. He sees his career in financial time-series analysis and indexing for international markets as anything but a humdrum coda to his youth. He advises the very rich, and declares with delight that he has sold out. Luck is also, of course, a matter of parents. Wu may have been saved by his mother's support of his less-than-obvious academic interests–buying him thousands of carnivorous plants, taking him on frequent trips to the library and allowing him to mix with the "normal" kids in the neighborhood. Wu's best friend growing up was a NASCAR enthusiast, whom Wu cajoled to come along on treks through the swamps by promising the opportunity to steal a few carnivorous plants.

Buoyant ex-prodigies like Wu and Haimovitz and their dour opposite numbers raise the same question: Why do some succeed, while others don't? And why do some of those who do succeed despise the parents who made that success possible?

Some scholars promote mainstreaming gifted children, as Wu's parents did. Dona Matthews, coauthor of *Being Smart about Gifted Children: A Guidebook for Parents and Educators* and the director of the Hunter College Center for Gifted Studies and Education, is a strong proponent of that approach. When I sit down with Matthews, she stresses that children be sent to schools where they are "not segregated like hothouse plants, like houseplants that cannot be put into the world, plants that can't exist in weather like this." As she says this, Matthews gestures toward the cold New York City winter beyond her windowpane, and then at the fragile, exotic orchid on her desk.

There are also personal qualities that allowed Haimovitz, Wu, and a few other early successes to continue succeeding into adulthood. Those mysterious qualities, which are hard to measure or teach, include intrinsic motivation, resiliency, and mental independence. Such qualities are not the sole province of gifted kids who are extensively nurtured and thoroughly educated–indeed, they are often missing even in these children. They can also be found in adults who were never "discovered" or otherwise prepped.

America is struggling to navigate the dilemma of giftedness. On one hand, enriched education can promote high achievement. At the same time, "hothousing" children can hurt them.

Some of this hothousing consists of faddish and tricky lessons and classes that have, at best, no real effect on their recipients' later lives. Moreover, all of these classes shave resonant hours off free and self-directed play, which will always be important to children. Fifteen years ago, the great majority of American school districts reported giving students at least one recess period per day. Today, according to the American Association for the Child's Right to Play, many school systems have eliminated recess altogether, out of fear of disrupting children's schoolwork. America is experiencing what one scholar calls "the recession of recess." This is not just un-fun. It can be academically counterproductive. Recent studies have shown that young schoolchildren grow increasingly distracted the longer recess is delayed–and are more attentive on days when they have had recess.

And the unpleasant element of economic class rears its head amid the new hothousing. While the emphasis on testing children applies across income strata, the benefits of true scholastic enrichment are far from equally distributed. The children of the wealthy have so much more access to strong learning programs, while lower-class and even middle-class kids are being increasingly deprived of gifted education.

Parents who push their children to strive for golden performance may view the resulting achievements as a form of insurance. Such pressure can also be a sort of projection–the cliché of parents pressing their wishes onto their kids, demanding that their children achieve what they themselves could not.

And what is the value of so much achievement so early, after all? We tend to assume that it will translate into higher achievement later, but that's not necessarily so. An overemphasis on early achievement has caused many to forget that achievements can also come later on–that not everyone accomplishes at the same velocity.

Take Maurice Ashley, chess's first black grandmaster, a true late bloomer. Ashley learned chess at the age of fourteen, long after the prodigy age. Nonetheless, he beat the odds to become highly ranked. "I was fourteen when I took a chess book out of the school library," he recounts. "And from then on, I would look at something once and I would understand it. I was surprised that there were books about it. I fell in love with it. I was a crazy black kid talking about being a GM [grandmaster]."

Today, at thirty-eight, Ashley is suave, with a square-shouldered athlete's build. A father of two, he lives in a middle-class section of Queens, where he gives inspirational lectures about chess. Sometimes Ashley uses chess as a metaphor for politics, and vice versa, comparing George W. Bush to "a king blocking up the middle of a chess game," where the other side is the Iraqi forces. Ashley fantasizes about starting a reality show about chess prodigies: "Can't you see it? A little kid battling against an adult on TV: The question is, who will get the queen? Right now, chess is seen as anti-sport and wimpish, but if we had a real corporate sponsor, and made it a battle of the sexes, maybe? Or had eight prodigies playing in an international competition?"

Ashley's relationship to chess prodigies is complicated. He has sought to discover and develop chess prodigies in public schools in Harlem, and wants to pitch their stories to cable television. He thinks he could have been a prodigy if only he had learned chess earlier, and he feels the loss. "My mother disapproved of chess," he says. He recalls her asking him all the time how he was going to make money. He went to "random weekend tournaments," though, and started winning. "I soaked it up like a child prodigy would have, even though I was older, in my late teens," he explains. "In six years, I became a chess master. I competed against people who started before they were eight. I was already a senior master at twenty-one. I studied with a famous Ukrainian coach at his home."

Ashley embodies the paradox of the gifted child/prodigy, the cultural desire to be one of them, to be naturally special when one is young, while at the same time knowing on some level that it is fine to mature or come into one's powers at a slower pace. In Ashley's case, his more drawn-out germination might have been all for the best. Not having been a chess prodigy or a hothouse kid or an enriched kid–not having been forced to become good at chess or anything really early–may have been good for him, says Ashley.

Was it? That's one of the questions this book seeks to answer. Of course, some hothouse kids do not suffer later. They are lucky: earmarked early and properly trained, some can effloresce into truly extraordinary and also well-adjusted adults. In this book, you will meet some of them. The book will take you into the world of hothouse kids, from their allegedly intelligence-enhancing videos to born-again preacher prodigies to Math Olympiad winners who go on to create complex investment vehicles at large banks. It will offer portraits of those who, like Larisa Stephan, were pressed to become prodigies when they may have been simply bright, talented, or precocious. It will ask questions of today's world of advanced toddler education: Who will make it–and who will buckle under the pressure? How much enrichment, testing, and time awareness is actually good for children? Will it harm us in the long run if increasingly organized infant life, highly academic preschool programs, and avid enrichment are allowed to keep widening social inequities between the children of low- and high-income families?

And if parents are oriented toward enhancing their children, how can they ensure that their children can obtain Stephan's brightness, without her resentment or somber memories? Can you get the achievement without the debility?

Where is all this aggressive early learning taking us?

TWO

The Baby Genius Edutainment Complex: The New Smart Baby Products

"She's ten months old, for God's sake," I said. "I know," Seymour said. "They have ears. They can hear." The story Seymour read to Franny that night, by flashlight, was a favorite of his, a Taoist tale. To this day, Franny swears that she remembers Seymour reading it to her.

J. D. SALINGER, "Raise High the Roof Beam, Carpenters"

One DVD is full of images of children big and small, all holding violins, recorders, guitars, and cellos–while a song in the background insists that when playing music, children should "Do your best! And never less!" Another contains images of toddlers on a putting green or wandering around a basketball court and a baby with a golf ball, all set to bouncy music with words like *teamwork* flashing on the screen, in the hopes of inspiring a generation of toddler athletes. Another features a puppet called Vincent van Goat that introduces an infant to six primary colors and then to the colors as they appear in van Gogh's paintings *The Starry Night* and *Wheat Fields with Reaper at Sunrise.* Yet another DVD contains colorful, high-contrast imagery of babies playing with blocks and balloons, counting tomatoes, and sibilating words in English, French, and Spanish.

These infant and toddler DVDs may be cute or even visually striking, but their selling point is that they offer the youngest viewer–intended age sometimes as young as newborn and up–a great deal more. The *Brainy Baby Left and Right Brain* DVD set, from a company whose motto heralds "a little genius in the making," claims to "engage your child's whole brain (logic and creative) to help boost your baby's intellect." The *Right Brain* disc features classical music and focuses on "cognitive skills," among them "Rhymes, Spatial Reasoning, and Imagination, Intuition, and more!" The *Left Brain* disc has bright visuals, patterns, and shapes in red, black, and white, with letters of the alphabet, and voiceovers offering words in Spanish and French. The *Baby Prodigy* DVD claims to do nothing short of giving a child "A Head Start in Life!" The disc's back copy reads, "Did you know that you can actually help to enhance the development of your baby's brain? The first 30 months of life is the period where a child's brain undergoes its most critical stages of evolution . . . together we can help to make your child the next Baby Prodigy!" The *So Smart!* two-disc set, suggested for infants of nine months and up, features Mozart and Vivaldi and interactive alphabet games the infant can play on the television using the remote control, while the *V. Smile* video game system promotes itself with the catchphrase "Turn Game Time into Brain Time."

Perhaps the best known of these products is the Baby Einstein series, which offers promotional materials swaddled in the rhetoric of stimulation: the word *multi-sensory* appears frequently. These DVDs tend to feature the alphabet or musical scales or colors, demonstrated through toys and lights and, of course, classical music. In fact, almost all of the company's DVDs are named after a crew of infantilized dead white male geniuses: *Baby Galileo, Baby Shakespeare, Baby Wordsworth,* and *Baby Van Gogh.* The Baby Einstein PR rep explains the product name by saying, "Albert Einstein exemplifies someone who was truly curious about the world around him." Her remark unwittingly undercuts the very premise of the series, suggesting not that babies can be made into Einsteins but that Einstein remained, in some sense, a baby. Additionally, I couldn't help but recall that Albert Einstein was not an early bloomer.

These videos are part of a DVD and toy fad that I call the Baby Genius Edutainment Complex. What I mean by the word *complex* here is two things. The first is as in "military-industrial complex": as Webster's has it, "a whole made up of complicated or interrelated parts," and "a group of obviously related units of which the degree and nature of the relationship is imperfectly known." The second is the psychological sense of the word: an exaggerated reaction to a situation. The complex is the first stage of the American passion for raising gifted children, reflecting the faith that, exposed to enough media, typically in tandem with equally stirring classes, bright children can be invented, and that precocity is the best insurance policy for one's children. The complex is also composed of products and companies now promising to urge on children's precocity.

This complex is relatively new. Until 1997, there were no Baby Einstein videos. By 2003, 32 percent of our nation's infants owned at least one Baby Einstein video. Ten percent of kids aged six months to two years have a television remote designed for children, according to a 2003 report by the Henry J. Kaiser Family Foundation, *Zero to Six: Electronic Media in the Lives of Infants, Toddlers and Preschoolers.* Forty-two percent of children in this age group watch a videotape or a DVD each day. According to the 2005 Kaiser report *A Teacher in the Living Room? Educational Media for Babies, Toddlers and Preschoolers,* on the average babies six months to three years spend an hour watching TV and forty-seven minutes a day on videos or computers, all despite the American Academy of Pediatrics' 1999 recommendation of no screen time at all for babies under two and no more than an hour or two of highly educational screen media for children ages two and older. No wonder, then, that developmental videos and DVDs in 2004 brought in profits of $100 million. That same year, videos and DVDs for preschool-age children earned $500 million. (From 2003 to 2004, overall sales of educational toys increased by 19 percent.)

One boon to the producers of children's DVDs is that the parent consumer appears more willing to buy rather than rent them because of their "repeatability"–that is, infants and young children, unlike adults, enjoy watching the same DVD over and over again. (The irony here is that babies and toddlers like doing a lot of different kinds of things over and over again, in a level of repetition that adults might find intolerable, especially repeated actions with objects that are bright and shiny.) Chasing this opportunity, studios such as Warner Brothers have spent the last decade adding children's programming with an educational component into the mix. Baby Einstein is owned by Disney. The toy companies have also gotten into the act: Fisher-

Price, a major DVD producer, is a subsidiary of Mattel. For the nation's biggest companies, the incentive to get into the edutainment DVD market is as clear as phonics. It's clear for smaller companies as well: as Dennis Fedoruk, president of Brainy Baby, says, "There's a bumper crop of new kids each month, after all."

But the impetus behind the Baby Genius Edutainment Complex's acceleration has not been just savvy marketing. The popularity of DVDs with classical music, pinwheels, and colorful imagery coincided with–and was also incited by–theories of infant and childhood learning that became fashionable in the early 1990s. As Liz Iftikhar, founder and president of Baby BumbleBee, puts it, the kid vid biz emerged on the back of the Mozart effect.

The phenomenon called the Mozart effect made its first appearance in a study done by Gordon Shaw and Frances Rauscher in 1993. One group of college students listened to ten minutes of a Mozart sonata, while another group didn't. Then both groups took a paper-folding-and-cutting test. Those who had listened to the music reportedly performed better than those who had not. Shaw and Rauscher concluded that listening to Mozart improved the students' very short-term spatial thinking. A second study in 1995 yielded similar findings.

The benefits of listening to Mozart soon became folk wisdom, and Mozart became even more synonymous with early learning and precocity. From the start of the renown of the Mozart effect and the tendency to refer to children with gifts as "little Mozarts," I recall being somewhat disturbed by any ambition to be Mozartian. While we can all imagine little Mozart playing blindfolded before Emperor Joseph, it is quite clear that the infant prodigy was raised by his father to be a high-rent stage show, "scattering his notes," as the music historian Paul Metzner puts it, all around Europe, and that he grew up to be a wildly creative yet also unstable young man whose incandescent exertions ultimately brought him physical deterioration and an early death. Nevertheless, the two Mozarts coexist, the parental fantasy and the Enlightenment wreck.

Soon the Mozart effect study's college students morphed into infants in the imaginations of kid marketers, parents, and Zell Miller, then governor of Georgia, who pushed his state to send a Mozart CD to every newborn. The idea that classical music played to infants, or even fetuses, would improve their ability to reason fed into the pitches of edutainment video companies, which in 1995 started to make ostensibly stimulating videos for babies, usually with a classical music component. One businessman, Don Campbell, even trademarked the term *Mozart Effect* in order to better sell "educational" CDs and books for infants. And the pitch has broadened beyond the music of the prodigious Wolfgang Amadeus–some of the newer videos are accompanied by the sonorous strains of Beethoven, and some offer random noise.

The catch to all these CDs and baby edutainment videos is that no psychologists, musicians, or musicologists have been able to duplicate the Mozart effect that Shaw and Rauscher described. Kenneth Steele, professor of psychology at Appalachian State University, was one of the scholars who tried. In 1997, a few of his graduate students conducted similar experiments and failed to reproduce the results. Steele presumed at first that the Mozart effect was the result of individuals' arousal after listening to music. But he did not discover this to be the case. Then Steele himself tried, and he wasn't able to replicate the results, either. He eventually became the effect's greatest critic, publishing half a dozen papers decrying it, chief among them "Prelude or Requiem for the 'Mozart Effect'?" published with coauthors in *Nature* magazine in 1999. To date, the Mozart effect has failed to replicate in scientific settings at least three dozen times. Many additional scholars have noted that if any such effect does exist, it could well be due to the increased arousal that music can cause, or to the testing conditions.

None of this scholarly debunking has stymied the spread of the Baby Genius Complex. In fact, the complex has only expanded since the middle 1990s. Now it includes mind-enhancing baby formulas: giftedness has become digestible. In 2003 a fatty acid, DHA, suddenly made news as a wonder ingredient in baby formulas. DHA-ARA oils (docosahexaenoic acid and arachidonic acid), extracted from microbial sources such as algae and fungus, are supposed to help formulas replicate breast milk more closely than non-DHA formulas, thus increasing infant intelligence. Now a host of formulas offer DHA-ARA: Similac Advance, Nestle Good Start, Supreme with DHA and ARA, and Bright Beginnings. The Bright Beginnings pitch tells parents that the lipids added "are associated with mental and visual development." Enfamil A+ claims to be "the only formula clinically proven to result in higher early mental development scores."

Apparently, the creation of baby geniuses begins not at birth, but in the womb. Expecta Lipil, a pill for pregnant women, offers DHA in a prenatal form. There are also auditory prenatal enrichment products. Brent Logan, inventor of BabyPlus and author of *Learning before Birth: Every Child Deserves Giftedness,* hawks the prenatal BabyPlus system, a speaker unit that pregnant women are supposed to place in a fabric pouch that is then strapped to their abdomens: the unit gives off sixteen "scientifically designed rhythmic sounds that resemble a mother's heartbeat," according to the BabyPlus company. "The rhythm of the sounds increases incrementally and sequentially as the pregnancy progresses. The BabyPlus sound pattern introduces your child to a sequential learning process, built upon the natural rhythms of their own environment."

In describing his product to me, Logan promises that BabyPlus's "auditory exercises" will produce a higher-than-average IQ. The key to his pitch is the logical technique of inversion: he mentions in an interview that infants in Romania and Russia who are deprived suffer as adults, and thus infants in America who are enriched by a product like his will blossom. BabyPlus's ad copy claims that "babies and children enriched with BabyPlus are more relaxed at birth, with eyes and hands open, crying little," that they "reach their milestones earlier" and "have longer attention spans."

BabyPlus may be a far-out product, but like so many others, it uses parents' fears that their child might not hit milestones early or at the "normal time." Like the edutainment DVDs, it is first in a series of products claiming to promote child development and a timely march of the infant toward multilingualism and early spatial acumen. For instance, just to make sure progress is indeed timely, there is the Time Tracker, a lighted test-timer for children aged four and up. Once you could get by with an egg timer or a stopwatch. But in the age of edutainment mass culture, that's not good enough. The Time Tracker is a plastic object shaped like a large cucumber standing on its end. It has red, yellow, and green stripes that can be programmed to light up after a certain amount of time has passed, accompanied by six sound effects. I bought it and programmed it. I was struck by a number of things regarding Time Tracker. For starters, there was the product's relative popularity–on Amazon.com it was in the top 2,000 the last time I checked. Second, I found the extension of time management–now such a concern among adults, as documented by a number of sociologists who study time use, and parents—to the toys of the youngest children meaningful. I was also struck by its similarity to a number of other objects: a lighted joystick, a miniature of the spaceship in *Close Encounters of the Third Kind,* and finally and somewhat disturbingly, although also somewhat amusingly, a sex toy.

The claims made by the producers of Baby Genius Edutainment DVDs and brain-feeding formulas may at times seem absurd. But the impulses that usher parents into the complex and drive them to purchase these products are utterly sincere, and the wish to raise flourishing children is so old it is practically biblical.

As Peggy Madsen, a parent of two in Colorado, put it to me, "Giftedness is a gift you can give." Madsen has always been terrifically determined that her children be the very smartest, and she continues to champion the use of flash cards to inspire early reading. She has written about wandering around the house, naming objects, when her children were still newborns, watching their eyes intently to make sure they understood. She believes it is thanks to her efforts that her children began attending college when they were thirteen.

The ambition to give "giftedness" may have quite a history, but other aspects of the complex are new. Today's complex yokes together two concepts of infant betterment—that those skills and aptitudes not provided through genetics can be worked at and developed, and that one must do so by a certain age, or the jig is up. Only in the last ten years have parents been inundated with flash cards, DVDs, toys, and games that promise to provide "just the right level" of stimulation. Parents are much more receptive to these ideas and pitches today because they are more anxious about their children's futures, which precocious achievement may assure.

One need only look at the history of toys to learn that educational stimulation has not always been the primary aim of children's and infants' playthings. Through the nineteenth century, children tended not to play with manufactured things. Toys were handcrafted and usually homemade, and most children had few or even no toys in the cupboard. Only the wealthy had a number of toys, and these were quite different from contemporary playthings. Diminutive replicas of women, babies, and furniture enabled children to engage the larger world at their own level, that of small bit players. Many children's toys were indistinguishable from the miniatures included in the reliquaries of the adult dead. Such toys were meant to help pass the time, not to create genius.

Early manufactured toys and games were a good index for how Americans conceived of childhood, and also of parents' more general wishes and impulses. The game Monopoly, for example, first produced in 1883, was an Industrial Revolution training ground whose promotional material described it as the site of "the struggle between Capital and Labor." In fact, "One of the most important changes in the play of children from large group ring games to small group board games represented the embourgeoisement of our society," writes Stephen Kline, a professor of media studies at Simon Fraser University, in his book *Out of the Garden.* For instance, the beginning of the twentieth century saw a rise of mass-produced toys dedicated to solitary play. Lincoln Logs (invented by John Lloyd Wright, son of architect Frank), boxes of crayons (first produced by Crayola in 1903), and Erector sets (introduced in 1913) all signaled an increase in time spent indoors for children in newly prosperous families.

Some of these toys for solitary play were the earliest precursors of the DVDs and similar products sold by today's edutainment complex. Initially, Parker Bros., Playskool, and Milton Bradley were three toy companies specializing in "education games." A notion of playthings as maturational devices for children was on the rise, but it remained very different from the ideas behind today's ostensibly intelligence-enhancing toys. These maturational playthings did not claim to promote a child's achievement or mental gain: they could simply be dolls that taught mothering, for example. (In an article in a toy trade magazine in 1927, dolls were termed an "Antidote to Race Suicide" in that they would encourage white girls to reproduce. The teddy bear emerged in Brooklyn, New York, in 1902 and soon became faddish. It, too, was thought to have maturational benefits, but not in the sense of making children or toddlers faster learners. Rather, teddy bears were thought to be objects that spurred children's emotional growth. Teddy bears also have the benefit of being tactile, tangible, and manipulatable in a way that today's Baby Genius Edutainment Complex's DVDs and videos are not.

DVDs, when playing on a screen, are by definition untouchable and mechanical. They encourage infants and toddlers to think while watching images on a box, rather than to invent and imagine a story around an object like a toy bear.

One of the aspects of the Baby Genius Edutainment Complex, the study of play and playthings' relationship to the development of children, also began in the late nineteenth century. Anthropologists started studying children's games as a sort of living folklore. One study of 15,000 kids in Cleveland in 1913 discovered that of a number of possible activities, "3171 were just fooling" while "531 were playing with kites," a bit of historical data that strikes me as particularly interesting in light of our contemporary attitudes toward children's mental development, where the "just fooling" time, seen as wasteful, has shrunk. At the turn of the century, toys were being used in kindergartens. The educator Maria Montessori used toys to teach math concepts, and promoted the enlightened notion that child pupils would be less obdurate about learning if work was more playlike, because when they were playing they were actively engaged. Montessori's ideas soon caught on among some educators. But the nature of toys was also debated, with academics championing free play and high-quality materials. In 1920, a professor at Columbia University's Teachers College informed a group of businessmen in the toy industry that they should make toys of better quality that appealed to the imagination–a plea not always heeded by manufacturers.

Complaints about toys stifling imagination rather than charging it have become ever more urgent with regard to the toys and DVDs of today. In an insolent, sparkling essay on the subject first collected in 1957 in the book *Mythologies,* the cultural critic Roland Barthes decried his era's playthings as products of "chemistry not nature." He was horrified that there were "dolls which urinate" and other toys "meant to prepare the little girl for the causality of housekeeping, to 'condition' her to her future role as mother." These toys, Barthes wrote, "are meant to produce children who are users, not creators." He was paraphrasing what was to become a central tenet of scholars of play: self-directed play is seen as superior play, and toys where children can improvise and imagine are privileged over those that are passive and preprogrammed. Prefabricated toys of this kind condemned the child to feel, Barthes wrote, that "he does not invent the world, he uses it: there are, prepared for him, actions without adventure, without wonder, without joy. He is turned into a little stay-at-home householder who does not even have to invent the mainsprings of adult causality; they are supplied to him ready-made: he has only to help himself, he is never allowed to discover anything from start to finish."

After Barthes, the psychologist Erik Erikson's insights into toys and development complicated the study of playthings. Erikson wrote of the earliest and most primitive play in a child's life, "autocosmic play," where infants play with their own bodies, and going on to a toy "microsphere" or "the small world of manageable toys," which is "a harbor" for the child's ego. Ultimately, according to Erikson, the toy "thing-world" expands into the "macrosphere" of group play, or play with other children. Erikson kept underlining the point that play and play with toys is a part of identity, and the children's world of manageable toys should be shaped or intervened with as little as possible to avoid any disruption in their social learning.

At least in Barthes's era, children's playthings were still primarily tactile in character. Today's DVDs tend to be images of toys emanating from a television screen in programs with goofy pedantry. Still, Barthes's notion of toys as totems of a prescribed and manufactured adult world held some truth, and would only become more true with time. Already by the middle of the last century, toys had become less arcadian. They were creations devoted to novelty and expendability–in other words, trendy and makeshift: yo-yos and Davy Crockett hats and the like. In fact, today's nostalgia for a simpler time, for a time when childhood meant frolicking in more innocent pastoral climes–romping through the yard rather than through parents' DVD collections–may be an attractive construction, but it is also almost always misleading, a sort of sentimentality for an idyllic childhood that may have existed a century ago rather than one or two generations past. Beginning as early as the 1950s, toys suddenly became spin-off gear from television shows or children's films: when a child wasn't watching television, she might well be playing with action figures or other toys based on television programs, products that would allow her to re-create, in her own home, scenes from her favorite series. Along with the ever more calculated nature of children's toys, there was inevitably an increase of market-driven toy testing and research conducted by toy manufacturers.

This isn't to say that the "maturational" ambitions of toys vanished. For instance, the construction toy Lego advertised itself as an "instructive game." And in 1969, the ultimate maturational television program, *Sesame Street* debuted, with a line of educational toys following in its wake. The lessons of *Sesame Street,* were strongly influenced by the educational philosophy of Maria Montessori, and from the beginning *Sesame Street*'s producers, the Children's Television Workshop, made a huge effort at outreach to young children and their families in low-income areas. The show was, in fact, considered to be an extension of the 1960s "War on Poverty," funded in part by the Department of Health, Education and Welfare, as if it were a social program.

But in a certain sense, the early debates that swirled around *Sesame Street* are echoed today in the debates over the Baby Edutainment Complex. *Sesame Street*'s critics argued that young children benefit from imaginary play rather than watching television. Similarly, the edutainment DVDs for infants regularly run afoul of the American Academy of Pediatrics, which suggests that there should be no television watching at all for children under two. But there is a crucial difference between edutainment DVDs and *Sesame Street. Sesame Street* was not intended for babies (until now, that is, as a *Sesame Street* infant DVD line is readied for release), while today's DVDs are made explicitly for children two and under.

Companies are making these products because parents want them. Parents want them because they are concerned about their children's mental lives, thanks to the hard-sell marketing. There are deeper reasons, too, for parents' greater receptivity to such products and toys. One is a contemporary mania for infant betterment and precocity. Another is an increasing fashion for gizmos and technological improving devices for people of all ages, starting in infancy. A third reason is harder to prove but seems to me to be widespread: adults' tendency to project themselves into infant and toddler experience, as an antidote to their inability to remember that time, and perhaps to remember much of childhood at all, given the pressure to live in the future rather than the past. The gap between adults' projections onto infants' viewing experience and the true nature of that experience is large–is the baby learning or just taking in a set of bright two-dimensional images that makes little sense? And if the infant is learning from the edutainment DVD, wouldn't she learn from any repetitive experience, since infants learn through repetition? DVDs are just easier to repeat than other experiences.

This is part of how the Baby Edutainment Complex is the beginning of the movement to invent gifted children: it starts with parental wishes and hopes, one of which is that the infant is getting as much out of a DVD as his parents. It's also part of another aspect of childhood that will be covered in more depth elsewhere in this book–directed play has trumped free play. This is one unspoken reason why babies are now the audience for educational products. According to Brainy Baby president Dennis Fedoruk, parents are concerned about their infants' mental lives. "Parents know about that preschool window of opportunity–it's very narrow," he says. "Parents want to maximize results in their children without causing their children trouble. Listen, you can't turn back the hands of time. Once they enter kindergarten they can't have the window of opportunity any longer. It's too late."

Similarly, CEO and founder of the Athletic Baby Company Karen Foster tells me that her *Athletic Baby Golf* and *Athletic Baby All-Star* DVDs help parents give a head start to their kids, so that when they are actually old enough to play a sport or even to walk, "they will succeed at it." She likens her DVDs' potential effect to the effect of his father on Tiger Woods: "Everyone has heard about Tiger's imprinting from an early age by his father. . . . The earlier the age, the more successful they will be." Foster gives the standard edutainment-complex line: if infant deprivation creates negative effects, inversely, "enriching" products must automatically produce a positive effect. She mentions the child obesity epidemic frequently, as if her *Athletic Baby* DVDs are a sure cure. Even as many researchers tie obesity to sedentary habits, Foster wants parents to sit their babies down in front of a DVD to prevent–well, to prevent them from sitting around. By this logic, adults would be encouraged to keep in shape by watching the NFL on TV each Sunday afternoon.

The makers of the smart-baby formulas also sell their products by promising bright children. "The difference between the children who received formulas containing this ingredient and other children can be observed from each group's reading of one line on the eye chart," claimed Angela Tsetsis, director of marketing for Martek, the company that produces the "smart" fatty acid and sells it to the companies that use it in their baby formulas. "At eighteen months, we looked at the mental acuity of babies who have received the nutrient, and those babies scored higher."

"BabyPlus helps with imprinting," Brent Logan, the inventor, claims. "And soon, the imprinting window shuts off for the pre-infants and it is too late. When they are pre-nates, they are in an unusual different time and they are learning in a different mode." Logan and BabyPlus are extremes in the edutainment market–Logan does an unironic star turn in a British television documentary program entitled *Brave New Babies,* which he proudly sends me. But his prenatal interventionist ideology is not a fringe belief. Real mothers are buying his product. Rather than a radical maneuver, Logan's move into prenatal marketing seems like the next logical step.

All of these are pitches that could make a parent nervous enough to run out and buy the product. But are any of them accurate? To better understand the answer to this question, one needs to first cleave the popular ideas of infant "crucial stages," "brain cell death," "windows of time," and "brain plasticity" (today's scientized buzzword for "ability to learn") from the science and cultural history underlying them.

The notion that the first three years are key ones for emotional and intellectual development isn't new. Americans have long sought to command and control natural processes so as to accelerate them. This is part of our faith in man's ability to harness nature and to use time shrewdly. As Benjamin Franklin said, time is money, and the stuff life is made of. Child development pioneer Jean Piaget was famously disturbed by Americans' fixation on their children's educational velocity. A story was told to me anecdotally by Charles Nelson, a professor of pediatrics at Harvard Medical School, of Piaget's tour of American universities in the middle of the last century. When the Swiss psychologist described the cognitive stages children pass through as they mature, his American listeners asked him how they could make their children go through those stages faster. (Piaget was displeased.) In 1964, those who founded Head Start, a federally funded program for disadvantaged preschool children, emphasized the urgent nature of education in the earliest years, an undertaking that was seen as determining these children's entire futures.

In the last decade or so, a focus on early development and the necessity of intervention for disadvantaged children, once a social welfare plank, fueled a popular awareness (and sometimes misunderstanding) of the crucial period from zero to three. Vociferous celebrity advocates for infants, a White House conference on the subject, and the Mozart effect theory ultimately gave rise to a rash of baby products promising infant precocity.

As John Bruer recounts in his clear-headed derogation of the early enrichment movement, *The Myth of the First Three Years,* texts from the 1990s like *Rethinking the Brain* tended to suggest that critical periods pervade all areas of learning. In the mid-1990s, the actor Rob Reiner's national "I Am Your Child" campaign, with its slogan "The first years last forever," disseminated the zero-to-three worldview. Reiner claimed at the time that parents who don't read to their children in those first three years were diminishing the growth potential of their brains, and that by the age of ten "your brain is cooked and there's nothing much you can do." While Reiner and his campaign claimed to address an infant's intellectual development, Bruer notes correctly that it was theories of emotional attachment as outlined by child psychologists in the late 1950s, '60s, and '70s–most famous among them the legendary British child psychologist John Bowlby–that gave Reiner's campaign its true ballast. A second event that egged the craze onward was the 1997 White House Conference on Child Development, which emphasized the effect of early childhood events on the development of a child's intelligence. A third element was a series of studies on rats and enrichment conducted by Mark Rosenzweig at the University of California, Berkeley, and William Greenough at the University of Illinois in the 1970s and '80s. Both researchers looked at how rats' brains benefit from experience. They conducted studies on the brains of rats raised in enriched environments with toys and with other rats–cages akin to the rats' natural habitat–versus the brains of rats in bare cages more akin to prison cells. The rats in the enriched cages were found to have more dendritic area in certain regions of the brain: basically, these rats were more mentally enhanced than their deprived colleagues. This research was ultimately absorbed by the popular press and applied to infants and children.

And then there was the Mozart effect.

But in the years since the middle 1990s, scholars have cast aspersions on the credence of zero-to-three as an absolute time frame. William Greenough of rat-enrichment fame was a vehement critic of the new overemphasis on early learning: he argued that his research supported the idea that the brain continues to be plastic after infancy, rather than the opposite conclusion that the time for development is limited. Indeed, many in the neuroscientific community now dismiss the idea that adult brains lose plasticity, viewing the brain as an entity that continually remodels itself. The trend in current research is to study in earnest how individuals execute cognitive tasks from ages six to ninety, and observe mental dynamics across the life span.

"It's important to point out that windows of development do not slam shut, as the earliest versions of 'Parents' Action for Children' and the 'Birth to Three' movement suggested," says Bradley Schlaggar, a pediatric neurologist at Washington University. "When the development windows are thought to slam shut, a parent may feel that he or she must try again with the next child. While the motivation was very justifiable–a desire to make sure every child had access to good nutrition–the message was so harsh."

Schlaggar and other neurologists, cognitive scientists, psychologists, and child development specialists I spoke with questioned the idea that educational toys or DVDs accomplish what their makers claim. As Professor Charles Nelson, a professor at Harvard Medical School and a preeminent scholar of the infant brain, puts it, "There is no proof of the value of the early enrichment toys and videos in terms of brain science." Nelson also consulted for Mead Johnson for a year regarding "smart" food additives and says that while DHA and ARA have been shown to improve babies' auditory and retina responses, they have not been shown to improve reading skills.

Scholars have also argued that the idea of hard and fast "critical periods" is overplayed. For one thing, there is a difference between brain functions that are "experience-expectant" and bound by critical periods, and those that are "experience-dependent" and not so bound. Experience-expectant means, for example, that the brain requires exposure to light so that vision can develop properly. This experience does, in fact, need to take place at a particular point in the development of all infants. Experience-dependent learning, by contrast, is how an infant or child learns things individual to her environment–reading or weaving or dumpling-making. This sort of learning is less time-governed. As John Bruer puts it, "critical periods are less likely to exist for traits and behaviors that are unique to the experiences of individuals, social groups, or cultures."

According to Fred Dick, a developmental cognitive neuroscientist and a lecturer in psychology at the University of London, starting to learn second or even third languages early can be a good thing. But early doesn't mean infancy. Furthermore, teaching a child language with another child may be preferable to using videos, because a normal environment with another child "holds more information than any multimedia film." Experts tell me that today's edutainment DVDs or language-blurting toys are generally untested in how effective they are in teaching children a second language. The DVDs tend to offer only disconnected French or Spanish words; additionally, a child must be exposed to a language continuously to acquire it. Studies have shown that the ability to learn the grammar of a second language begins to decline in puberty–quite a while after the age of three. And ultimately, says Dick, one can be a successful language learner well into adulthood. "It's not as easy, but I can take up a new language when I am twenty," says Michael Merzenich, a neuroscientist at the University of California and a preeminent expert on brain plasticity. "It's not as easy *not* because I am less plastic, but because I became so damn proficient at my native language."

Many infant DVDs are hawked with questionable promises about time-limited opportunities for learning. Some head straight for the parental panic button, selling themselves by gesturing at the specter of "infant brain cell death." Charles Zorn, a neuropsychological education specialist, told me that he often has to reassure parents that numbers of brain cells are not a measure of a child's intelligence, knowledge, or ability to learn. The brain deliberately makes too many, then lets a bunch wither; the specific ones that wither depend on the environment the newborn encounters. In fact, cell death is actually a part of the learning process. "When you learn to read, you are killing cells to create a pathway," he says.

Indeed, reducing infant brain cell death is counterproductive; cell death is the main way the nervous system refines its circuits. One scholar used the example of a toddler flying an airplane and asked rhetorically, Wouldn't you rather a trained adult pilot it, even if the toddler may have more exuberant brain cells?

Academics who study cognition also question the value of prenatal enrichment products. Gary Marcus, a professor of psychology at New York University and author of *The Birth of the Mind,* says that while it is possible to learn something in the womb, it also isn't good to give a fetus too much stimulation. And given the paucity of long-term research on the subject, it's hard to gauge what would be overstimulating, says Marcus: "We don't know enough about early brain development to say."

In truth, scant neurobiology is dedicated to gifted children, and there are also few studies on the value of edutainment videos. The 2005 Kaiser Family Foundation report *A Teacher in the Living Room,* underlines the point I have heard time and again from researchers of infant brain development and education on the effect of the bright baby videos: there is little adequate scholarship on these products' value over time.

What researchers *can* comfortably assert is that a false set of assumptions is at work. According to the blurry logic I described earlier, the total neglect of orphans is shown to be bad, and therefore superstimulation must be good. This is a false conflation, says Nelson; deprived infants who benefit from a move to an ordinary environment are being used to indicate the benefits of enrichment to children who grow up in ordinary or even "super" environments. "For many infants, there's an a priori enrichment in their daily lives," says Nelson. "What they see in *Baby Einstein,* and all of the edutainment DVDs, exists in the baby's ordinary environment." As long as you don't put a child in a closet, nutritionally deprive him, or cause trauma to his developing brain, he will naturally learn.

The proposition is that, say, if disadvantaged children are helped by exposure to age-appropriate enrichment, then advantaged children will be even more enriched by exposure to supersonic educational stimuli. Data on the value of early learning intervention for disadvantaged kids is also mapped onto the value of pumped-up learning for advantaged children, including a study in which three-year-olds in Early Head Start programs performed significantly better cognitively, linguistically, and emotionally than a similarly disadvantaged control group not enrolled in Early Head Start. But just because a child who lacks the ordinary stimulation of an everyday childhood and gets a great deal of negative stimulation may experience permanent damage, that does not mean that more stimulation is better for all kids. To put it in hothouse terms, a lack of water will kill an orchid–but so will a flood. Nevertheless, the makers of baby edutainment use a blurry syllogism in their efforts to beguile parents: Deprivation is bad; therefore, the opposite of deprivation is good.

The final criticism that researchers have made of the Baby Genius Edutainment Complex goes beyond the fact that the DVDs are not as educational as they claim: their widening use may actually prevent more effective learning from taking place. A University of Massachusetts researcher had one sample group of infants learn to use a puppet from a live person, while the other learned by watching a DVD. The tots who received live instruction learned to use the puppet immediately, but the infant video-watchers had to repeat their viewing six times before they learned the same skill. A number of scholars have also started to investigate whether the millions of infants and children who have grown up watching educational videos have actually been damaged by their new orientation to the television. One such scholar, Rhonda Clements, a professor of education at Manhattanville College and the former president of the American Association for the Child's Right to Play, recently conducted a study that found that 70 percent of the sample's mothers said that they themselves played every day outdoors when they were children, typically tag, hopscotch, and jumping rope, as compared with 31 percent of their children. And of the mothers who said their children played outdoors, only 22 percent played for three hours at a time or longer. The study concluded that today's level of indoor activity and play, even if it involves "learning," is deleterious to the children's young bodies and minds. (The study was financed by the detergent maker Wisk–perhaps in an effort to promote an increase in dirt and grass stains.)

But despite negative findings about time spent watching DVDs indoors, and the fuzziness of the edutainment product makers' claims, even the most sophisticated parents can be drawn to the Baby Edutainment Complex.

"There are some guarantees with these products," says Lynne Varner, a forty-two-year-old newspaper writer and mom who resides in Seattle. "There aren't guarantees in the world. My son may not see all the colors in the prism every day. He may go outside and see a green tree one day and a roaring bus the next day, but I have to hope that nature and life offer everything to him. I want our child to always be doing something that stimulates him. And so does everyone I know."

Varner's accumulation of educational toys started with Baby Einstein and grew from there to Baby BumbleBee toys purchased at the Imaginarium and the now-defunct Zany Brainy. The stores and products made reassuring guarantees that her kid was going to be smart, she says: Baby Einstein markets itself this way to the "überparents" she knows in Seattle and Palo Alto.

"I do believe that the brain has a certain clump of neurons firing, and that by the time he is five it will be too late," one women, an educated professional who is an avid consumer of these products, told me. "It sounds panicky, I know, but if those neurons are dying off . . . you have to get in there during the first three years. If my baby doesn't use it with a stimulating game or class, he is going to lose it." But her baby's neurons are going to die no matter what she does. They're supposed to die.

On Amazon.com, reviewers likewise emphasize that the videos are part of their responsibility to adequately enhance and stimulate their children. One writes about *Brainy Baby Left Brain,* "I come from a Montessori background and have very high standards regarding my child's education. I am discriminating about what I expose her to. The formative years are a crucial time in every child's development. . . . Now that she is three years old, she enjoys the more cognitive lessons in the video (even though it is all review for her!). . . . No longer do parents have to tolerate the use of mindless videos to 'occupy' their young ones. We now have the opportunity to actually EDUCATE our babies with a video. The child will LEARN something while watching this."

Another reviwer writes, "My 1-year-old is growing into a Brainy Baby, herself! How many 18-month-olds can tell you what an orangutan is, or the difference between a circle and an oval, or that the color of our van is 'silver'? My son could–from watching these videos!"

Of course, parents don't entirely trust the pitches from the companies. The Seattle mom recognizes that many of the pitches she receives for toys play upon her worst fears–that her children's brains will stop growing, that her children will become adults who fall through the cracks. "Unless something cataclysmic happens, our children won't be prisoners, or even drug addicts," says the mom. But she still buys *Baby Einstein,* Leapster, and the rest.

Many parents buy these products even as they remain skeptical about their claims. In 2004, I attended an educational-toy party in New York. The party's emcee, the self-proclaimed "Discovery Toy Lady," was named Simone Weissman. Weissman is an enthusiastic woman with curly hair, a loud girlish voice, and a more-than-passing resemblance to Bette Midler. She sold her products Tupperware-style: plastic toys, plush toys, and flash cards in a sea of primary colors, laid out before her on a table in a sunset-suffused thirtieth-floor apartment. The partygoers, women of thirty or fortyish, wore stretchy comfort clothes–not a plunging shirtdress in sight. As they drank wine, a wailing baby provided the party's sound track from behind a set of screens. While the baby cried, Discovery Toy Lady Weissman pointed out the products that provoke "fine and gross mental skills." She moved on to a toy that used to be merely sentimental: a stuffed bear. But this teddy was named Classical Casey, and played famous melodies from six classical composers. He wasn't sold as being all about love: he also strengthened an infant's "sensory capacities," Weissman said. The mothers looked on, seemingly unimpressed by Classical Casey. No one reached for their purses, even when she showed the group flash cards called Think It Through Tiles. The cards, Weissman said, were good for studying for the ERBs–the Educational Records Bureau test for private preschool admission, tests that are given to children as young as three. The mothers at this particular party weren't planning on sending their children to private schools, but upon hearing that other mothers were using these flash cards and had seen great improvement in their children's scores, they perked up. They didn't want to fail to do due diligence for their kids. Weissman said that the cards' buyers wanted their children to have an edge. "These moms worry that their children aren't doing the right things, you know?" she said.

But doing things "right" isn't the whole story. It seems to me that the Baby Genius Edutainment Complex exists, in part, out of a deeper fear than that of infants losing their learning opportunities. It responds to adults' fear of children's boredom. The edutainment products are, at bottom, meant to reduce unproductive boredom.

But what exactly is boredom, especially in infancy and childhood? The psychotherapist and writer Adam Phillips writes in *On Kissing, Tickling, and Being Bored* that the bored child is waiting "for an experience of anticipation" and that being bored, rather than an inadequacy, is an opportunity and perhaps even a capacity: boredom is "a developmental achievement for the child."

"It is one of the most oppressive demands of adults that the child should be interested," writes Phillips, "rather than take time to find what interests him. Boredom is integral to the process of taking one's time." But taking one's time and waiting for desire or interest to return goes against the grain of the new improved infancy, and the regimen of infant stimulation.

Talking about childhood boredom is not boring–I find this out discoursing on dullness in the sun-filled office of Dona Matthews, coauthor of *Being Smart about Gifted Children: A Guidebook for Parents and Educators* and the director of Hunter College's Center for Gifted Studies and Education. Matthews is fifty-something, clad in a stripy sweater. Her office has the upbeat atmosphere common to those who work with children: a blue plate full of bright orange nectarines, an orchid, a colorful poster, and Matthews herself, with a bright smile and winningly tousled hair. "Parents are always saying, 'My kids are bored or understimulated,'" she says. "Sometimes it is a parent-induced boredom, where the parents are centered on entertaining the child." Like many in the gifted business, Matthews has the air of a Boomer Vivant. "Boredom is essential. It's important to encourage children to find things to do, and a commonality with others. We call it do-nothing time. It is necessary to be bored to find out what you really want to do." Buddhists call it non-doing.

There are even experts who argue that a certain amount of boredom is important for kids' development. Fred Dick, the developmental cognitive neuroscientist, notes that babies' emotional states tend to change, and thus an infant's caregivers should attend to a child but should not feel obliged to provide *constant* stimulation to their children.

One specialist in gifted education suggests that an adult finger can be just as stimulating for an infant as the whirling dervish of rainbows on a *Baby*

Einstein DVD. Charles Zorn, the neuropsychological educational consultant, suggests that parents who aren't sold on the need for stimulating DVDs can see that the perfect educational baby toys are everywhere: keys on a chain. They jingle. Babies get excited, are aurally and visually stimulated, and learn to identify a shape that will have lifelong application. Others suggest playing with a broom and dustpan.

Such simple pleasures, which adults find boring–and this is part of it: our inability, as adults, to remember how easily we were entertained during our own infancies–are often just what infants need. Their systems are ready for simplicity, not for a deluge of diffuse stimuli.

Why the aversion to boredom? It belongs to a larger fear of emptiness, a fascination with whirring cities, technologies, a distrust of the "dull" repetitions of experience. As Patricia Meyer Spacks writes in her book of literary criticism, *Boredom,* "The diagnoses (self-diagnoses and evaluations by others) of middle class adolescents and housewives as sufferers from boredom exemplify the imaginative functions boredom serves in our culture. . . . The claim of boredom now locates the causes of conduct firmly outside the self."

"If sleep is the apogee of physical relaxation," writes philosopher and cultural critic Walter Benjamin, "boredom is the apogee of mental relaxation. Boredom is the dream bird that hatches the egg of experience. A rustling in the leaves drives him away. His nesting places–the activities that are intimately associated with boredom–are already extinct in the cities and are declining in the country as well."

Indeed, a number of childhood edutainment products are equivalent to a mechanical rustling in the leaves, a buzzing, bleeping thing called computerized enrichment that drives away the dream bird that could otherwise have hatched the egg of true human experience. What is that experience for infants? Perhaps it's keys on a chain. Perhaps it's what they see between the rails of their cribs. But it is also letting the infant alone with her thoughts, her own developing self, rather than providing external stimulus.

The fight against boredom, the insistence on external stimulation whenever possible, is clearly tied to a concern about time. This concern–or, perhaps, fear–drives the Baby Genius Edutainment Complex: the fear that time is being wasted, that windows of development are slamming shut, that time for learning is running out.

. . .

In the Baby Genius Edutainment Complex, the palliative for childish boredom or time-wasting is always a new product, and it can seem that price is no object. In effect, these products are mostly intended for the reasonably well off. The Time Tracker, for instance, costs $35. BabyPlus runs $150. The Leapster Multimedia Learning System is $70. The LeapPad Plus Writing and Microphone System is $59.99. The by now classic Baby Einstein videos–*Baby Mozart, Baby Bach, Baby Beethoven, Baby Einstein Language Nursery,* and Baby Einstein Language Discovery Cards–come as a special set at a cost of $69.99.

Like a number of other elements of precociously gifted childhood, which may include private school admissions, overstructured activity, protoprofessional training, and participation in competitions, edutainment products are the first items in a two-tiered system where children are divided into have and have-less. The infants inculcated with the early-reading DVDs and flash cards are supposed to ultimately deploy their precocious knowledge to get ahead of other reasonably affluent children. The paradox is that infants whose parents have the wherewithal to purchase these products are most likely already ahead of other children. Of course, some of the products, like "smart" baby formulas, are marketed to working-class parents as well–taking advantage, perhaps, of parents who also want to help their children succeed but don't have the money to send them to private schools or live in a place with good public schools or spend a lot of time with them because they have to work. In the United States, breast-feeding rates are rising, and the formula market is shrinking. The smart-baby formulas have thus offered formula manufacturers a much-needed edge. Marion Nestle, professor of food studies at New York University, told me that this is why the formula companies now "do everything they can get away with to convince moms that breastfeeding is inconvenient or impossible. They fought hard for permission to add the new nutrients because they can use them as an additional sales strategy." Now a large share of formulas contain them, up to 50 percent of baby formulas by some counts, and mothers of all social classes are buying them. The smart formulas' popularity seems to me to indicate that many of the mothers who can't afford the classes and the schools and the tutors, or even

DVDs and toys, still want to imagine that they are "giving" their children the gift of giftedness.

The DVDs and the range of toys are just the beginning of the expenditure. After all, the educational-kid-toy-and-video industry is the equivalent of a gateway drug into the larger giftedness culture, the first stop on the voyage on which children of America are shaped into champions.

THREE

The Educated Infant: Classes for an Improved Childhood

As I stared awe-struck at the infant, Tom spoke wistfully of her future. . . . "She should have a musical discipline and she should learn to speak French." On hearing this, my spirits soared. "Let me teach her the cello!" I said without a moment's hesitation.

CLAUDE KENNESON, *Music Prodigies: Perilous Journeys, Remarkable Lives*

On a weekend morning in May, a group of four- and five-year-olds run in an orderly row, chasing a soccer ball. One boy kicks the ball, and his teammates, clad in yellow vests, scrimmage with their rivals, who wear blue-and-white jerseys. As they race around the grass in a Redmond, Washington, sports arena, the young crew is markedly deft and calm, without the tears or clumsiness that would seem natural to this age group. But then, this is no random game. It's a soccer micro-league. And these four- and five-year-olds are not novices to the sport. Many here have played soccer since they were eighteen months old.

Across the country in New York City, a dozen toddlers are similarly hard at work. It is a weekday morning, and they are greeted with the exhortation, "Good morning, Broadway Babies!" by three pretty young women. Trained actors outfitted in cowboy hats, the women then boom out their musical greetings to the tots: "Hello, MacKenzie! Hello, Sebastian! Hello, Heather!" At Broadway Babies, a pianist bangs out show tunes from a different Broadway musical each week, as parents, nannies, and infants sing along. The program describes itself as offering "a carefully written curriculum guided by highly accredited teachers and pediatricians" in order to "develop motor skills, color and letter recognition, counting, socialization, etc. At Broadway Babies, a 7-month-old is already tapping out rhythms to 'Lion King' while a 3-year-old is doing the hand-jive to 'Grease.'" Broadway Babies enrolls infants as young as a few weeks and kids "graduate" from the program at age three or four.

During the class, the teacher trio tries to make good on that promise. They make jazz hands, and the babies accompany them, Fosse-style. Various baby stimulation materials are handed to the tots intermittently, to go along with the "musical"–plastic suns, microphones, egg shakers, and the like. These are, according to a Broadway Babies teacher, implements and prods for the infants' tactile development, visual and audio stimulation, and color development.

This week's show is *Annie Get Your Gun,* so each Broadway Baby is also given a cowboy hat in red, green, or yellow to go along with the egg shakers et al. Donning their hats, they "begin a relationship with the musical." The three young actor-teachers are sure earning their SAG member fees, belting out snippets of songs in thick, assimilated western twangs, then hooting and hollering and finally making horse, cow, and chicken sounds. On an easel near them, a sign declares, "I'm just a Broadway Baby / Walking off my tired feet / Poundin' Forty Second Street / To be in a show."

Today's infant and toddler classes certainly are a show.

Like the edutainment videos and toys, these classes, courses, and tutoring services have exploded onto the scene in recent years. They now dot the landscape of early childhood all over America, and have become a key part of the giftedness industry. The classes aim to stimulate infants' and children's minds and bodies. The idea is to start children's training so young that they are likelier to discover and nurture notable talents, and be set on the path to excellence and specialness. But these classes are not, as they might have been in the past, envisioned as the first stepping-stones to an adult specialization as a musician or a soccer player or a musical theater thesp. A rhetoric of "roundedness" tends to accompany the classes–the idea that toddlers and kids should be given classes in as many areas as possible, and stimulated in classroom settings as early and often as possible. Parents I spoke with considered one class a season to be too limiting. *Their* toddlers should be exposed to soccer, music, baby sign language, karate, *and* French–in concert, and as early as possible. Lurking beneath the surface of this obsession with classes is a nearly Hellenic notion of the total child who will become an adult of superior ability and mastery. It means that eighteen- and twenty-four-month-olds and their two- to three-year-old elders attend toddler soccer classes at the national franchise Lil' Kickers at venues around the country, from Valley Forge, Pennsylvania, to Hillsboro, Oregon. Once a week, for forty minutes, the younger soccer students walk backward, stomp on bubbles, and swerve around red parachutes, working on "gross motor skills." The two- and three-year- olds are encouraged to pretend the net is a hungry hippo that they are feeding watermelons–a Mommy-and-me nice way of getting them to learn how to score goals. They balance on one foot and kick a soccer ball, and they dribble the balls down the field–actions intended to promote foot-eye coordination.

Though wildly popular, soccer provides only one of many physical training grounds for the creation of better babies and children. Gymboree starts accepting children at the age of ten months: the Gymboree infant struggles with early walking skills, among other things. The My Gym chain in Los Angeles offers the Tiny Tykes program for babies aged three months and up, which "focuses on your infant's natural movement abilities" until ultimately they graduate to the development of those much-touted "fine and gross motor coordination" skills.

Infants are now also taking classes in second and third languages. In New York City, they go to Musical Kids, where they learn songs in English, Japanese, Spanish, Korean, and French. A preferred school in Los Angeles is the Baby-Genius Art & Languages School, which offers English, Spanish, French, Italian, German, Hebrew, Farsi, Russian, and Chinese. The students start their regimen at ten months. The school has been jokingly referred to as "UCLA for babies." Some instructors have master's degrees or Ph.D.s. The school even offers a trilingual preschool alternative program.

And while music classes have always existed for the young, today even newborns are taking them. Broadway Babies is one example. Another is Houston's Suzuki Baby Music program for newborns, which, like the edutainment companies, calls upon unnamed studies to support its claims: "Current research shows that babies who are exposed to music form stronger neural connections and are therefore more able to handle higher-level thinking skills later in life." (The Pre-Natal Music and Relaxation class appeals to pregnant mothers with great aspirations for their yet-to-be-born kids: the school claims this class is a must because "a sense of hearing is strongly developed in the womb.") Music programs range from noncompetitive, open-enrollment classes like those at Broadway Babies to music schools and programs that emphasize infant talent development. One of the preeminent programs is the Diller-Quaile School of Music in New York City, which teaches students as young as one year old and has an application process that begins a year before classes–which for some applicants means right after birth. A class of two- and three-year-olds at Diller-Quaile displays the idyllic appearance a parent might seek in such a school. Most of the young girls are decked out in bows, floral cotton dresses, and shiny Mary Jane shoes. The teacher has a classically trained voice adorned with a touch of vibrato, and she is using it, and its musical accompaniment, purely for the toddlers' enjoyment. "Five little ducks: Quack, quack, quack," sings the teacher, Karie Brown, with a luscious trill. "The big black cat goes stalking, stalking."

Brown then does a light-opera rendition of a rather prosaic line: "We have some fishies for the children." Brown wields a box of goldfish crackers. The children look up eagerly, by all appearances more stimulated by the promise of a snack than they are by the music. I wander into another room, where Diller-Quaile tots are encouraged to paint a free-form notation of the live piano music they are hearing. They draw waves to signify the movement of sound. At three these children learn Eurhythmics, a method that introduces them to symbolic representation, or, as the school's director puts it, "meaningful, invented forms of notation." When they are four, the school interviews its wards to obtain a portrait of how ready each is to start formal music lessons. An early childhood development expert fills out the picture with an emotional assessment.

Enrichment classes for music, art, languages, or sports operate alongside the growing field of preschool academic tutoring. Big tutoring chains are now expanding their reach to take in younger pupils. Kaplan Inc., long known for its SAT classes, now operates a chain of educational centers called Score. In 2005, 20 percent of Score's students were between the ages of four and six. In the same year, the educational tutoring chain Sylvan launched its preschool-age Beginning Reading program. And the youngest children of all attend the junior program of the tutoring franchise Kumon North America–they can be as young as two years old. Kumon was founded by the Japanese educator Toru Kumon fifty years ago and now operates worldwide: 130,000 students attend their U.S. centers alone, and 20,000 of them are five and under.

Soon after the program started, I visited one of the Junior Kumon classes. A gaggle of three-, four-, and five-year-olds circled words in workbooks. They drew their lines, concentrating fiercely. Two young Japanese-born teachers reviewed their responses, murmuring encouragement.

Junior Kumon students take a standardized curriculum: they must finish a timed assignment without error. They take twice-weekly lessons of fifteen minutes in length in math or reading or both. Kumon ultimately publishes a list of its twenty most proficient students per age level, starting with the two-year-olds: at the Kumon school I visited in New York City, the walls were posted with the names of the children who were achieving the furthest above their grade levels. These names were tacked up beneath posters meant to inspire the children, with slogans like "Math Reading Success" and "I Want to Be Prime Minister." According to the Junior Kumon administrator for New York City, the parents she meets want their three- and four-year-olds to learn "organization, discipline, time management!"

Finally, there are the ubiquitous baby sign language (BSL) classes, where hearing infants learn a communication system based on American Sign Language (ASL), and sometimes even learn ASL itself. The idea of teaching ASL to hearing babies derives from the 1970s research of W. Joseph Garcia, who recognized that deaf infants who used sign language to communicate expressed themselves in a more refined fashion than same-age hearing infants did by speaking. The movement sprang up around best-selling books by Garcia and others, such as *Baby Signs, Sign with Your Baby: How to Communicate with Infants before They Can Speak,* and *Baby Sign Language Basics.* The expansion of baby sign language–now there are classes all around the country–had a lot to do with the heady claims of BSL teachers Joan Acredelo and Susan

Goodwyn. In their book *Baby Sign Language,* they describe a study funded by the National Institutes of Health, published in their paper "The Long-Term Impact of Symbolic Gesturing during Infancy on IQ at Age 8." The study used the intelligence test known as the WISC-II to measure infant development, and found a 12-point advantage among a rather small sample of children who had learned to sign. Adherents believe that baby signing leads to intelligence enhancement because the brain is working long before speech arrives. Ostensibly, learning sign language can help infants communicate more effectively, thus rendering them less likely to cry or whine: an infant can learn twenty signs by the age of one, and eighty signs by the age of two. Its practitioners claim it also helps children's long-term language development, leading to better reading skills, and that BSL and baby ASL are a particular boon to bright children, as an active infancy is better than passive infancy. BSL, they say, can give infants a sense of being someone who can cause an effect, and thus helps them early on to see themselves as effective in the world.

Each city has its own premier class. In Houston, Texas, there's BabyCanSign. In Seattle, the local favorite is ASL teacher Nancy Hanauer. When I visited her class, a toddler was showing a group of parents and infants what he had learned. He did the sign for *more:* both hands in a semi-flattened O and then put together. In the sun-filled room, his fellow infant pupils looked dazed, perhaps impressed by the infant's mastery. His nanny–a youngish white woman with incredibly long hair, a 1990s grungy demeanor, and a tattoo of a wedding ring around her fourth finger–rewarded the young scholar with a biscuit. Hanauer reviewed the signs for *cracker* ("cracking" an elbow by brushing one hand against one's bent elbow) and *more water* (putting the right hand in the shape of the letter W and touching one's mouth with the index finger, then repeating). Then the parents and caregivers displayed flash cards depicting a gorilla, a sheep, a squirrel, a snake, and a frog, accompanied by the American Sign Language sign for each animal, while their infants looked on.

I wondered what the teacher and the parents thought their children got out of it, and asked Judith Anderson Wright, who runs baby sign language classes in San Diego and taught sign language to her daughter. She believes learning baby sign language has given her daughter a much longer attention span than that of other children her age. "If I had had to wait until she could talk to explain something like a chick being born to her–I explained how a chick is born from an egg with sign language–a little learning opportunity would have disappeared," said Wright. What Wright and other practitioners of baby sign language have in common with those of the other baby-class disciplines is a belief that there is brilliance locked within every preverbal child. The infants are unable to articulate their dazzling visions due to a stumbling block: infancy itself.

Infant and toddler classes and schools and the aspiration to improve the preverbal or quasi-verbal child can seem harmless. But they also do have their ominous side, as understood by Aldous Huxley, whose classic 1932 novel *Brave New World* depicted the Central London Hatchery and Conditioning Centre, a toddler school of a sort that predestines, conditions, and "decants" babies as socialized human beings. In *Brave New World,* children come preranked, from Alpha to Epsilon, from future world controllers to future sewage workers. The infant nurseries in *Brave New World* are called Neo-Pavlovian Conditioning Rooms, and the center's children are conditioned by being forced to memorize rote information and phrases.

The recent real-life history of precocious childhood learning and advanced early instruction is, of course, more well-meaning than the dungeon-like hatcheries of *Brave New World.* Starting in 1964, advocates for Project Head Start and then Early Head Start argued the value of early education for disadvantaged kids.

At around that time, the Japanese pedant Shinichi Suzuki also popularized teaching toddlers music. He called his method "Talent Education": the child must listen to music, practice with parents or kin, and play for an audience whenever possible. One of Suzuki's acquaintances, an American named Glenn Doman, was also part of the construction of the idea of the educated infant in the early 1960s. It was in 1964 that he published his multimillion-copy-selling book *How to Teach Your Baby to Read: The Gentle Revolution.* In its pages, Doman set down the watchwords of his "gentle revolution": tiny children want to learn to read. Of the period from birth to five, Doman writes, "It is during this period that [a child] can learn to speak a foreign language, even as many as five, which he at present fails to learn through high school and college. They should be offered to him." Doman also describes the newborn child as "an exact duplicate of an empty electronic computer. . . . A computer is able to place such information in either permanent or temporary storage. So is a child." Doman's thinking and pedagogy is one clear precursor of today's giftedness industry. The computer metaphor for the bright baby's brain continues to get a lot of play, famously in a 1996 *Newsweek* article that exemplified early-learning mania. (According to that *Newsweek* cover story, childhood experiences "wire the circuits of the brain as surely as a programmer at a keyboard reconfigures the circuits in a computer.")

Glenn Doman ran a school for children with brain injuries in a suburb of Philadelphia, and in 1978 he extended his program to "well children," with courses for parents and infants called How to Multiply Your Baby's Intelligence. Since then, nearly ten thousand parents have taken this course in the United States, and it is "also offered in Italy, Japan, Mexico, and Singapore." The programs and the school itself now go by the name of the Institutes for the Achievement of Human Potential–and are run by Janet Doman, Glenn Doman's fifty-something daughter.

The IAHP's ideology runs in curious parallel to the one used to sell BabyPlus and products like it–studies of deprived or damaged infants are extended to "normal" or well children to encourage the parent to buy the enriching product. The Evan Thomas Institute–the part of the IAHP devoted to "well children"–helped to popularize the notion of "balanced development" for the very young: according to the institute, a child's brain grows rapidly until the age of six, and then the ability to absorb information slows down drastically. By this thinking, it becomes crucial that instruction in reading, math, encyclopedic study, foreign languages, and music and gymnastics all begin long before six. The Domans argue that gymnastics, in particular, enhances the brain by developing what they call the "vestibular mechanism"–the neurological and inner ear functions responsible for balance. Development of this mechanism, they say, improves "coordination and control of the body. . . . This development of the vestibular mechanism can then be applied to any physical and/or academic activity. The Institutes teach that when one area of the brain grows, so does the capacity of the other areas." In the IAHP parlance, great gymnasts are "vestibular geniuses."

In addition to courses that teach parents how to make their children smarter, in the Evan Thomas Early Development On-Campus Program toddlers are schooled in all of the vital disciplines, plus things like violin and Latin. They compete in a triathlon including running and swimming. One of the school's most prized adult graduates was brought into the fold through a How to Multiply Your Baby's Intelligence course when she was six months old, and within a year was learning reading and mathematics, encountering Bit of Intelligence cards, taking music, walking and running, swimming, Japanese, and gymnastics. At two, she spoke in full paragraphs and recited the "The Owl and the Pussycat," and she began to play the violin at two and a half.

Upon entering the IAHP, a neo-Gothic school building littered with images of mothers and children–for instance, a 1960s wood sculpture of a mother and child embracing–I was immediately drawn into a class where babies were learning eighth notes, octaves, clefs, musical notations, and the sounds "Lulu, Lulu, Lulu" as their mothers sat near them. Colleen Kumpf, the music teacher and an Evan Thomas Institute and IAHP graduate, led the students on the violin. The mothers called out their children's names–and here the children's names seemed to be even more unusual than the Parkers and Dakotas one might find elsewhere: one was named Remington, while another, a graduate, was named Marlowe, after the Elizabethan playwright. All around the school building, I saw very young children performing handstands without the wall. "What's your goal? To straighten arms and straighten legs!" barked the instructor. If they didn't manage to do this, then they had to perform a thirty-second handstand against the wall. (The Domans also have happened to publish a book on the subject, *How to Teach Your Baby to Be Physically Superb: From Birth to Age Six; The Gentle Revolution,* which presumably should be used in tandem with *How to Give Your Baby Encyclopedic Knowledge: More Gentle Revolution* and *How to Teach Your Baby Math: The Gentle Revolution.*) These children are five or so; most began attending as infants.

During my visits to the institute, I would recall briefly Jodie Foster's film *Little Man Tate* and the hothouse school where six-year-old prodigy Fred Tate did his advanced math experiments, surrounded by equally bright albeit strange peers, his easeful childhood a distant memory. But the IAHP philosophy does not seem to acknowledge the possibility of any negative social or emotional effects for all this hard-core training. In fact, its promotional materials state, "It is now very clear that the children who are truly bright, knowledgeable, capable, and confident are the nicest and kindest children. They are full of the characteristics for which we love children."

In another classroom, a mother volunteer was drawing a Cartesian plane. A nurse who lived in New Jersey, this mother drove her kids back and forth to the school for two and a half hours each day. She was not teaching at the school purely out of passion or altruism: while the institute is free, the terms of entrance are that parents work there and also wear a uniform: black pants, white shirt, and a tan blazer. All the students also wear uniforms–white shirts, blue pants, and stripy rainbow sweater vests, along with armbands connoting their rank. One highly skilled child's colored armband reads "shakijin" in honor of her high achievement, and when students "graduate" from certain programs, they begin to wear armbands with Japanese writing upon them.

A similar regimentation extends to teachers and administrators. For instance, Janet Doman is called *sensei,* the Japanese word for both master and teacher, by her students. I speak with Doman after her class in what she calls "Daddy's office," although Daddy Doman is retired. Doman's hair is severely pinned back, in a 1950s style. With her pink-red lipstick and matching skirt suit, beige pumps, and hose, she looks dressed for an Eisenhower-era melodrama–ready to play a neighbor, perhaps, in a Douglas Sirk film.

Doman's emphasis is on parental involvement, heavy-duty intellectual and physical stimulation, and a balanced curriculum. "Mother needs to stimulate them from an early age, to open those pathways," she says. "Yes, I mean 'Mother,' in as much as it is culturally accepted that children should be raised by their mothers!" Doman insists on the necessity of a maternal presence rather than–as is the case for so many children in a complex world–a father, a nonrelated caregiver, or nonmaternal kin. She almost seems to be waiting for me to flinch. "Mothers have to justify what they do," she says. "A mother of three babies who is extremely healthy doesn't have to be a cardiac surgeon as well."

Doman has equally strong opinions about the programs and products she names as pale imitations of the IAHP: "It's troubling that others are saying it now, and we've been saying it for forty years. Now Baby Einstein and the commercial world are trying to cash in on it, but you can't buy a device and make it happen," she says. She stresses the importance of the first three years once again. "We say, 'Teach a baby to read.' Those who say, 'Don't push kids'? That's an argument for mediocrity, that's an argument against differentiation."

Whether or not she is accurate in positioning the institute as the progenitor of today's educated baby movement, Doman's conjunction of her school's cosmology and the Baby Einstein product line certainly makes sense. There is an obvious link between enrichment classes and videos and the like. Today, parents who send their children to these programs sometimes subscribe to the same thinking about brain "plasticity" and "absorbency" that the companies selling DVDs and toys promote, what educator Maria Montessori might have called "the absorbent mind," although it sounded better when she wrote it in Italian. Both the bright-baby DVDs and the better-baby classes depend on a valorization of the absorbency of toddler minds.

They both also depend, I think, upon some things that are going on not in the minds of children, but in those of the adults who care for them. First there is the worry that we adults are insufficiently flexible or speedy, accompanied by the fantasy about educating our offspring so well that they won't be stymied, as we seem to be, by their limits of mind and body. Just as some wealthy people dwell on the miseries of the poor to make themselves feel rich, or men compare themselves to women to feel more masculine, the infantile fluidity of mind and body can reassure an adult of her own stability as well as provide an illusion of escape from her own adult limits. And better still, if a child is infinitely moldable, then we can claim the right to decide what that child is, and what kind of adult he will become. No wonder, then, that Doman uses the word *options* frequently, saying her programs reflects the desire of parents "to give their kids options." In fact, the IAHP makes even more comforting, if grandiose, claims about the potential of its programs, promising that making better babies (presumably, in the IAHP mold) will make a better world: the objective, it says, of its "Gentle Revolution" is "to give all parents the knowledge required to make highly intelligent, extremely capable, and delightful children, and by so doing, to make a highly humane, sane and decent world."

So much of the cant of baby classes and toddler tutoring is designed to appeal to adults, not children. The premise is that these classes are providing children with choices, and with instruction that will lead to new capacities for the child. Of course, whether a toddler or a child would choose these classes independently is not always so clear–after all, what is existential choice for a newborn? And while giftedness culture advocates developing a full palette of sharply honed skills in childhood, is being a Renaissance kid, rather than playing or even focusing on one childlike passion, the best way to spend one's early youth?

The contours and limits of a young child's free will remains an open question. But there are plenty of scholars of early education–and adults who were educated intensively in special classes, starting in early childhood–whose accounts complicate the sunny promises of the infant schools and classes.

Some experts critique the notion that toddlers and even older children should strive to be well-rounded. According to Tracy L. Cross, a professor of gifted studies at Ball State University, one of the "myths" of giftedness is that a child should or must be balanced in his talents and interests. The "introverted gifted student" with a talent for computers can inspire adults to "drag the child away from her passion to get her to participate in something she may loathe," Cross writes, as if channeling the anger of the prodded child into prose. He concludes: "Much of the research on successful gifted adults has revealed that they spent considerable amounts of time, often alone, in their passion areas as children."

One of the most renowned experts in elite performance, Florida State University professor of psychology Anders Ericsson, notes that adults who are excellent mathematicians, musicians, hockey players, Scrabble players, and occasionally even writers tend to have been dedicated practitioners of their crafts early. Elite performers in domains with a heavy motor component, like skiing, skating, and music, started at even more extremely precocious ages. Ericsson believes, for example, that perfect pitch can be obtained only if a musician started playing between the ages three and five.

Even so, Ericsson doesn't think such instruction is always felicitous. In recent years, parents have sent him videocassettes of their children performing exceptionally, among them a sixteen-month-old swinging a golf club. Ericsson was not sure infant putting was such a good idea. Ultimately, Ericsson has come to the conclusion that parents who decide what their children should do are working against themselves. "It has to be the individual who wants to do it, or they won't reach a high level, because they have to be committed to continued improvement and deliberative practice," he says. "What sets apart people who are successful from those who are not is internal motivation. Nursing that motivation is key. The 'giftedness' perspective doesn't have means to explain how important that is."

Her own internal motivation, even despite her parents' wishes, is particularly important for Jennifer Koh, a former music prodigy and now, at thirty, a highly accomplished professional violinist. The *Strad,* the classical music industry journal, called her "a scorching talent that should on no account be missed." Her first CD hit the stores when she was only twenty-four. Her second CD, 2004's *Violin Fantasies,* garnered raves for Koh's interpretation of Robert Schumann's Fantasie in C Major for Violin and Piano, Ornette Coleman's *Trinity–Fantasy for Solo Violin,* and works by Schubert and Schoenberg.

Koh's performing life started early. She took classes in multiple areas as soon as her parents could send her, and by the age of eight she was competing not only in local music competitions but also in rhythmic gymnastics, ballet, ice-skating, and swimming. She also learned French and Russian– "anything my parents couldn't do in Korea during the war," she says. Her musical training certainly paid off. Wearing a light pastel Easter dress with puffy sleeves, she played a solo with the Chicago Symphony at the age of eleven. When she was fourteen, the great violinist Isaac Stern urged her to go to the Curtis Institute of Music.

Nonetheless, Koh felt herself to be a source of *han,* the Korean word for unhappiness. According to Koh, her parents didn't see her achievements as positive because they did not view music as a viable career. She was intensely pursuing what had become not only her natural talent but her own "passion area." But they resented what they regarded as her musician's impracticality, and were reluctant to reward her for it.

Koh is contained and slim, with impeccable dark lipstick, spiky short black hair, and a well-cut cardigan buttoned almost to the top, so fashionable that her violin, at times lying in a case at her feet, looks like a modish accessory. Yet her polished appearance belies a tumultuous past. Koh left home at sixteen to strike out on her own. She gained early admission to Oberlin College, including a scholarship with free room and board. At the end of the year she tied for the top prize awarded that year in the famous Tchaikovsky competition, earning a few thousand dollars. Her family did not celebrate this achievement. When Koh left home, she stopped speaking with her parents for a while, and to this day her relations with them are strained. She describes with incredulity people who talk to their parents as often as once a week.

"It was very difficult for my father to accept that I was an American and a musician," says Koh. "My parents don't see kids as individuals. Sometimes parents think of children as just an extension of them. When people would compliment me as a child, my parents would say, 'Oh no, she's not smart.'"

Her mouth turns down at the corners, an expression of unhappiness cracking the glaze of refined good taste. But it's just a momentary mood. Paradoxically, Koh sees a positive effect in the fact that her parents pushed her intensely to succeed as a child, but then gave up on her as a teenager because they did not approve of music as a line of work. Her parents' unwillingness to see her as a musician allowed her to become one, she says—even as it exacted other costs. "Music was something I owned myself. I was always doing it for myself. It was my own world, the way I escaped from everything. Music gave back to me," she says. "Music approved."

Koh's success fits with what Anders Ericsson asserts about the role of early and adult deliberative practice in the creation of elite talent: parents must foster a child's independent interest in a domain. A child should be able to continue with the activity after the parent "no longer has power over them," as Ericsson puts it. "The child must have agency," he says. "They have to have confidence in their ability to keep improving."

Parents raising children, "gifted" or otherwise, want them to become successful adults—to grow up happy, without deformed characters. Koh's parents inadvertently ensured her long-term success by opposing her prodigy. It was not, she says, the worst thing they could have done for her.

Ericsson notes that even the child who is allowed to find her own internal motivation and dedicates herself to her lessons with fervor will likely wind up disappointed. As he puts it, "Even the most highly skilled musicians, who have spent twenty-five years trying to become solo performers, have to settle for playing in the orchestra." Ericsson has heard from his research subjects that it was so much easier for them to be considered remarkably gifted or to have an unusual level of mastery over a domain when they were young.

Having been special when one was young, and never as special again, can shadow the former child pupil. I thought of one woman, Donna Lynne Champlin, now thirty-five. Champlin is a theater actor whose physical quality and singing voice, a belting soprano, makes her a "Judy Garland minx," as she rightly describes herself. She started taking tap-dancing lessons at three, then moved on to jazz and lyrical dance lessons, and by four she was competing around the country. She added piano lessons at seven, flute at ten, and voice at eleven. When she was very young, Champlin enjoyed competition and lessons because she excelled at them. "I was three years old going on thirty-five," she says. "I wondered about other children: Where was their drive, damn it?"

By her own account, she grew into an extremely competitive young adult, the sort who would cry at a play not because it was phosphorescently tragic or oh-so-gorgeous, but because, she says, she herself was not up there onstage. Today, Champlin is a working actor; she gets plaudits for performances in plays and musicals. Yet there is still a sense within her that, given her years of lessons and labor and her early rewards, she ought to be at the forefront of contemporary theater–a feeling that makes ordinary life and work pale in comparison.

Some experts object to early learning on other grounds. Beyond setting in motion a lifetime of searing and most likely unrealizable ambition for greatness, they believe such classes are actually bad for infant development. Kathy Pasek-Hirsh, a developmental psychologist at Temple University and author of several books on early learning, including *Einstein Never Used Flashcards,* has been looking into the classes' developmental value, and has concluded that not only do they tend to be a waste of money, they also "go against developmental psychology." Infants don't learn in class settings, she says, but rather from negotiating the world–stretching, reaching, conversing for the first time with their peers. She echoes many of the criticisms lodged against the baby edutainment products: "With the classes and the DVDs, we have substituted passive learning for active learning." Pasek-Hirsh is even more cynical regarding the more refined intellectual and physical claims of the classes. Baby sign language teachers often suggest that their classes improve an infant's IQ: Pasek-Hirsh asks how that is possible, given the impossibility of accurately tabulating a newborn's or young toddler's IQ. She also believes playing in the backyard is a superior activity to soccer or gym classes. "A parent who takes their child to these and other classes outsources parenting to activities and experts," Pasek-Hirsh concludes.

Toddler class instructors are familiar with criticism like Pasek-Hirsh's. They see aggressive parents as the ones at fault: parents who imagine their children will hop over developmental milestones, and those who like to create invidious comparisons between their own and other children. While they advocate for early learning, even they acknowledge that many things are not developmentally right for very young children–a fact, they say, that some parents refuse to accept. "We are educating the parents when the parents are asking, 'Why aren't the kids playing soccer yet?'" says Ty Redinger, director of the Redmond, Washington, Lil' Kickers. "These are parents who can't wait to get their children involved as young as eighteen months. At seventeen months they are saying, 'Only a month away' about Lil' Kickers enrollment. Some of the parents have this idea that their kid is going to be the next Pelé. They don't get it. They are telling us there's not enough soccer here. We know what the kids need. We know parents that are on the extreme side and are asking, 'Why aren't they scrimmaging more?' We tell those parents: Your kids, they are three and four, they don't understand teams, they don't understand 'my side,' 'your side.' Being competitive is slowly developed–at four and five, some are ready, some are not."

"Sometimes, parents will tell their two- or three-year-old to copy the way the teacher is doing it and quash the child's own creativity," mused Karie Brown, a Diller-Quaille toddler music teacher. "The parents guide their hands and hold their hands and get them to play it this way to the beat. We have to teach the parents that their child doesn't have to copy the perfect way Claire plays. We like to affirm the way all the children hit the sticks together to a beat."

But the instructors don't only see competitive parents. They also see parents attending classes for the community and sociality they offer. One of the bright-eyed young lovelies on the Broadway Babies staff explained to me of her students' mothers, "These moms want to get out there!" The mothers I spoke to at Lil' Kickers met friends there, they said. ("The parents are doing it because all of their friends are doing it," agrees Redinger.) In fact, some of the early learning programs even resemble unintentional social communities, coalescing around toddler achievement. As Robert Putnam described in *Bowling Alone,* historical American communities have fallen away–all the Lion's Clubs and the Rotaries–and adults have had to create their own newfangled communities in various ways. For instance, at the Seattle baby sign language class I visited, much of the class work seemed intended to amuse the parents in attendance, helping them cohere into a mini instant community, especially when the teacher taught the parents and nannies the sign for "divorce."

But the most obvious parental desire of all behind these infant classes is the creation of a well-rounded, high-achieving kid. A father of a four-year-old Junior Kumon student explained why he and his wife started taking his son there at age three: "Math takes repetition. My son is gifted, but there's just not enough math at preschool. So we've been coming here once a week in the year since he was three. Now he is doing the reading. He has homework every day. My wife is very involved in learning, both reading and math. We use LeapFrog, videos, words, exercises, repetition, and reading."

At the Institutes for the Achievement of Human Potential, the parental ambition was even more striking. The parents told stories of having moved to towns and cities near Philadelphia so their children could attend the school as toddlers. For many, the school was the center and pinnacle of their own lives. One mother told me that upon arriving at the school, when her son was one year old, her husband cried because he felt they had "wasted a year of our baby's life." The couple "decided to make up for lost time, to introduce them to everything, to open up options," she says. "By six, their brains are the same size as adults, but you can grow brains up till then. My son is like, 'Why, why, why?' He takes in information, memorizes, and then presents information."

Another IAHP parent, Moisha Yakov-Feldman, relocated to Philadelphia, along with her husband and daughter Masha, now eight, so that Masha could attend the institute. "I want Masha to have balanced development," she said. "I missed out. I am starting all over. I am now here all the time so I know what's going on. I am assisting teachers. I also teach Masha at home. I see the benefits."

For Yakov-Feldman and other Evan Thomas parents, the perceived benefits are so great that the parents will pay with their labor. Usually, parents pay in cash, and sometimes lots of it. Broadway Babies class runs forty-five minutes and costs $41. Junior Kumon costs up to $110 a month. At the music school Diller-Quaile, the weekly classes during the school year go for up to $1,730. More and more parents feel obliged to spend substantial money to put their infants into "enriched" environments, or risk feeling like parenting failures. (These classes can involve hidden costs as well, as in gifts for the toddlers' teachers–parental suggestions for appropriate presents included a $200 gift certificate or Lindt chocolate in a ruler-shaped box.)

But for the parents who believe their infants should attend one or many classes, no cost is too great. "We are respecting our son by teaching him sign language," one mother at a baby sign language class told me. "Our son is not dumb. Shouldn't everyone be considered gifted? And we are just trying to unlock his giftedness."

Standing amid the baby sign language workbooks and ziplock bags of snacks, this mother was expressing a substantial democratic ideal, an educated baby's Bill of Rights: that every child should have the right to access their "giftedness."

Still, wanting all infants to be considered as having "equal" talents and possibilities runs smack up against the truth of the matter–that not all families can pay for such instruction. A democratic and sometimes faux-democratic rhetoric runs through the baby and toddler classes–IAHP says, "The Institutes proposes that *every* child has the *right* to be intellectually, physically, and socially excellent" (emphasis theirs). Once again, though, rights belong to those who can afford the classes, give up work hours to volunteer as schoolteachers, and even move house to be closer to these schools and classes. By doing this, parents may assuage trepidations about their children's futures and their own. Such reassurance is a privilege, however: even the dream of precocious giftedness and talent is available only at a cost.

FOUR

Child's Play or Child Labor? Preprofessional Kids

The child plays at being not only a shopkeeper or teacher but also a windmill and a train.

WALTER BENJAMIN

Now in myth and ritual the great instinctive forces of civilized life have their origin: law and order, commerce and profit, craft and art, poetry, wisdom and science. All are rooted in the primaeval soil of play.

JOHAN HUIZINGA, *Homo Ludens*

Marla Olmstead swings on a multicolored hammock, jabbering with her brother Zane, who swings on another hammock alongside her. They are in an apartment in upstate New York, a place that resembles a zealously kid-friendly pediatrician's office: there's a giant stuffed panda on a beanbag chair; big glass containers of candy, gumballs, and peanuts; an aquarium overloaded with Day-Glo fish; clown collectibles; and a washboard emblazoned with the word "Midget."

Marla's relaxing right now, but she's one hardworking person. Her dozens of oil paintings have brought in $300,000, a figure that will soon rise to millions. The *New York Times* has published three articles about her. The Oprah people have called, as have the David Letterman and Ellen DeGeneres people. Talk-show host Tony Danza's people called, too, although their calls were not returned. Marla's originals bring in $15,000, while her limited-edition prints sell for up to $800. Two thousand people attended her opening in the summer of 2004. At the start of 2005, the waiting list for her work was two hundred people deep.

Still, Marla remains oblivious to her improved fortune. That makes perfect sense: she's only four years old.

Mark Olmstead, who is thirty-eight, a night manager at Frito-Lay, and the sixth cousin to Frederick Law Olmsted, the nineteenth-century landscaper most famous for crafting Central Park (apparently Olmsted gained an *a* along the way to becoming Mark's last name), told me his daughter started painting with brushes, and graduated first to spatulas, then fingers. Her use of fingers came last, which is why Olmstead chose to name one finger-heavy piece *Digits*. According to Olmstead, Marla began painting while still wearing a diaper, and has almost always painted on canvas. He and his wife encouraged Marla's initial foray into the public eye, asking a friend who owns a café in their hometown of Binghamton, New York, if he would like to display one of their daughter's paintings. The café owner obliged, hanging a few of her works in the café in 2003. It was there that Marla was "discovered" by gallery owner Anthony Brunelli. Brunelli, a strapping red-haired man who is now thirty-nine, says he was struck by one of Marla's paintings. Interested in showing the artist's work in his own gallery, Brunelli approached the café owner, who was also a friend of his, about getting in touch with her. Only later, Brunelli says, did he learn that the artist was three years old.

Ever since, Brunelli has been plotting the ascent of the girl with the sandy blond hair and chocolate-colored eyes, grooming her for long-term profitability. After all, Marla Olmstead exhibits naturally what art historian Jonathan Fineberg has termed "strategic childhood," a childlike aesthetic that for more than a hundred years adult artists have intentionally deployed, availing themselves of the primitive techniques of youth in their art for resonance and profit, among them Keith Haring and Jean-Michel Basquiat. Artists have also long exulted in children's art. After viewing an exhibition of children's drawings during the 1950s, Pablo Picasso reportedly said of child painters, "When I was their age, I could draw like Raphael. It took me many years to learn how to draw like these children." Children's art also influenced the post-Symbolist generation of European masters, such as Paul Klee, Joan

Miró, and Jean Dubuffet. As early as 1917, the art critic Roger Fry wrote that children's drawings should be extolled for their sincerity and their play. In 1938, critic Robert Goldwater wrote that one of the most striking characteristics of modern art is its likeness to children's art.

But while children's art was being reconceived as a teacher of spontaneity to adult painters, children's artworks themselves were rarely signed. In fact, that lack of signature–which implied a lack of ego, no motive but pure creativity and self-expression, and no consciousness of audience beyond, perhaps, the viewers of a grandparent's refrigerator–was part of the reason children's art was so valued. Today it's a different situation, evinced by the crumbly capital letters spelling MARLA, now the key to child-artist-as-brand. It's also different in that some of the well-remunerated artists using Pop art–like childish techniques are, in fact, children like Marla. In a variation on the way that the art world has always extolled the purity and authenticity of the very young, today's "strategic childhood" in visual arts is created by actual children who actually profit from it. This partly explains why Marla's professional ascent was so fast. The Guggenheim Museum spoke to Brunelli about putting a Marla on its 2004 Christmas card (it didn't pan out). Crayola considered making her the company's spokesperson, although they, too, ultimately dropped the idea.

Marla's aesthetic style is clearly superior to that of the average four-year-old–critics have noted its abstraction, consistency, color sense, formal balance, and maturity. The high prices her work fetches, however, are very much the doing of Brunelli and her parents. Those who buy Marla's work insist on its brilliance and sincerity. Their numbers includes West Coast art buyer Stuart Simpson, who owns Renoirs and Matisses, and now runs a gallery that sells Marlas.

Marla's paintings are uniformly bright. They tend to feature swirls, and truncated, murky triangles and rhombuses in carmine pinks and ocher oranges, brick reds, and Mack truck yellow. They bear friendly titles like *Camp Fire, Face, Frenzy, Lollipop,* and *Fire Now.* A recent one, *Fireworks,* is composed of the graffitiish blues and reds of 1980s subway tags. It is composed of lines reminiscent of Jackson Pollock, layers of squiggles apparently squirted onto the canvas. Another features primitive shapes in almost cacophonously bright colors. A third has a folkloric feel, with animals and homunculae scratched onto the canvas. A fourth is a painting whose dark blue background is interrupted by white sketchy arcs and doodles, giving the impression of an insoluble math problem.

Marla has something in common with eight-year-old Mitchie Brusco. He also works for money at something that began as play: skateboarding. Mitchie, a regular kid with cute ears that stick out, has nine corporate sponsors, one of which named a skateboard after him. The sponsors' motives are clear: seeing another child sponsor a product inspires kids–it's a powerful seal of approval.

One day in the summer of 2004, Mitchie skated at Manhattan's Jacob Javits Center for Mattel's Hot Wheels, his biggest sponsor. Mattel created a ramp out of poured concrete so Mitchie could do his tricks before a hundred children's toy professionals in business attire. Half the height of his audience, Mitchie does a kick flip here, a twist there, speeding on the ramp like a human go-cart. The scene embodied Gen X cross-branding weirdness–theme park authenticity. Klieg lights illuminated Mitchie as he performed his stunts.

The transformation of Mitchie's play into work began long before he made a deal with Hot Wheels. When he was three, Mitchie's parents began a relationship with the Olympic and action sports division at sports management firm Octagon. At four, he was sponsored by Jones Soda, which gave him T-shirts and wristbands. He got shoes, backpacks, and pants from DC Shoes, and helmets from Triple Eight. At five, Softrucks rewarded him for his tricks. Lego Sports gave him Lego clothes to wear on the ramps. Today he gets royalties for the Mitchie Brusco skateboard line. And he has lost two sponsors, but this is no cause for sympathy: he lost them because Mattel's Hot Wheels and Lego signed for an undisclosable but clearly generous "semi-exclusive" agreement. Television correspondents wait outside Mitchie's school to interview him. He goes to a celebrity bowling event in Los Angeles, where he skates in front of an audience of adults at a huge warehouse. Jones Soda gives him free brightly colored soda so he will hold parties at school, thereby tethering him to the name of Jones. Although Mitchie turned seven in 2004, much of his future has already been determined. As a professional, he is no longer eligible to skate against kids his own age. Instead he competes in the sponsored division of skating competitions for skaters of all ages. The older professional skaters are usually better than he is, by dint of their adult strength and their years of training. Consequently, despite the talent that brought all those sponsors, Mitchie doesn't get to win.

A four-year-old star painter and an eight-year-old skating celebrity might seem mere novelties or simply emblems of kitschy Americana. But Marla Olmstead and Mitchie Brusco are part of a larger phenomenon: that of kids' activities turning into professional pursuits, proto-professional training, and means to later-life achievement. Marla is one of a number of professional child and teen painters, forming a relatively new market that can earn their parents and their galleries thousands of dollars. In the case of child artists, there's a particular cast of talent-spotters: in addition to parents themselves, this includes gallery owners and even art therapists, who suggest that parents should keep their eyes peeled for young talent from the age of six months. At least half a dozen art dads and moms have sent JPEGs of their children's work to Brunelli in the hope that he will make their children famous as well.

Children's art is but one of a growing number of childhood domains that used to be all play but are now tied closely to money, with a growing number of kid professionals that have been discovered in recent years. For some kids, childhood has become Play Incorporated. Children's extreme sports like skateboarding and snowboarding are increasingly professionalized, with child athletes sponsored, like Mitchie, by companies like Lego and Burton. But more traditional sports like soccer, hockey, and baseball are proto-professionalized, their games superorganized events with equipment and uniforms that cost thousands of dollars.

Rather than play pickup baseball or basketball games in vacant lots, many kids attend all-day sports training programs each summer. The professional end of these traditional sports has also started its recruitment at earlier and earlier ages. Young basketball players with professional aspirations try to get spotted by sports recruiters as early as the fourth grade and want to speak to recruiters as early as age twelve, according to Clark Francis, editor and publisher of the HoopScoop Online, a Web site that gives recruiting information and player rankings for both high school and junior high school basketball players. The earlier the recruiters get to their talents, the likelier they are to seal the deal. Recruiters tend to now believe–as parents sometimes do–that the earlier one invests in a child's talent, the greater the payoff. According to this perspective, a precocious start is thought to increase a child's mastery and, in some cases, his adult economic viability. Companies like Adidas, Reebok, and Nike are also waiting in the wings to sponsor the choicest young basketball players; Nike begins looking for teams and players in the seventh grade.

In addition to the activities that have been professionalized or proto-professionalized at younger and younger ages, there is the related phenomenon of hard-core training for higher achievement, as in the case of chess: children's chess championships are also considered career moves. Chess dads I have spoken to talk about chess as a route into college and, possibly, money. Seventeen colleges and universities now offer chess scholarships, and they recruit from the youth chess-championship pool. One chess dad told me he used to worry that his son was too focused on chess. Then he realized what his wins against adults might mean: going to college on his chess abilities, as the University of Texas at Austin and the University of Maryland offer full four-year tuition-and-board chess scholarships. The common wisdom for chess parents is that if a child wins the Junior Open, he can get such scholarships automatically.

Chess is a skill that is often associated with early learning and intelligence in general, and has long produced child prodigies. But today, all sorts of skills are seen as a ticket to later-life success, and children now train at them with the aim of gaining expert status. There has been a growth in specialized summer camps where children may polish their robotics or SAT or digital filmmaking skills. The trend of specialized camps has become so pronounced that it has been credited with driving up camp attendance among American kids in the late nineties and early noughts.

The precocious proto-professional training happens in nonscholastic domains. But it also happens within schools. Schoolwork, most notably test preparation, has now eclipsed play from preschool onward. The growth of structured work lives for American children has been accompanied by a drop in the hours apportioned to play. Between 1981 and 1997, children's nondiscretionary hours increased significantly. In a 2001 article published by Sandra L. Hofferth and John F. Sandberg of the University of Michigan entitled "Changes in American Children's Time, 1981–1997," the scholars looked at samples of the time use of children between the ages three and twelve in that sixteen-year period. According to the report, children's participation in passive leisure declined 24 percent between 1981 and 1997, from 66 to 50 percent, while the proportion participating in sports increased 21 percent, from 59 to 75 percent, and participation in art activities increased 37 percent, from 19 to 26 percent. Most tellingly, play time for children decreased 16 percent—only a little less than the diminution of free time for children overall.

Many parents don't need a study to tell them that children's play has decreased, and not just at home. A lot of parents are grappling with a real increase in their kids' schoolwork, as well as the elimination of recess in a lot of K-6 public schools as these schools face both fiscal cutbacks and constant pressure to ready children for national tests. In Georgia, for example, many school systems don't have recess at all, according to Olga Jarrett, a scholar of early childhood education at Georgia State University. Children's activities that were once considered play are now professionalized and quasi-professionalized. The classes described in the last chapter, as well as training in chess and computers and academic preschools, are a subcontinuum of this childhood professionalism. This trend raises some serious questions: When should a parent—or a society—worry that child's play has become child's labor? How do you know when a child has become professional, or too professional? How much adult direction of children's play is too much direction, overdetermining children's activity and sucking the spirit out of it? Is there something wrong with the transformation of play into work among child professionals, and with schoolchildren having their recess taken away? Are there long-term psychological and physical ramifications? Is there a danger of exploitation by managers and parents? Or is it a necessary part of the new economy and a more competitive job market?

In some cases, what's wrong with the professionalization of children is all too easy to see, as when a kid is blatantly exploited by adults. Some of the managers get greedy with their golden geese. Texas-based "prodigy" art promoter Ben Valenty has for a decade been selling art buyers on the "Child Picasso" and the "Child Dalí." For example, Valenty promoted Olivia Bennett, a pretty blond preteen cancer survivor who paints large, simple oils of flowers. He pitched Alexandra Nechita, now nineteen, as a tiny ambassador of the former Eastern bloc.

Ultimately, Valenty's representation of the art prodigies took a dark turn. Some of the families of Valenty's stable of child painters sued him for the money they believed he owed them. When I spoke with Valenty in 2004, he admitted to no wrongdoing, and instead implied that Bennett lacked talent. "The best analogy that can be used is that Olivia [Bennett] is the Monkees. Alexandra [Nechita] is the Beatles," he said. The suits against him were settled, Valenty says, although he remains tight-lipped about their terms. He does, however, no longer handle any prodigies: he is still an art broker who offers to pick up a Peter Max painting for potential clients. But recruiters in art and sports–including the neighbors of young basketball talents–just keep rising to take his place on the gifted-kid gravy train. Clark Francis also cited a few instances of extended family members attempting to get children recruited for basketball in order to gain profit from the children.

There are subtle but nonetheless possibly negative effects of the professionalization of kids' play. Gianine D. Rosenblum, a psychologist who specializes in early childhood at the Institute for the Study of Child Development, says that children who have been defined as gifted and then do not practice and "live up to their potential" can wind up feeling guilty. Rosenblum has the pleasant, calm speaking voice–the gentle, lullaby-like intonation–that is ideal for someone who works with children. But this lesson of her clinical experience–that the new proto-professional kids may well also be guilty kids, blaming themselves for their incapacity to master a skill–is a far from soothing one. Rosenblum suggests that parents take a hard look at their child's resiliency, not just their talent and discipline, before training them: directing play into culturally valued activities like painting or music or sports can further test a child's equanimity.

For those children whose participation in sports resembles a sports career rather than free play, another downside is the growing incidence of child sports injuries. The rise of golf for young players, for example, has resulted in a growing number of children suffering head injuries. Pediatric sports doctors report that the overly intense culture of organized youth sports has created an epidemic of overuse sports injuries among the very young, with stress fractures, cracked kneecaps, and back conditions, once the nearly exclusive province of adults, more and more present among children. Specialization in one sport and obsessive, year-round training from an early age are the cause.

Psychologists, doctors, and parents are not just worried about the professional or proto-professional kid end of the continuum. Some are concerned with the reduction of play not just for the gifted and athletically talented, but for all children. They point to the diminution of recess in public schools as the most visible sign of a disturbing and damaging trend. Many scholars with links to the respectable and expanding academic field of play studies have joined the activist "pro-recess movement," along with parents. The movement even has its own magazine, *Play Rights,* and an advocacy group that calls itself the American Association for the Child's Right to Play. Anthony Pellegrini, a professor of psychology at the University of Minnesota, is well known within the movement for his book *Recess,* and for the book's message: children have the right to play, and this right is endangered. Pellegrini's book contains his research on the attentiveness and achievement levels of students who had had recess and those who had none. He reached the conclusion that a recess environment helps children learn social skills and bevel their interaction capacities, and also helps children fidget less in the classroom. To ensure that there be adequate time for recess as well as for increasing academic demands, Pellegrini advocates a longer school year with many more breaks during the day. According to a study based on University of Michigan data, homework has increased to two hours and eight minutes a week, from fifty-two minutes a week, for six- to eight-year-olds between 1981 and 1997.

For scholars of play and child psychology, one of the key points here is that recess–unlike PE or any other subject in school–is child-directed or nondirected play. Play that is not adult-directed, and activity that is not explicitly goal-oriented, they argue, is a necessary component of childhood.

A founder of play studies and its "great man" is octogenarian Brian Sutton-Smith, emeritus professor of education at the University of Pennsylvania and the author of *The Ambiguity of Play,* among dozens of other "play" books. Sutton-Smith puts the whole thing in terms that every adult can understand: "When you take away children's recess, you are taking away from a child the adult worker's equivalent of a coffee break," he says. He asserts that play is an activity meant to improve one's ability to work. He calls it "educational parenthesis"–the pause in a child's day that motivates the child to learn more. It's an elegant phrase. Sutton-Smith goes beyond the purely practical arguments, suggesting that play is a right, albeit a pragmatic sort of right, that helps both adults and children work harder, among other things.

And he is a man whose persona is true to his lifelong fascination–he is playful. He speaks in a rollicking fashion about his childhood in New Zealand. He makes jokes about his advanced age. While explaining that recess is the time for a child to pick up qualities like social aplomb, he says that President Bush would be nowhere if he hadn't been good at playing and learned all those playground social tricks.

It may seem as though Sutton-Smith, and to an even greater extent Pellegrini and his fellow right-to-play advocates, are waging a campaign of the obvious. But for these advocates, the loss of recess and child-directed play, the turn toward career-directed and adult-directed work, is nothing less than a baleful redefinition of childhood. It could even be seen as a return to earlier periods in history. Indeed, I think part of the drive among parents to encourage giftedness is the legacy of children as workers and our current confusion about children's social roles.

In past centuries, children were neither free nor innocent. They were laborers, and were hardly distinguished from working teenagers or even adults. Medieval European children were apprenticed rather than educated. And as historian Steven Mintz writes, for the Puritans, "children were adults in training who needed to be prepared for salvation and inducted into the world of work as early as possible."

For them, childhood was simply a time of training for adult work lives. Children worked on farms, and later in mills and factories. The notion of childhood as a time that ought to be free of labor was not in evidence for many then; this concept did not arise until the late nineteenth century. In her classic book *Pricing the Priceless Child,* sociologist Viviana Zelizer writes that the 1870s to 1930s saw the emergence of an "economically 'worthless' but emotionally 'priceless' child." The child labor law reforms of the nineteenth century meant that children's work had become schoolwork or chores–for their moral betterment, rather than for immediate economic gain. The conception of the "long childhood" emerged only then. The long childhood was a time and place separate from the demands of the marketplace and adult worries, and from distinctly adult varieties of power and powerlessness.

If childhood and even infancy has again become a time for determining and engaging in the adult work life, we can see this preoccupation as an ironic return to the nineteenth-century practice of child apprenticeship, which existed before labor law reforms and mandatory education were instituted. One key difference is that today's preprofessional kids (although not your everyday kid without recess) tend to be decently paid for their work. Another is that they know that their peers are not expected to work. Today's star kids may be envied by their peers, but the demands placed on them go far beyond what most children would want for themselves–and what most parents would want for their children. Today's overstructured, hardworking children are in a sense a strange echo of the idea of childhood in earlier centuries, except now it is the upper and upper-middle classes who labor so young, rather than the other way around. They are like Baruch Shemtov, a teen tie designer, who in 2004 had his first trunk show at a high-end department store, calling his ties, which he works on in addition to his hours of schoolwork, "haute couture." (Baruch's "career" started when he collected Gucci catalogs as a child. His first clothing line, designed at age eight, was named BYSH, after himself.) "Because I have school, I can't expand as much as I'd like," he told me.

Parents of child professionals–and also some of the millions of American children with shrunken recess and play hours–don't all think the reduction of play is such a terrible thing. They say their children really *want* to work, and that devoting nearly all school hours to schoolwork, as well as many hours to homework, is far from draconian. Furthermore, if children's work is painting or skating or basketball or chess, perhaps their careers could be considered what play studies scholars call "play-work," a combination of the two and thus free of harm.

Mitchie Brusco's mom wants me to understand that her son's whole career has been his idea. Mitchie started out on the foot ramp when he was four years old, she says. He wakes up in the morning and rushes off to skate all day of his own volition. He even practices his skating moves in the living room, jumping into chairs. Skating-as-career is all her son's choice, Jennifer Brusco says. Like Mark Olmstead and other parents of kid wonders, Brusco describes Mitchie as an unstoppable force, tearing through equipment, begging to start skating right after he wakes up. He has been like that, with no parental or coach goading, since he was small. "Now he is on a fourteen-foot ramp," says Brusco, who is thirty-seven and, like Mitchie, small, tan, compact, and very muscular, with bright white teeth. "Mitchie's the same person. I mean, there was a photo of the star 'Mitchie Brusco' on the phone booth right outside of our hotel room here in New York City, but Mitchie hasn't seen it yet and didn't want to see it.

"Look at our official Mitchie skateboard," says his mother as we stroll around the Hot Wheels booth at the Jacob Javits Center on the day Mitchie performs. She picks it up and hands it to me. "It's wicked light. We got to choose what it would look like. The Liberty Group hired Mitch to design the Hot Wheels Board for a good reason, because they realized little kids have a voice and that other little kids listen to them.

"If he was in eight-and-under competitions, he'd have won the competitions and he'd have gotten the prizes," says Jennifer Brusco. "So we get him a DVD or another gift, instead of the prizes he would have won if he had been able to compete.

"Kid athletes today have total organization, afterschool programs, gymnastics," she continues. Mitchie's drinking a Dr Pepper upstairs: although Jones Soda is a sponsor, he is not abiding by the rules that apply to fellow kid skater star Skyler Bothell, who as one newspaper noted can't "drink a Pepsi in public because it would violate his contract" with Jones. Mitchie's playing a Hot Wheels video game with his sister. Now and again, sounds of fighting drift down. "When I grew up, you just got home and ran with the neighbors," Brusco says.

In Jennifer Brusco's memories of unstructured after-school play, one hears the hint of a sort of freedom to which Mitchie–and most children, for that matter–have lost access. But it wasn't as if Jennifer and her husband lived without a care. She went to college on a college basketball scholarship, and a baseball scholarship helped put her husband through college. They did quite well, but the financial rewards and public attention Mitchie has brought in are beyond anything they experienced. "This opportunity with Mattel is opening up so many other doors," Jennifer says. "I played tennis really hard, my older sister played, and I was taken to all the meets. But if I had been sponsored, I would have lost eligibility to compete in those sports in college, so I was never sponsored. I didn't have Mitchie's opportunities."

The Bruscos feel that they are ensuring Mitchie's later life with his success now, with money for his future. "He's made enough money now so he won't have to make the choice to go to his kids' baseball games or go to work," says Mitchie's father. "We live in insecure times. Look at the job market. Look at terrorism. Who knows what these kids will be up against when they will be my age? I am glad he will have savings and he will have choices. He'll not have to lay roofs like his dad."

Marla's dad, Mark Olmstead, strikes similar notes to those of the Bruscos. A handsome brunette with a genial smile and the muscular physique of the college football player he was, Olmstead tells me the impetus for the work comes wholly from Marla. "I really am only Marla's assistant," he says. "People are suspicious: 'How much do you assist her?' they ask. They say, 'Marla is too good to be a four-year-old painter.' Sometimes when she talks about her paintings, Marla says, 'Look, I painted it, and it wasn't easy.' People ask me, 'Did you teach her?'

"Marla can really paint," he continues. "Still, she'll make something really beautiful, and critics will compare her to a turtle." (As in, "A turtle could have painted that.") "I cringe at that. Marla's conscious. She is a thinking person. She's neither an elephant nor a turtle. Comparing her to animals is an insult. I'd like to see a turtle or an elephant do what she does.

"I think adult artists are threatened by child artists and I feel for them." As an art aficionado who works as a night manager, Mark probably *can* feel for adult artists. He completes the thought by remarking, "Ninety-nine percent of adult artists don't get to have fun doing what they are doing. People who have knowledge of the art world, people who know things, are taking her seriously.

"Is this thing exploitation?" he asks, rhetorically. "If people say it is exploitation, I ask them if it is exploitation when they stick a football in a kid's hands. I say, 'Stick your kid in front of an easel. Let them paint over and over again.' " Olmstead claims that Marla just wants to paint all the time–he can't pull her away from the canvas.

Although Marla's parents brought her into the limelight, they remain protective. Laura Olmstead, Marla's mom, her platinum hair cut in a bob, her eyes bright blue and her temperament steely, tells me she feels uncomfortable that Marla's progress should be recorded for posterity in a book.

"We are private people," Laura Olmstead says. "*The Daily Show* called, for instance, and we didn't do that." (They did do *CBS Sunday Morning* and the *Today* show, however.) "I don't like the word 'giftedness.' We have been getting hate mail. I don't know what she'll think when she's twenty-four if she's in a book about gifted kids. To say she's a 'phenom' is fine. You could stomach that. But to use the word 'prodigy' puts it in a whole new light." The words *phenom* and *prodigy* are synonyms, for most of us, but to Laura they feel somehow different. She makes a similarly personal distinction between her daughter's appearing on a television show and appearing in a book. Laura wonders aloud what the possible reward for participation in a book project could be. She seems to want to know whether the reward will be financial, or a more abstract promotion of the Marla brand.

Her father's approach to promoting her brand is more straightforward– he points out her oeuvre's attributes while circling Brunelli's gallery. "Marla's works . . ." Olmstead gestures at his daughter's pieces on the Brunelli walls and trails off, looking out the window of the gallery, which is abutted by downtown Binghamton's few stores and the occasional grimy diner, the dingy Greyhound station, and an empty lot full of rocks, and fringed by the city's grand, underutilized municipal buildings. "Well, it's funny to call them works," he continues. "They were play, but now we call them work because they are art."

The confusion between play and work here brings up the key question about Play Incorporated: Are kids being forced to work at the expense of their childhoods? In the case of Marla, it was hard to tell. It was hard, that is, until five months after I met her, when the television show *60 Minutes* aired a report about her. Perhaps starstruck by the show's prestige, the Olmsteads had permitted a hidden camera to film Marla in the act of painting. The resulting television clip revealed that Marla's father had indeed helped the tot by painting one of her canvases red. The television clip also showed that her father was present when Marla painted on that red canvas. The sound track recorded Mark telling Marla what colors she should use and how she should paint. At times he appeared to urge Marla to keep painting, even after she gave signs of wanting to stop.

The story of Marla, and to a lesser degree Mitchie, begs the question: Can parental backing of child professionalism or proto-professionalism be exploitative, or is it simply parents vouchsafing their children's future? It is not always easy to tell the difference. The disappearance of recess and the expansion of homework are rife with similar conflicts: How can one tell how much work is necessary for children to achieve, and how much work literally removes every last mote of pleasure?

Many parents find the world terribly unpredictable. The risks to a child are myriad. Add to that the parents' own frustration–so common in today's world, which promises so much and delivers so much less–at their perceived adult failure, at being thwarted or not quite hitting the mark. Who wouldn't want their kids to have all the chances they themselves missed? There is a substantial reality to the perception that children are going to face increasingly tough competition for knowledge work. The parents who are pressing their children forward, who are intent that their kids won't waste their time and who train their children for professional acumen, don't always have sinister, or even wholly misguided, motivations.

University of Maryland sociologist Annette Lareau, author of *Unequal Childhoods,* speaks with clarity, certitude, and bemusement about the professional parents she has studied, families that view the cultivation of their children's talents as their main parental goal. Families adhere to complex schedules to achieve this. Lareau argues that the calendar, rather than the hearth, is the new symbolic center of the American home. "Micromanaging is very common among some families," says Lareau. "There's a lurking worry among middle-class parents that their children won't do as well as they did, and they want to give their children every edge that they can possibly give them to cultivate them–so that they can succeed, and their wealth can be transferred. . . . That's why you see an exponential growth of specialized 'work' children's camps–to ensure that children succeed."

After all, most parents who wish to be assured that their kids aren't "wasting" their time are propelled by the desire to know that they're getting adequate preparation for success in later life. And they do so with the understanding that such success early on can form a sort of silken cushion for them unto adulthood.

Of course, an intensive focus on an activity is good for children only if the children are passionate about the avocation, as in the case of the former carnivorous-plant-collecting child prodigy Vezen Wu or the former musical prodigy Matthew Haimovitz we met in chapter 1, each wound up reclaiming his genuine interest in music as his own in later life. Artist Jonathan Lerman is an extreme case of this kind of concentration: he is both autistic and mentally handicapped, and from his early childhood on, his painting has allowed him to express himself. Now seventeen, Jonathan is represented by Manhattan gallery owner Kerry Schuss of KS Gallery, who sells the fascinating and profound drawings he has been producing for years.

Jonathan's drawings go for about $1,200, while his paintings fetch $2,500. His work features men and women with giant eyes, noses, and lips. They look like very innocent Picassos. They have a dollop of naive Pop as well–they are often portraits of celebrities like John Lennon or the MTV cartoon icon Daria. But Jonathan's range is wider than that. He has produced Renaissance-style portraits, in charcoal, of remarkably sensual overstatement–the lace cuffs extra thick, the facial features extra languorous. And there's Jonathan's "art box," adorned with images that Jonathan has painted of faces, always faces. Difficulty reading facial expressions is often an element of autism; perhaps for this reason, there are faces in every corner of Jonathan's images. One particularly moving, mysterious charcoal has three decades–"1920's, 1930's, 1940's"–scribbled on it. Another bears a giant twisted face and reads, "The God is Wrong." The wonder of an inarticulate child rendering his experience in charcoal and oil makes Jonathan's case stand out.

He paints in a gloomy basement room of a studio school. Adding to the grimness, the studio school building is met on one side by a cemetery and on the other by a pile of debris. But in the studio itself, Jonathan is aglow. He wears a red polo shirt, loose jeans, and three different macramé necklaces. A small brown braid–a tail–winds down the back of his neck. One day when I visit, Jonathan is listening to grunge music, as is his wont, and painting a portrait of the actor Joey Lawrence, who is his favorite actor of all time. A photograph of Lawrence hangs near his canvas on a bulletin board.

Of the child artists I've met, Jonathan best embodies the ideal: children's art as total and almost transparent expression of self. Indeed, art is often the only way he *can* express himself and be understood by others, as language often fails him. His play-as-work has given him plenty of new tools and skills that appear to give him not only an activity but a sort of semi-rapture.

Jonathan's father Alan, a gastroenterologist, even goes so far as to say that the drawings describe Jonathan's experience of not being able to express himself. Alan tells me that the piece inscribed with the phrase "The God is Wrong" means that Jonathan feels that "God is wrong for trapping Jonathan in himself." I tell him I'm less sure what it means.

"Too purple, too purple," says Jonathan, manically mixing a would-be pale flesh tone, as if his brush were a whisk. He has dedicated his day to the pursuit of the right color for his portrait, a search that might continue through tomorrow. For Jonathan, the line between work and play is blurred, as are the lines between process and outcome, external reward and self-directed inclination. It is a flow state of work-play that anyone, adult or child, might envy.

Of course, some of the children who achieve a "work-play" flow state are still confronted with whether or not to go pro. A case in point is the Kitchen family. When I visited them they were trying to decide whether turning their daughter's predilection into a career was the best move for her.

At six and a half, the Kitchens' only daughter, Alexa, is a remarkably avid cartoonist. She has written and illustrated two cartoon books, *Alexa Kitchen, the Early Years, Volume I (Age 5) Comic Book Art* and *Volume 2 Age 6*. Her father, Denis Kitchen, sixty, published both books and would like Alexa to get published more widely. Her mother, however, has argued against this. The Kitchens' dilemma represents a more extreme version of what many parents struggle with: Should I let my child go public with her talents, honing and training them? Or should I let her "just be a kid" and enjoy her hobbies undisturbed?

It makes sense, given Alexa's predilections, that her father is a major figure in the world of comics: Kitchen Publishing has published many of the hottest comic talents, including R. Crumb and Harvey Kurtzman. The family, though dwelling in Shutesbury, Massachusetts, twenty minutes from Amherst, at the end of a long and isolated road, gets its share of visits from arts professionals. Denis, a tall man with black-rimmed retro nerd glasses, a thick mustache, dense black hair that is graying around the temples, and a plaid flannel shirt encasing his barrel chest, tells me these cartooning dignitaries went wild for Alexa's work, including the late elder statesman Will Eisner, whose Spirit Publishing was crucial to the growth of cartoon art.

"Will looked at the art of many, many kids before," Denis says. "But he had never even seen a fourteen-year-old who could do the cartoons like Alexa. This is more than a father's pride. She has instinctive talent."

As a form of proof, Denis displays a sheaf of Alexa's drawings, pointing out their attributes. "Look at that thrown popcorn. Look at that hand clearly reaching for a doorknob. Look at the skeleton, the sweat beads, the look of the hair . . ."

While Denis is enthusiastic about going public with Alexa and her art, her mom, Stacey Kitchen, thirty-two, is far less thrilled. Muckety-mucks in the comic world may describe Alexa as singularly talented–*Underground Comix Price Guide* author Jay Kennedy called her "the Tiger Woods of cartooning"–but Stacey has her reservations. She understands the Icarus effect from the inside: Stacey was a child beauty queen.

"I was the little kid, gimmicky and cute," she says. Stacey remains pretty, in the round-faced, button-nosed way of a soap-opera ingenue. She regrets her own emotionally difficult experiences of being pushed to perform early. "My mother capitalized on it," she says. "It is painful inside and out to watch the TV shows now, with kids singing and dancing. JonBenet [Ramsey, the murdered child beauty queen] makes me ill. I grew up in that. It was a huge southern thing. From Alexa's age on, I was in beauty pageants. At eight, I was in a metallic string bikini. I was like Bo Derek, with the braids and the swimsuit. It was horrifying."

Stacy didn't just look cute. "I sang really well for my age," she explains. As a girl, Stacey had naturally good pitch. She took lessons. She sang a song that sounds like it was simultaneously campy and cringe-worthy: "I May Be Little but I Am Loud."

"I am an average well-trained singer now, but I was a novelty act then," Stacey says. With impeccable hostess manners, she offers me some more cold cuts, with three different varieties of mustard. Then she returns to her memories of fame. "I was trying to get on TV. I did opening shows for the headliner in Nashville. I wrote my own songs starting at ten. At twenty-three, I left Nashville. I realized I was not going to be able to do it. There was a huge spark lit inside me, but nothing happened. It haunts me."

She gestures toward the wall, which holds a cheesecake poster from the 1980s of a girl who resembles the sitcom actress Valerie Bertinelli. It's Stacey in her teen-dream phase, clad in white thigh-high boots, ornamented by big hair. Stacey knows from experience that a child can perform well on the outside while feeling vulnerable on the inside. And Alexa is vulnerable, Stacey emphasizes. She looks edgily at Denis, registering his pride and his wish to take Alexa to the masses.

"I forced her to go to a birthday party, and it didn't go so well," says Stacey. "Alexa wrote on the card for the girl, 'I like you all the way to Pluto!' Alexa meant, 'The best things in the world are out of this world,' and the birthday girl was one of those out-of-the-world things. The girl didn't get it. Alexa is geeky, but not in a pocket-protector sort of way. I know she's embarrassed about her experiences at school. She doesn't like to talk about it. She says, 'Mom, I am feeling very melancholy, it's a strange feeling.'"

It's clear that Alexa is isolated. The question is whether her obsession with cartooning did the isolating–in which case public success could make her even more solitary–or whether she would have spent a lot of time alone anyway, so that cartooning, rather than hampering her, gives her a much-needed outlet.

Alexa doesn't seem melancholy when I meet her. She runs in and makes a point of hugging everyone in the room. She does, however, appear wonderfully peculiar: if she particularly likes you, she rubs against you and presses her face to yours. She is twitching with energy–a fountain of facts, vocabulary words, and associations.

"My name starts with an A and ends with an A," she says. "Like Africa and Asia. Europe is attached to Asia, which is not attached to Africa. Do you want to hear the capitals of countries?"

Her eyes glitter. Her hands flap like the wings of birds. She's thin, with sandy hair and large brown eyes. According to her parents, Alexa goes through a ream of paper a week for her illustrations. According to Alexa herself, her room is a "nest of paper." And indeed, a dizzying number of image-covered pages lie on the floor.

"I want to be an artist. Is there a difference between artist and cartoonist? What is the difference?" Alexa asks no one in particular. "I do no cartoons using lower-case letters," she explains. "I write all the sentences in upper case. I fought with the teacher. I said I don't want to do lower case. My teacher chastised me. I did it anyway.

"Linch is in Kirsy Lirsy Land," Alexa then says, referring to an invented place that is prominent in her drawings. "I can show you the index I made for KLL. Linch was discovered in 1849."

When Alexa leaves the room, presumably to draw, Denis plays down Alexa's unhappiness. He also plays down the risk that celebrating Alexa as gifted could make her more of an outsider than she is already. He says lightly that Alexa gets so nervous she starts to shake, and that he remembers going through the same thing. The gap between the parents' notions of whether Alexa's play should become work lies, as it so often does, in their own origins. "My mother knew nothing about cartooning," says Denis. "I was in grade school, illustrating texts. By the time I was thirteen, I sold them. I was a publisher. My mother was a widow. I focused on survival. There was no recognition for me at home."

Unlike Denis, Stacey doesn't believe that the solution lies in turning Alexa's main solace–the thousands and thousands of stories she illustrates–into a professional career. Stacey's concern comes from her firsthand experience of the perils of play becoming work, of childhood becoming adulthood, and of youthful fame fading into adult obscurity.

Unlike Marla's paintings, Alexa's "work" isn't abstract in the least; it teems with human forms. Could that be an antidote to loneliness? There are carefully wrought images of horses and girls. There's a naked Alexa getting an X ray at a doctor's visit. Alexa prefers curious titles that carry a precocious poetry, like, FOUR SCARY ITALIAN GIRLS WHO SPEAK ENGLISH, LIFE AND BEAUTY: A BEAUTY GUIDE AND A LIFE GUIDE, CHILDREN CHAPTER ONE: HOW TO TEACH CHILDREN, and THE WEIRD HOTEL WORKERS.

At four, Alexa could incorporate words into her images, say her parents. Also at four, Alexa's imaginary friend "Kirsy" founded Kirsy Lirsy Land, or KLL. By five, her advanced vocabulary outpaced that of her parents–she would, they say, never again ask for assistance in spelling. She created several dictionaries to accompany KLL. Alexa frequently reads the dictionary and memorizes it, she tells me, and also the atlas. She is also into time zones, to the point that she knows the current time in both China and Alaska.

Sitting in the Kitchens' living room, her father says dotingly, "I look at

Alexa's drawing of a light switch and I know she did it in ten seconds, and that she did it fearlessly." Alexa peregrinates around the living room. "At two she drew a ladybug," her father continues. "It was an eighth of an inch, with wings that were a sixteenth, with dots and legs. Now, she's barely six and can do flashbacks. Even when I was twelve, I was a much more primitive artist. Alexa's work is inspired by others' art. And then she draws cubes. She can do perspective. First-graders can't do perspective. All her covers have cover pages, and she creates false collaborators to have authored them with her."

Denis is a professional artist and art-book publisher, but as a child, he was no prodigy. "I wasn't remotely as prolific," he says. "My mother never raved about my work, like I rave about Alexa's. I love the innocence of Alexa's work, the modesty."

In the Kitchens' home, one sees a whole host of cartoon-related paraphernalia: Shmoo dolls, spaceships, and plastic aliens. Among Denis's collectibles are hundreds of files of original cartoons, organized under categories like "Aliens," "Devil Girl," "Goldwater Buttons," and "Plastic Bob's Big Boy dolls." There are 3-D prints by Robert Crumb, and dolls of Nancy and Li'l Abner. In the basement there's an eight-paneled display case, roughly six feet high, filled from top to bottom with Shmoos.

One also sees a quiet parental war over what is to be done with their gifted child. Although the children's gifts vary widely–from skateboarding to shooting a basketball to programming a computer to looking pretty in a competition–the same argument takes place every night, in small towns and big cities all across America.

"I think of sending Alexa's work to *Nickelodeon* magazine, and I am 90 percent sure they'd accept it," muses Denis, patting his daughter's head. "If I did that, I would have turned Alexa into a novelty, I know. But we would be getting $350 a page for her college fund."

Denis has already started Alexa's public life, although in a less extreme fashion than Marla's parents. At a book-sale event, Alexa sat with her book next to the other cartoon books among her father's offerings. Above her hung a big, carefully lettered white sign, declaring: "Youngest Professional Cartoonist! 2 New Books!" When discussing the youngest-professional-cartoonist college fund, Stacey looks uncomfortable. "This is so you can be a proud papa?" she asks. She's joking, but with an edge. Alexa may be brilliant, Stacey says, but she doesn't get along with kids her own age.

"My wife was the victim of a stage mother," says Denis.

"Publishing Alexa would all be about you, a gloat for you," says Stacey, the former child beauty queen. Denis shrugs.

Stacey is proud of her daughter, recounting visits to the zoo that were cut short by Alexa's desperate need to write and draw, and she scrupulously maintains Alexa's Web site, which contains Alexa's biography and work. But Stacey also has her doubts.

"Alexa is six," she says. "What does publication mean to her?" Stacey completes the thought by explaining what going onstage meant to her when she was a child, when her play first became work. "I was mortified by the way my mother had me perform," she says. "Like the organ grinder's monkey."

FIVE

Gifted and Left Behind: Enrichment in the Public Schools

May books and Nature be their early joy!
And knowledge, right honoured with that name–
Knowledge not purchased by the loss of power!

WORDSWORTH, *The Prelude*

He was spoilt from childhood by the future, which he mastered rather early and apparently without great difficulty.

BORIS PASTERNAK

Mrs. Bauer throws a plastic, oversized eyeball. Inside the eyeball is a red liquid: fake blood. A petite girl with tiny glasses catches the eyeball. "The verb is 'export,'" she says a bit primly, and tosses the eyeball back.

Bauer, a small woman of late middle age and nearly cliché "kindly schoolteacher" looks–bobbed hair, crinkling smile, round rimless glasses–accepts it, sliding over in her non-schoolteacherish sequined clogs.

We're in a gifted classroom in Springfield, Illinois. Mrs. Bauer had asked the 25 nine-year-olds to come up with the verb that means "to send goods to another country." Now she's thinking of an adjective that could describe the area near the equator. Her hand wriggles along Ecuador and the Sahara Desert on a giant classroom map of the world.

Arms go up around the room. Bauer spots one belonging to a boy in a blue sweatshirt and throws him the eyeball.

"'Equivalent'?" he says, his mouth screwed to the side and one eye squeezed shut in a slapstick expression of concentration. "No," says Bauer. The boy in blue throws the ball back, and she throws it to Nick Wilson. He has been writing the answers to a homework assignment in pencil in a precociously achieved cursive. Looking up in time to catch the eyeball, he says, "The adjective is 'tropical.'"

Toward the end of the lesson, Bauer returns to "export." The concept rivets the children, perhaps because it involves sharing, taking, and giving all at once, on a grand scale. These are themes that children tend to find fascinating–taking "this is mine, this is yours, let's trade" to the global level.

"'Import' is export's opposite," says Bauer. "It means, 'to accept goods from another country.'"

"Like imported oil from Iraq!" squeals a boy.

The children excitedly start to check where their clothing is from. One kid's shirt was imported from the Dominican Republic; another's, from El Salvador.

This is fourth grade–traditionally, the grade kids pass through just before the disappointment sets in.

This is a gifted school, and Mrs. Bauer's class is what a good enriched class looks like. It's playful, with more games than a regular class and fewer students. The teacher has been trained to work with gifted kids, and knows how to engage them in self-directed learning. She shows them how to work together and learn from one another in groups. She does not become angry when they are hyperactive–one child plays incessantly with the cord hanging off the map until she takes it out of his hands. She challenges them with lessons like this one, where they discover, to their delight, that their clothing is manufactured in countries around the world, and learn that twenty years ago, none of their sweatshirts or flip-flops would read "Made in China," as so many do today.

The softness of the environment had become clear to me earlier that morning, when the nine- and ten-year-olds said "Hello" to the children beside them, shaking their classmates' hands and delivering compliments like "Nick has nice shirts and glasses." Students are encouraged to write poems about their experiences, and the poems, along with children's drawings, line the hallways. One boy has written, "I pretend to be dumb. I feel falling pianos. I worry about the apocalypse. I cry when chopping onions. I am funny in a strange way. I understand algebra. I say I will rule the universe."

Mrs. Bauer talks of each student's talents and peccadilloes, and about their families' hardships or lack thereof. She relates this information while standing beneath a ceiling covered with mobiles, where adjectives dangle from plastic airplanes among puffy white clouds. The classroom could fit nicely in a swanky private school–except for the fact that private-school children would likely be tapping their homework into a G4 computer, rather than at a hulking donated Apple workstation of early 1990s vintage. And at a swanky private school, few, if any, students would be eating a subsidized lunch, as many do here. The students at a swanky private school could probably look forward to attending a swanky private middle school. Their middle school experience would be a continuation, rather than a radical shift to overcrowded classrooms with upward of thirty-five students each. And such students would have been unlikely to witness a man being shot across the street from their school or to attend a school surrounded by houses known as excellent drug venues.

But Mrs. Bauer's class is at Iles Elementary, a public school–albeit a public school that has been called the seventh best elementary school in Illinois. It has been particularly commended for its slender "achievement gap," that euphemism used to describe the difference between the academic performance of children from lower-income, often minority families and everyone else. The school's skill at navigating the "achievement gap" is particularly necessary in a city's with a 15 percent African-American population–17,000 people–who for the most part tend to live on the east side of town, where Iles is located.

And Iles, as a gifted school, is under attack.

Iles principal Susan Rhodes, a fifty-something round-faced, feline blonde, wants to bring a school psychologist to Iles. She wants to ensure a linkage between the Iles curriculum and the one in the middle schools the children will attend after Iles, and see that "gifted kids at risk"–children with learning or behavioral disabilities or children from low-income or neglectful homes–will still get adequate and specific attention in middle school and high school. Like many of her colleagues in gifted education, Rhodes does not have the resources to ensure any of these things. She says that teachers are no longer being given professional development for teaching gifted education, which means training in the traits and needs of the gifted population, and in how to teach gifted and talented students in underrepresented populations, meaning poor and minority.

Four years ago, Illinois' gifted programs received $19 million in state funds. Now they get none. The state of Illinois used to sponsor gifted education training, with seven to eight days' worth of concentrated area education for teachers. Now it trains no one. Worse still, in the eyes of Illinois' gifted educators and irate parents, two years ago, all mention of gifted children was eliminated from the Illinois school code. (As of this writing, the language but not the money has been returned in Illinois.) Since 2001, it has become increasingly common for gifted students to be moved back into "regular" classes after middle school, where they repeat the same lessons they learned two years earlier.

Educators and administrators in Illinois are putting together programs on one-third of the money gifted programs had come to expect. Their funding is entirely derived from shuffling around nongifted money to cover their expenses, or from local sources. This, inevitably, means that the quality–and even the existence–of gifted programs depends upon the wealth of a particular school district. This is in stark contrast to 1979, when Illinois first earmarked state monies for gifted students: $4.5 million to start. After that, individual school districts wrote grants each year for the amount of money they thought they needed.

Jane Clarenbach, director of public education/affiliate relations at the National Association for Gifted Children, is quick to describe Illinois and Michigan as the two most dramatic examples of defunding. Illinois once mandated gifted education, and Michigan, while it did not mandate it, spent $6 million at the state level during the 2002–2003 year. By 2004, however, both states had eliminated funding, and Illinois its mandate. But Michigan and Illinois were far from alone. A survey by the association conducted in

2004 discovered that fifteen other states did not contribute toward gifted education and six contributed less than a million dollars.

The cuts in funding to gifted programs are part of a larger pattern of education funding cuts–which in turn reflect decreasing government support for social programs in general. But gifted programs face some specific obstacles, as well. In some communities and districts, one of the culprits in the cutbacks was clear: many gifted advocates blame this loss of funding on the federal program known as No Child Left Behind (NCLB). The 2001 NCLB Act's mandate was to fully fund basic-skills education, so that no child would slip through the cracks. In theory, the goal was, and remains, laudable. But many educators argue that NCLB's specific requirements have yielded widespread negative effects. There are broad problems with NCLB, they say, in particular its emphasis on standardized tests. Educator Deborah Meier writes in *Many Children Left Behind* that the emphasis on tests has moved schools "further and further from their publics and put the important decisions in the hands of a few large test and text publishers. . . . NCLB forces local districts to engage in one-size-fits all practices that ignore the needs of these children [children of color, the poor, handicapped kids, or kids who need ESL]."

Another negative consequence of NCLB has been the shifting of dollars away from gifted education, especially in poorer districts, as schools struggle to meet the requirements of NCLB. It's hard to measure the damage done to gifted education since the passage of NCLB, since gifted programs are funded on a state-by-state level, but according to Rebecca Eckert, the gifted resource specialist at the National Association for Gifted Children, "Programs are being cut because budgets are being reallocated." Today, 61 percent of classroom teachers have never received any training in gifted education, and just .00029 percent of the federal education budget goes to gifted and talented students.

NCLB exemplifies the deep ironies that are at work when it comes to our thinking about and support for gifted education. During the presidential race of 2000, education was one of the only real planks in George W. Bush's domestic platform. He presented himself as a compassionate conservative–one who cared about educating all of America's children. The "compassion" part would be demonstrated by insisting that all students meet minimal federal standards in reading and math skills. The "conservative" part was that no new federal money would be found to pay for this new emphasis–yet states would be punished if they failed to produce the desired effects. Given this situation, the easiest thing for Illinois and many other states to do was to cut public financing for gifted education. After all, what politician would suffer for such a cut? Gifted students were a small minority of the school population. And parents with wealth and influence were likely to be sending their gifted children–along with all their children–to private schools, or to schools in affluent suburbs where a strong local funding base could make up for state-level cuts. Failing to address the needs of gifted public school children held few political risks: it was a politically expedient solution to a sticky financial problem.

Some critics of America's educational system, including educator and writer Jonathan Kozol, detect ulterior motives behind NCLB, among them to catalyze the privatization of education. As Kozol told the *New York Times Magazine*, NCLB's "driving motive is to highlight failure in inner-city schools as dramatically as possible in order to create a groundswell of support for private vouchers or other privatizing schemes." Kozol and others see NCLB as a maneuver in that longer-term war.

And indeed, privatization is the key word. Growth of enrollment in private schools has been considerable. In 2004, six million students–11.5 percent of the nation's elementary and secondary school population–attended private schools, according to the Department of Education's National Center for Education. Enrollment in private elementary and secondary schools increased 18 percent between 1988 and 2001, and is projected to increase another 7 percent between 2001 and 2013. Additionally, the voucher system that offers parents a choice of where a child's share of government education funds can be applied, including private schools, has grown. Such trends have a significant bearing on the subject of gifted education, producing what I call a "privatization of talent" for children, where increasingly, only affluent families can afford the sobriquet "gifted."

Rather than raising a national alarm, these cutbacks in gifted education have been met with divergent responses. In part, this is because the cutbacks are not evenly distributed, and many districts–as well as private schools–are not feeling their heat. But the varied responses also reflect myriad views about the value and appropriateness of gifted programs. In fact, there are many sharp critics of the whole notion of gifted education. The rationales behind the criticism are various. Some education experts say that the gifted system serves middle-class and upper-middle-class students while underenrolling minority students. Others don't think the educational needs of the gifted should be given priority when so many American children are struggling in subpar schools, many without the benefit of natural gifts. A third strain views giftedness, like intelligence, as a social construct: if it exists at all, they believe, it reflects what kinds of thinking and behaviors we find acceptable, more than any inherent youthful brilliance. A fourth critique draws on plain old resentment at the whole idea that some kids should be selected out for special treatment.

Professor James Borland of Columbia University's Teachers College, perhaps the most radical gifted-education scholar, is one of those critics. At times, he seems to dislike his own specialty. He is as famous in his field for an essay praising the "death" of giftedness as literary critic Roland Barthes once was for declaring the "death of the author." In conversation, Borland asserts one of his overall criticisms of gifted education–that it is a subtle form of social control, with giftedness as a category with certain ethical and practical claims. He also argues that its programs have served primarily children of high socioeconomic standing, and thus the programs tend to be unjust and elitist. Borland says that there are "liabilities" in putting "a bunch of bright kids together." By this, he means that these children are guaranteed to do well because, he believes, they tend to already have many inbuilt advantages that students in "normal" public school classes may not, like being the products of homes with higher socioeconomic standing. Separating them out of the general school population only privileges the already privileged, which condemns the less advantaged students to mediocrity.

Borland is not alone: an entire genre of education writing is dedicated to critiquing giftedness not just as an elitist instrument but also as a way of enforcing social divisions, both of class and race, from an early age. In *Dividing Classes,* Indiana University professor of education Ellen Brantlinger writes that separating students does more harm than good "in light of the tenets of the American dream," and accuses gifted education of blocking diversity. In

Standardized Minds, education writer Peter Sacks renewed the critique of tracking, or grouping students in classes according to their skill, as sometimes involving institutional racism in early 1990s New Jersey, which, he writes, "amounted to the academic lynching of children of color."

The fairness problem, as Borland says, may be inherent in the whole idea of giftedness. A true assessment of giftedness–of a child's intelligence, talent, and potential–would require a level playing field, and "such a notion is impossible within the inequities in our society." Cultural capital is transmitted through families, with some families having what some sociologists call "accumulated advantage," a tradition of networks and behaviors and knowledges that prepare children for a professional elite, but it is also transmitted through schools. In this sense, gifted programs are really the icing on the cake in the creation of social class difference.

The arguments in support of gifted programs, however, are similarly vehement. Gifted psychologist Julia Osborn argues that the more extreme a child's intellectual ability, the less likely it is that the child will be able to bear with a standard curriculum. If some children can excellently decode words and comprehend printed passages and understand math processes, Osborn writes, they need to be in classes where these abilities are honed at earlier times than those of their peers.

In *Genius Denied,* Jan and Bob Davidson, founders of the Davidson Institute for Talented Development, a nonprofit for gifted children, write that gifted students in accelerated classes "advanced as much as a whole year compared to students of similar age and intelligence. In other words, for every year a highly gifted child is left in a regular, unenriched classroom, she loses a year of what her intellectual capabilities in that subject could have been. This is a very high price to pay in the name of equity."

According to the National Association for Gifted Children, there are three million academically gifted and talented students in the United States, and those in elementary school already know nearly half of the material to be covered in the regular class before the school year begins. Familiarity with the material–and the boredom that inevitably results–is part of the reason why around 20 percent of gifted and talented students, usually those from poorer backgrounds where extracurricular programs are far less available, drop out of schools. Advocates for the gifted point to this dropout rate to counter the common assumption that "the gifted," left to their own devices, will come out all right in the end. Entropy and a lack of interest can lead gifted children to perform poorly and ultimately drop out–an improperly nurtured gifted child can die on the vine.

Teaching the gifted, experts say, requires that there be gifted education services all the way through, from kindergarten to twelfth grade. A really adequate gifted program also requires flexibility: tiered assignments, elastic grouping, room for students to accelerate, and dual enrollment, where students can take college classes in high school. Teachers may use a range of tools: pretesting, whereby an instructor will test a child to see if she knows the material and then let her jump ahead if she does; and curriculum compaction, which means a teacher will give a gifted student fewer problems if he shows that he knows the material. Busy work that simply reiterates rather than advances students' knowledge can make gifted students very oppositional–what one gifted education expert describes as "real pills in the classroom." At the high end of the gifted spectrum, at programs like Johns Hopkins University's famous Center for Talented Youth, a student can complete a year's worth of math in three weeks at a ferocious clip.

I too think gifted education's techniques can be necessary and useful and that some children will suffer and be stymied without it, although one would like the sort of attention and enrichment that these programs at their best deliver to be available to all students,

But the argument that gifted children really need specialized education, where the schoolwork is accelerated and not repetitive, doesn't really dent giftedness's most fascinating enemy: social resentment. The resentment is understandable. Any time a select group is singled out for specialness–or worse still, singles itself out–resentment is inevitable. In Springfield, for instance, as in so many places, other people's specialness is not a source of delight. Springfield may even be extraordinarily committed to the ordinary. In a few conversations, it became clear to me that the city's residents actually want their town to be the Anywhereville Springfield featured on *The Simpsons:* when one passes the blinking power plant, three or four souls tell me it is the model for the Springfield nuclear power plant on the show. Springfield is the state capital, the longtime home of Abraham Lincoln, full of lobbyists, health insurers, lawyers, and chain restaurants that serve sandwiches with both cheese and fries in between the bread slices, as well as the nation's largest carillon (sixty-seven huge bells housed in a giant tower in a city park). That carillon, and memories of Lincoln, are the city's pride–not the programs for advanced learners in its public schools.

But the resentment of the gifted and of gifted education can be more nefarious than a general distaste for those who think of themselves as special. Some of it can be chalked up to anti-intellectualism. Parents of gifted children may fawn over them, and documentaries and films may represent an enchantment with "genius kids" (or perhaps it's just a morbid fascination). But ultimately, America dances with the cool kids rather than the smart ones, and seems to prefer them.

The resentment can seem an essential one, an angry and covetous response to those who are privileged, whether by nature or by nurture. It makes sense: the "gifted" label is elitist by definition, if we define elitism as the dictionary does, as advocacy for a choice part or segment of the population, or consciousness of being part of a socially superior group. Americans tend to have a culturally imbued respect for superiority that's achieved through hard work, or as a triumph over adversity. But the very word *gifted* suggests something unearned; even though gifted children may work hard for their achievements, they've had a head start based on chance rather than on deservedness. Those who are gifted are gifted by luck, by the good chance of genes and an environment that primed those genes for optimal intellectual performance. The word *gifted* also suggests the verb *to give.* The implication is that something has been given, and thus a debt has been incurred–and as with all gifts, a demand for reciprocation. But how is a child to reciprocate? There is, I think, a buried sense that the gifted child already owes the world something in exchange for the gift of her "natural" abilities, and to give her more classes and more funding would only deepen that debt. Social resentment toward the gifted stems from a basic aversion to the notion that some children are better than others; the selecting out of gifted kids can be seen as irritating, high-handed, or even unjust. If all animals are equal, how can some animals be more equal than others? If some are born better, why should their reward, their "gifting," continue? If they are "made," why should the public pay for their continued improvement? There's an inchoate sense that locating or building a "gifted class" of children cuts against the American ethos. As a society that is loath to acknowledge that there are social classes, Americans are disturbed by the notion of a group of kids that is entitled to a higher and more specialized tier of learning. And given that those who have "a gift" are often taught to think of themselves as special, some gifted kids do bear out the worst fears of the normal kids, thinking of themselves and defining themselves as better than their peers in school, and in some cases continuing to do so later in life.

Finally, being "gifted" has become something so cherished over the years that the designation of giftedness itself, and not the specialness it implies, has become the primary object of desire–and its own cause of resentment. An increasing number of Americans, including adults, seek out the label such programs confer, and judge themselves–and others–accordingly.

In 1981, psychoanalyst Alice Miller's book *Prisoners of Childhood: The Drama of the Gifted Child and the Search for the True Self* was published in the United States; it was retitled *The Drama of the Gifted Child: The Search for the True Self* when it was published in paperback in 1983. Despite its title, the book was not about academically gifted children; instead, it recounted the wounds inflicted on sensitive children by narcissistic parents, and was quite poignant and intellectually substantial in its attempt to do so. As Miller wrote after her book's publication: "When I used the word 'gifted' in the title, I had in mind neither children who receive high grades in school nor children talented in a special way. I simply meant all of us who have survived an abusive childhood thanks to an ability to adapt even to unspeakable cruelty by becoming numb. . . . Without this 'gift' offered us by nature, we would not have survived." (In the U.K., the book was published under the more subdued title *The Drama of Being a Child.*) American book buyers did not seem to mind seeing themselves as damaged, as long as they could also see themselves as gifted. Miller's diagnosis promised to explain why, despite the reader's gifts–as demonstrated by his or her ability to identify with the pain felt by the children described–he or she has not become rich and famous.

The craving for giftedness inspires some parents, like the mother who insisted to me that her seven-year-old daughter was highly gifted. When I met her and watched her slowly read a book from the Harry Potter series out loud, her finger tracing each word, her mother explained that she and her daughter both had "special mental talents." At the end of her reading selection, the daughter offered me one of the gold star stickers. I felt I was witnessing a kind of Munchausen syndrome by proxy–in reverse. Instead of presenting her healthy daughter as ill, the mother was presenting her gentle, relatively ordinary daughter as brilliant. Parents like this one, and others I have encountered who are so eager to wrap themselves in the giftedness cape, are one cause for social resentment. They can make it seem as if having a gifted child is essential to the parent's identity as well as the child's. The social resentment in this instance doesn't derive from the fact that they are narcissistic but rather from the fact that they are willing to publicly exalt in their children, although they would find exalting in themselves to be socially unacceptable.

As neuropsychologist and gifted specialist Nadia Webb has said of some of the parents she encounters in her practice as an intelligence evaluator, "These can be narcissistic parents, who see their children as an extension of themselves: that their child's accomplishment is their accomplishment." (Ironically, this is precisely one of the damaging parental behaviors described by Miller in *The Drama of the Gifted Child.*) While I basically support the idea of gifted education, I have my own misgivings about "giftedness" for children who are the objects of social resentment toward the gifted and also for those children whose giftedness is trained and refined incessantly at home or in costly extracurricular programs.

The history of gifted education reflects these tensions, containing conflicting crosscurrents of thought and emotion. The American public education system was premised on the notion of equality, and yet meritocracy is also a strongly held American value. The irony is that giving gifted kids–whether poor or middle class or wealthy–enriched education can be understood as both a fundamentally meritocratic practice and as an elitist one, all at the same time.

Giftedness had its antecedents: in *The Republic* Plato suggested that a handpicked child elite should be raised by teachers rather than their parents after the age of ten, and that this child elite should be composed of all classes. Eventually, its members would be ready to rule. In America, the blueprint of a merit-based elite found sponsors in men like Thomas Jefferson and

Ralph Waldo Emerson. Jefferson wanted the new country to locate and educate a "natural aristocracy" based on merit, rather than favoring privileged children. "There is a natural aristocracy among men," said Jefferson. "The grounds of this are virtue and talents." Of course, in the time of Plato, slaves were in abundance, and Jefferson was himself a slaveholder. During the late eighteenth century, the German philosopher Immanuel Kant imagined genius as unique imagination, aligned with a spirit. By the beginning of the twentieth century, the myth of Romantic genius had altered into the idea of a gifted child who can be culled from the assembly line of mass education and educated in a special but still reproducible fashion. One could see "giftedness" as a sort of mass-production model of genius, like the Ford automobile, or Frederick Taylor engineering experiments. Our school system, and especially its system of hierarchical tracking, was modeled on the German one. Early education reformer Horace Mann pushed for "Prussianized" schools in the 1840s. These schools "efficiently separated those bound for the factory from those headed to the office," writes historian David Nasaw. In every school, each group received "differentiated schooling adjusted to its probable workplace destiny."

Gifted education began as "advanced learning" in American public schools. It did not entail separate classes, but simply acceleration: smart children skipped grades. The superintendent of schools in St. Louis, Dr. William T. Harris, wrote in the 1870s of the benefits of accelerating gifted students through the grades, and he presented a plan for doing so, as well as for giving "bright pupils" more challenging work. Other ways of dealing with gifted children developed over time: in the late 1800s, a school district in New Jersey divided all of its lower-school classes into three sections based on ability. And in 1900, New York City established Rapid Advancement classes in one of its schools, and the first gifted program appeared in 1918. To this day, however, grade promotion remains the most common way to handle bright students; attempts to create tracking and enriched classes are scattershot by comparison.

Skipping grades was the first way that children got to use their gifts in the public schools without "taking away" anything from their struggling peers, and it continues to hold favor in some quarters of the gifted parent community. For instance, Susan Fenton, founder of Advocacy for Radical Acceleration, is a parent who sees grade-skipping as the solution. Fenton is a fifty-nine-year-old mother in Los Angeles whose eighteen-year-old son Michael just took the Law School Admission Test, or LSAT. Michael started attending an early-entrance college program at thirteen.

"He was a PG [profoundly gifted] kid who was not happy in seventh grade, so I arranged for him to go to a college," Fenton told me. "Before that, he was intimidating the teacher by using big words. He got 1100 on his SATs then. He's been a huge investment in time and money."

Fenton, a sturdy woman with hair cut in a black bob and the zeal of a woman twenty years her junior, was most intent on my understanding that she had accelerated her son because she didn't want to "normalize him" or force him to fit into standard schooling or curricula.

Fenton is part of a passel of parents who prefer acceleration to enrichment. Among today's parents, on Web sites for the gifted, and at events for the profoundly gifted, acceleration is the new dictum, conceived of as the best prophylactic against young boredom. Perhaps because acceleration seems to solve the problem of asking for special treatment without taking anything from children who are already deprived, the Internet teems with pro-acceleration essays. In one such essay, Carolyn K, parent of a gifted child, instructs other parents to not mention the word "skip" to skittish educators: "The myth is that children cannot 'skip' a grade because they might miss some valuable learning. But our children aren't missing anything, or at least not much. . . . The word we should be using is 'align.'"

In most of these parent-crafted essays, teachers and administrators are the villains. But the strongest voice for acceleration belongs to Nicholas Colangelo, the tanned, toothy, absurdly media-ready editor of *A Nation Deceived: How Schools Hold Back America's Brightest Students.* Colangelo, a professor of gifted education at the University of Iowa, is a devout fan of all forms of scholastic acceleration. Colangelo wants such decisions to be based on the Iowa Acceleration Scale, "so it's not up to mom or dad." He believes that reliance on this tool would reduce the impact of particularly bumptious or imperious parents.

The biggest obstacle to his plan, as he sees it, is that the public in general doesn't like acceleration, and educators have the most negative attitudes, "all because it doesn't fit with their philosophy that all kids ought to be treated the same. At colleges of education, they never take a class on gifted education. They see themselves as progressive . . . , that all kids are gifted, that all kids should have the same things. The attitude is that when we accelerate, we are forcing them to have something they are not ready for."

Acceleration is certainly the cheapest answer–far cheaper than hiring special teachers or building new buildings to house gifted programs. And because it costs little, it is far less explosive politically than, say, demanding ample federal funds for gifted education. But does it damage children to remove them from their peer group? The answer is not entirely clear. Advocates of acceleration point not only to Colangelo's book but also to a 1992 meta-analysis by University of Michigan researchers, who crunched twenty-six studies conducted internationally of accelerated students, and found that such students not only do better academically than their peers but also have nearly the same social abilities as those peers. But another study conducted with data gathered from children who attended the Center for Talented Youth at Johns Hopkins confirmed the ambiguities of acceleration: it found that while 95 percent of the 175 youths in the study regarded their acceleration positively, 50 percent reported some negative effects. At the same time, though, only 2 percent reported only negative effects.

Sometimes skipping is simply elevating students in a plebian manner–simply speeding up their educations rather than improving them or transforming them to meet the needs of gifted kids. When children skip a grade, after all, the teaching style of the instructor remains the same, as does the general pace of learning; the only difference is that the material is one grade or more further along.

The most authoritative voice for radical acceleration in recent history was Julian Stanley, the late founder of the Center for Talented Youth, a math and science summer program for exceptional junior high schoolers. He compared the suffering of the nonaccelerated child to a Procrustean bed of Greek legend, where presumably the mind of a bright child is like the body cut to conform.

Stanley, however, wound up questioning the practice later in life, writing, "A danger of starting early is that you may get into the wrong field. If you're good in math and science, you get moved into physics, etc. At each stage, you get moved up. But if you do it too early before you've thought it out, you might settle for a career that you end up not being happy with."

Some of Stanley's former students agree with his later opinion, including Stephen Menn, forty, now a philosophy professor at McGill University. At fifteen, part of a wave of child mathematicians recruited by Stanley, Menn attended college at Johns Hopkins as a simultaneous candidate for a B.A. and Ph.D. Menn speaks to me from his home in Montreal. His voice rises as he recalls the way Stanley would look at students' transcripts without permission and then, Menn says, dolorously, send notes of unsolicited advice. Stanley also dictated that Menn and other young students should stock up on math and science courses–in order, Menn believes, to make Stanley look good by doing well in subjects the students already knew intimately. Menn accuses Stanley of doing this so he could "take credit for our achievements. He was just interested in churning students out, proving his idea that you can educate bright students starting young."

While Menn ultimately was glad he had been accelerated, his story illustrates the risks of being propelled ahead too early: a child's path can be extrinsically rather than intrinsically defined, to the child's ultimate detriment. A writer friend of mine who skipped a few grades was even more vituperative about the experience than Menn. To be fair, though, a number of the adults I have spoken to who were accelerated were quite sanguine about the practice. Suzanne Conklin Akbari, now a forty-year-old professor of English and medieval studies at the University of Toronto, who started college at Johns Hopkins at fifteen, said she was thankful for the head start and the early escape from high school drudgery. So was twenty-one-year-old Monique Okumakpeyi, who started high school at eleven, attended the University of Virginia as a young teenager far from her immigrant family in Brooklyn, and ultimately graduated from UVA with a master's degree in accounting at the age of twenty.

Acceleration has now become the favored strategy for educating gifted populations. This will most likely change, as gifted education tends to alter its methods cyclically, a microcosmic version of the concerns of Americans at large, as well as larger trends in education. Lewis Terman, creator of the Stanford-Binet test, was interested in studies and psychological tests in the 1920s, one heyday for such tests. His longitudinal study of high-IQ children helped to define the "gifted" as a school population. Gifted educator Leta Hollingworth formed a curriculum based on a longitudinal study she conducted of students with IQs over 155, and then in 1936 established the Speyer School for gifted children, where the children studied common life as well as academic subjects in the hopes of helping them live in the world, reflecting the educational tactics popular in that period, among them progressive education. Another example of Hollingworth's progressivism for the gifted: Hollingworth thought role models would help such children find their way, so she assigned biographies to the students in her enrichment classes.

An atmosphere of national pride influenced the next wave of gifted education. Twenty years later, gifted ed would get another infusion of energy, not from individuals with a passion for psychological tests or for locating and enhancing bright children, but from nationalist anxieties. Sputnik, the satellite that the Soviet Union lofted into orbit at the height of the Cold War in 1957, caused Americans to panic. The USSR had beaten the United States into space, and according to the conventional wisdom, American schools were largely to blame for this humiliating and dangerous failure. One response was that America's education administrators launched a new effort to shore up scientific education in general, and in particular science for gifted children, who would be the astrophysicists of tomorrow. Gifted children would repay America for giving them a superior education by making our nation stronger. This new focus led to the Great Talent Hunt, a national search to uncover and educate gifted children. During the Cold War, the gifted student plucked from the masses, who had long symbolized American democracy, also came to stand for America's ability to defend itself against the Communist menace.

These were halcyon days for gifted education. By the late 1960s, however, they also became halcyon days for a backlash of criticism against gifted education. It was a period when all sort of programs that were seen as serving "the Establishment" or building "the Elite" were attacked. Tracking and other armature of gifted education were widely perceived to be important maintainers of elite privilege, and as such were also assailed. A decision against ability grouping in the district schools in Washington, D.C., written by U.S. Appeals Court judge Skelly Wright in 1967 and quoted in the book *Gifted Children,* asserted that "the aptitude tests used to assign children to the various tracks are standardized primarily on white middle-class children," and thus relegated "Negro and disadvantaged children to the lower tracks from which, because of the reduced curricula and the absence of adequate remedial and compensatory education as well as continued inappropriate testing, the chance of escape is remote."

Rather than abandon gifted education, some initiatives sought to expand it–to offer its advantages to a wider and more diverse body of students. The Marland Report, the result of research on gifted programs, was delivered in 1971. According to the report, gifted education was not sufficiently available or accessible, and the report advocated federal action to address such inequities. By the late 1970s, gifted education had become far more accessible, and had ceased to be an enemy of political progressives. Ironically, the liberal and Left arguments of the 1960s against gifted education and tracking–that it was racist, classist, and societally divisive, and that educational resources should be placed with weaker learners rather than stronger ones–would be employed by conservatives to promote No Child Left Behind. Forty years ago, the case against tracking often also was a case against testing. This is clearly no longer the case.

Yet it's hard for me to dismiss the critiques of gifted education made in the 1960s, still being made: ability grouping can be just another way to reify class privilege, and it's also easy to find it more fair and perhaps more socially valuable to support weaker learners over stronger learners. The critique of gifted education articulated in the 1960s had some merit. What's so wrong with America condoning cutbacks?

My visit to Iles showed me what is wrong with the cutbacks in gifted education: these programs don't only serve a wealthy elite–or in some cases, even the middle class. They also give bright kids from poorer families a much-needed boost. In Springfield, for instance, for a good number of the families I met, gifted education was the only way they could hope to educate their children as they wished to. They did not create their gifted children in a home laboratory, and they could not afford to send their children to private schools. For them, public gifted classes provided the only way ahead.

This was the case for one of the parents I met, Mary Beth Alejandro, who was born into a family of factory workers in central Illinois and never graduated from high school. Alejandro's daughter Sarah, an Iles graduate, is now in seventh grade.

"I was a rebel," Alejandro says raspily as we sit in the chain restaurant known as Chedda's, eating bread, cheese, and grease. Married at twenty-two, giving birth to Sarah at twenty-three, Alejandro had already started drinking heavily when her husband, Sarah's father, was killed. She drank so much, she says, that at her lowest, she literally fell on her face and her daughter was taken care of by others. Ultimately, she sobered up to the point where she could care for her daughter again. Even so, it was a surprise when her luck turned around and her daughter obtained a high enough score on the Cognitive Assessment Test, known informally as the Naglieri, to be admitted to Iles. The Naglieri–a nonverbal test using brightly colored materials–is administered to all first-graders in the district, because it is believed to be less culturally biased than other intelligence tests.

"You don't know what they have unless they blossom," Alejandro tells me, popping fries into her mouth. She's small and thin, with feathered, sandy hair. One of her blue eyes is lazy, and she has a lurching strut of a walk. She and her daughter are physically unalike–while the mother is fair and her face looks weather-beaten, as if etched by her early life, Sarah's skin is dark and smooth. She has dark eyes, and is taller and fuller bodied than her mother. Her bearing is proper, and at times she seems disconcertingly motherly, correcting her mother gently and even calming her down. She's dressed neatly, in a ladylike purple and green outfit, while her mother is wearing unisex, functional clothing. Sarah keeps her black hair combed back sleek and flat in a ponytail.

Mary Beth Alejandro picks me up in a new car she bought earlier this year. It's her first car, and at thirty-six, she is also in her first year of driving. Before now she'd been "a walker," as she puts it–someone who walked forty minutes to work as a substitute school lunchroom server because she was afraid to get behind the wheel. When Alejandro expresses concern about her driving, Sarah reassures her–but is sure to catch my eye as her mother inches nervously down the cornfield-and-chain-restaurant-lined highway. She bought the car on an installment plan using the money left behind in her husband's life insurance policy; she really couldn't afford it, she tells me. But there is a longer backstory to her lack of driving skills–and her determination to acquire them. This involves a viperous stepmother who told her she was incompetent, "in order to make me dependent," says Alejandro. Alejandro has spent twenty years getting the "emotional junk off" her just so she can do basic tasks, she says. But she has a good sense of humor about it: "Don't laugh," she says. "I'm reading a book called *Insecurities.*" She then laughs at herself for feeling insecure about insecurity. She is now a car owner and a driver in part because members of her church community–newfound in her sobriety–taught her how to drive using their cars.

In a sense, gifted classes for Sarah have functioned like driving for Alejandro. "They put Sarah's artwork up at Iles," Alejandro says. "She plays the flute. I know that higher opportunity comes with higher-level thinking skills. For Alejandro, the opportunity is the key: she and her daughter live together in a mobile home, an '83 Windsor that she has had for ten years. She got a GED in 2000, pays the bills with $1,400 a month, has no insurance, and is, she says defiantly, in the lowest tax bracket.

"My daughter's on track, she'll have taken high school algebra by eighth grade and gotten an early start on college. When I was a kid, I was hating authority, and that comes into the school, into work," says Alejandro. "It's my job, I brought her into the world: I have to make it best for her. When she was real little, I read to her. I saw a parent educator. I knew I had an at-risk kid. The parent educator told me, 'Call me. I'll always give you a ride, call me.' Now Sarah wants to be a veterinarian. She wants to go to college."

At all ends of the spectrum, from a verdant costly private school for the "severely gifted" in Los Angeles to the Iles School in Springfield, parents, in particular mothers, are gifted education's foot soldiers. The common refrain among mothers I have spoken to, more than thirty years after second-wave feminism, is that they, rather than the fathers, take care of their children's education. Liesl Smith Mulder is one of those mothers. Parent of a seven-year-old named Marlie who attends Iles, Mulder is concerned that in sixth grade, when she leaves Iles, her child will "backtrack," losing the mental edge she got from her gifted program at Iles. Despite Mulder's efforts, Marlie almost certainly will lose that edge when she moves on to a middle school that isn't equipped for gifted students.

Mulder, who is African-American, grew up on Springfield's rough East Side as one of seven children, and credits education with her own transformation; she is now a university professor at Lincoln Land Community College. Her faith in education is part of why Marlie now reads three hours a day; even at Iles, the reading requirement is only twenty minutes a day. Liesl Mulder is a very involved parent, and intent on her daughter receiving enrichment she deems adequate. "The older I get, the angrier I get," she says. "Are we ever going to individualize education? This is a capital city, and yet the only option for my kid is one crowded middle school. I don't want Marlie to stagnate."

At Iles, Marlie was not stagnating, said Mulder–and in my days there, I saw why. It was in the classrooms, but also in the lunchroom and at recess. Iles was special–an intense fourth-grade class on hurricanes and natural disasters and another on how information is organized showed that to me. But Iles was also warmly ordinary, a necessary combination for the gifted population, who can so easily descend into isolation. At lunch, the kids discussed vivisection and a rock band a few of them had formed. They look up from pooling ketchup on their trays to give a brief performance, replete with air-guitar flourishes and harmonies. One boy tells me he is working on a novel called *Frankendude,* whose main character is "freakish and cool." In the hall, a sign reads "Bully-Free Zone."

Without these classes and this environment, there is a risk for gifted kids. They can tune out in school and backtrack, as Liesl Mulder worries: some kids really do require unique modes of teaching to reach their full potential. But for children like Sarah Alejandro, the early intervention and the support Mary Beth Alejandro received from the gifted program made all the difference. That's because for committed teachers and administrators like Iles's Susan Rhodes, getting the Iles children onto the marigold-colored school buses and supervising the loud lunchtime intake of skim milk and Tater Tots coexists with a more particular set of concerns, like getting special accommodation for gifted kids at risk–ensuring that her staff knows all about the signs of attention-deficit hyperactivity disorder, for example. Rhodes got her teachers to learn about ADHD, and also to attend to the children whose economically disadvantaged backgrounds may have led to gaps in their early learning. When I visited, she was not just attempting to get adequate care for children with "double diagnosis"–giftedness and a learning or behavioral disability. She was also trying to bring unusual extras to the school, like a literary festival. Rhodes had also recently fought for the ultimate "extra"–expanding her school so it would include a middle school, a gesture that brought Rhodes and her parental coconspirators into conflict with many of the citizens of Springfield.

The idea of extending Iles as a middle school, when there was already one middle school that served gifted kids in the city, went against Springfield's grain. A local paper noted that Iles's "success–again among the top in the state–in academic achievement among minority and low-income students" did not mean that Iles's parents should be able to keep their children at the school for junior high. The editorial argued that "spending huge sums to provide another option for a relatively small number of students is almost impossible to defend, especially in a school district that has had to make substantive cuts in recent years that affect large swaths of the student population. . . . While we understand the appeal of a K-8 program, the truth is that most District 186 students are not given that option."

This means that after Iles, parents like Mulder may not be able to retain an Iles-quality education for their children.

And this is happening for a reason that goes beyond a budget crunch and the reallocation of education funds. "Giftednessness" touches on a number of tensions in this country. We want to educate children to their fullest potential. Yet we may well resent that a sliver of kids is getting schooling that can be seen as more advantageous than "normal" schooling. Prodded by the pundits of our age to fret about international competition, we fear American students falling behind their peers in other countries. Yet schools teach to the mean under NCLB, primarily preparing children for routine tests rather than introducing more complex knowledge. An estimated 10 to 12 percent of students in Chicago are not meeting the testing standards, no matter what educational approach is used with them. Thus, the approach becomes a kind of triage: they exist in one corner, and the gifted children in another. The contrast is part of the dilemma of the gifted child. It's an American knot, where impassioned ideals of individual excellence and exclusiveness are tied up with our pride in egalitarianism.

My days at Iles showed me not just the importance of funding gifted education, now endangered by cutbacks, but the value of gifted education in general. So did my conversations with adults whose lives were altered by their gifted programs. Ruben Carbajal was one of them: without gifted programs, he would probably not have gone to college. Now thirty-four, he recalls being selected for a gifted program as a child in Racine, Wisconsin. He attended a Lighthouse program, which mixed some of the most academically talented and academically thwarted children in the same "special" classes. Ruben is the son of Latino born-again Christians. His mother dropped out of high school to have him when she was seventeen, and his butcher father, like the rest of his family, did not attend college.

"It's hard for me to separate who I am from the gifted program," he says. "I lovingly thought out lesson plans. I felt very special, although I disliked the idea of being better than others. I also learned how to work the system." Joining the gifted program in grade school gave Carbajal class status, friends, and a more imaginative learning experience. But when he got to high school, no such program existed, and he nearly fell through the cracks. It was friends he had met as a child, college-bound kids whose parents were managers at Johnson & Johnson, who by example reminded him to apply to college. It was through them that Carbajal realized in his senior year that he should have taken the SATs. He didn't attend college "on time," but he did go–thanks to his friends from the grade-school gifted program. As an adult, Carbajal found himself with so many good memories of the program that he wrote a play about it called, appropriately, *The Gifted Program.* A valentine to the originality of gifted kids, it's also a portrait of their nerdish freakiness.

Stories like Carbajal's, of which I heard a number while researching this book, brought home to me how effective gifted education in the public schools can be–if nothing else, it can help to bring children into broader social contexts where learning is valued. At Iles, kids I saw were flourishing in this environment in a way they probably wouldn't have in regular classrooms, especially in public schools in poorer areas. But the response is not adequate. Instead of fully funding education for both the gifted and those students who are struggling, we make kids fight a battle royale in which either the gifted or the academically straggling will lose–a battle where the children can only cancel one another out.

SIX

Gurus of Giftedness: Intelligence Testing and Talent by Other Measures

"Is my IQ okay?"

"More than okay."

"What is it?"

"I am not going to tell you. But it assures me that both you and Charles Wallace will be able to do pretty much whatever you like when you grow up to yourselves. You just wait till Charles Wallace starts to talk. You'll see."

MADELEINE L'ENGLE, *A Wrinkle in Time*

Linda Silverman's eyes widened earnestly behind rimless glasses as she addressed her audience of forty. "If you tell me a grandparent's IQ score," she said, "I can tell you their child's and grandchild's scores within ten points."

Then Silverman asked, "When you see a gifted kid, what do you see?"

The audience didn't know how respond. One muttered under her breath, "I love her." All looked at Silverman expectantly.

Clad in a billowing batiked purple-and-black shirt and skirt and a silver-buckled belt, Silverman strode over to the slide machine to present a graph of the standard deviations of IQ. Her manner and clothing gave the impression of a mystic bringing the Word to her disciples.

In a sense, that's just what she was. As the founder of the Institute for the Study of Advanced Development in Colorado, a consultancy that tests and assesses up to two hundred children a year, Silverman is a high priestess of giftedness, a matriarch of lost boys and girls. One can quickly see why so many are drawn to her: although I had known her only by telephone, upon seeing me, she greeted me with a grand hug. Seeing her do the same with a number of others, I imagined how consoling such a hug must be to the solitary gifted child. When I saw Silverman, she herself was far from solitary. She was with some 620 parents, educators, and other professionals at the World Gifted Conference of the World Council for Gifted and Talented Children, gathered in the New Orleans Hyatt Hotel in August 2005. Housed in a giant, anodyne building, the conference was a world apart from New Orleans's landmark nineteenth-century houses with iron gridwork and bougainvilleas, and just as far apart from New Orleans's many extremely poor neighborhoods. The World Gifted Conference, like so many conferences, took place in an antiseptic hotel, sealed off from the harsher urban spaces that surrounded it. The gap was not merely aesthetic. Even before Hurricane Katrina, Louisiana had the second lowest literacy rate in the United States.

The World Council for Gifted and Talented Children (WCGTC) is an international group, and the conference it organizes is a biennial event. Now based in Winnipeg, Canada, the WCGTC has been holding conferences for thirty years. It draws psychologists, university professors, secondary and elementary school teachers, school administrators and guidance counselors, academic psychologists, and a host of other private practitioners, as well as numerous parents–a small reflection of the members of the "gifted community." The WCGTC is actually smaller than other giftedness groups like the National Association for Gifted Children or the Association for the Gifted, and the World Gifted Conference is smaller than the gifted conferences of the state organizations of California or Texas, each of which brings in thousands of people. Nevertheless, the conference is one of the community's major events. Howard Gardner, a professor of education at Harvard University, the author of the *Multiple Intelligences* books (and the concept they are named for), and one of the intelligence field's true rock stars, wasn't there, but plenty of other giftedness demiurges were on hand, from Silverman to Joseph Renzulli, director of the University of Connecticut's Neag Center for Gifted Education and Talent Development.

The World Gifted Conference is also a trade show, and I found the peddlers of the giftedness industry an engaging supplement to the many talks. One could visit booths advertising Johns Hopkins University's Center for Talented Youth or purveying texts from gifted book publisher Great Potential Press. My visit to the trade exhibit punctuated my attendance of days of talks like edu-cute "Noggin' Nuggets: Mining Our Potentials" or the fashionably neuroscientific "Understanding the Gifted Brain: A Practical Understanding." (During the latter talk, a big blue image of the brain of a gifted child was projected on a screen, looking for all the world like an indigo boxing glove.) The attendees at the World Conference were indeed an international group. East Asian giftedness experts were there en masse from China, Singapore, and Taiwan, many with surprisingly emotive talks like "Helping Gifted Children Adapt Psychologically," and talk of gifted kids' "overexcitabilities."

This is the stomping ground of the highly idiosyncratic giftedness subculture, a subculture with its own quiddities. Among them is a penchant for conferences; there are dozens each year, and they are important enough to the community that I knew I had to attend one. It is also a culture with its own idiom. During the four days of the World Conference, participants referred to "the gifted" simply as "gifted" without an article, just as insiders and wannabes refer to the Central Intelligence Agency not as "the CIA," but as "CIA." (Sample sentence at the conference: "It's the best we can do for gifted.") Attendees slung diagnostic lingo with the comfort ordinary people use to discuss the romantic life of Hollywood's star du jour: instead of Angelina Jolie and Brad Pitt, they referred easily to "sensory modal," "visual spatial learning," "doubly exceptional" (a category that includes giftedness alongside another condition, like attention deficit disorder or Asperger's syndrome, a condition that is related to autism), and that old-time fave, "OCD" (obsessive-compulsive disorder). Creative–and even eccentric–behavior was generally encouraged: at one dinner, all participants were given complimentary feathered masks, pace Mardi Gras. A teacher sitting across from me would not rest until she found a bird mask, rather than the animal mask she had been given, and I watched the uninhibited giftedness professionals on hand do a line dance, their plumes swaying to the beat.

Silverman was one of a host of private intelligence psychologists at the conference. Over the course of my travels in giftedness, her name was frequently uttered, to the point that she had distinguished herself in my mind as *the* emblem of the contemporary giftedness movement, at its most zealous. She was one of its more well-known and splashy figures, and as such she would later that year be written about at length in the *New Yorker* as she assessed and counseled the profoundly gifted adolescent Brandenn Bremmer, whom I spoke to in 2004 and who committed suicide in 2005.

The favored evaluator for many in the PG community, Silverman also gained notoriety for being the tester of a child named Justin Chapman. In 2000, when Chapman was six, Silverman found the boy to have an IQ greater than 298–the highest ever recorded. Chapman was soon selling products like the Bell bicycle helmet, and interviewing New York governor George E. Pataki about age discrimination. Nearly as quickly, he began threatening suicide. He was hospitalized after suffering a nervous breakdown of sorts in November 2001. Subsequent testing showed him to be of average intelligence. Justin's brilliant performance turned out to be a deliberate hoax, promulgated by his underachieving, highly ambitious, but penniless young mother, Elizabeth Chapman. Elizabeth had created a delusional biography, and had supplied her only son with answers to the IQ test, fooling Silverman about her son's prodigy in the process. In another instance, Chapman palmed off her neighbors' son's SAT scores as Justin's own.

But neither dozens of years of testing thousands of children nor the tragic fates of two children she had championed seemed to have dampened Silverman's enthusiasm for IQ testing, and for extreme giftedness more generally. In both tone and content, many of Silverman's discussions of the phenomena of giftedness are imbued with a New Age sense of awe and mystery. She talks about the Flynn effect, which notes a rise in average IQs worldwide at a rate of 3 points every ten years in developed countries, and the apparent increase in the numbers of extremely gifted children. "There's no logical explanation for the fact that these kids are growing and multiplying," she told me passionately. Some of her statements are startling: "Something is different about them. These kids talk to animals and the animals communicate back." In many of her assessments of gifted children, she tends to advocate "vision therapy," the eye exercises for improvement of visual tracking that she believes increases one's intellectual powers.

Silverman may be one of the most visible doyennes of giftedness to express such New Age views–but she is far from alone. Time and again, I heard members of the gifted community mention the "Indigo Child" hypothesis, a New Age belief that unusually bright souls are coming to Earth today because the planet needs their talents. Indigo Children were first defined in the 1970s by a parapsychologist named Nancy Ann Tappe on the basis of their "indigo auras" and their acute consciousness. Among gifted psychologists and assessors and parents, it is relatively common to hear a child or client referred to as an Indigo Child, meaning he has a high IQ, special powers of intuition, and sometimes behaviors associated with attention deficit disorder.

Silverman's awestruck tone also made me wonder whether there is something in the desire to be near the extremely gifted that reflects a wish to be part of a transcendent category, to be adjacent to exceptional creatures not hindered by the ordinary rules of human existence.

Silverman and testers like her, of which there were quite a few at the conference, tend to focus on the "exceptionally gifted" and above. This is something akin to embracing a star system for youth intelligence. Intelligence here is the traditional one uncovered on IQ tests–a general unitary factor, referred to as "*g*," of mental ability. The general unitary factor can be measured to produce a number that is thought to predict a child's scholastic performance. This sort of test of mental ability is a product of the field of psychometrics or psychological measurement: while a psychologist could also measure an individual's personal psychology and attitudes with a psychometric instrument, the field of psychometrics not only tests personality and intelligence but also elaborates existent theories of measurement of mental ability.

Silverman employed her own demarcations, demarcations that were for the most part based on her testing using an older version of the Stanford-Binet test, the L-M, which a number of scholars believe doesn't provide an accurate assessment. She denoted children with IQ scores of 120 to 129 as advanced learners (some public school gifted programs require scores of 120 and up, and others 130 and up), 130 to 144 as moderately gifted, 145 to 159 as highly gifted, 160 to 174 as exceptionally gifted, and 175 and above as profoundly gifted. In other words, to be just "gifted," or approximately two standard deviations above the mean, means a child is in the 98th percentile of the population. To be "highly gifted," or approximately three standard deviations above the mean, is to be in the 99th percentile, while to be "exceptionally gifted," approximately four standard deviations above the mean, is to be in the 99.99th percentile. To my relief, those with IQs above 200–the "terrifyingly gifted," as Silverman calls them–were left out of most of the presentations. As I noticed myself relax at their absence, I wondered if these children intimidated me. (My potential intimidation is for others a sort of full-blown dread. As conservative critic Gertrude Himmelfarb wrote in *Commentary* in 1953, "Today's prodigy is looked upon less as precocious than as queer. . . . the prodigy no longer appears to be simply an adult in child's clothing, which would merely be a violation of convention, but a freak in child's clothing, which is an outrage against nature.")

Some of the conference was dedicated to the different ways that these scores could currently be obtained: psychologists see testing as a means of locating the best and the brightest. But a minority of them also think it's important to discriminate between a child with a 170 IQ and one with a 200 IQ. These testers thrive in part because some parents, and generally wealthier ones, have been flocking to psychologists willing and able to pay for intelligence tests out of pocket. Parents have been known to test children as young as two, although psychologists recommend they wait until children are at least three or four years old.

For instance, 1,500 private schools and suburban public schools around the country use the Educational Records Bureau tests as a basis of admission. The youngest to take one of the four tests developed and administered by the ERB are children of prekindergarten age. As with the Educational Testing Service and the SATs, the ERB is a private testing service that has established national standards, almost as if they were serving a public function. They tend to have something of a monopoly. In addition, they are less a choice for parents than a necessity. The ERB defines itself as an "educational service organization providing more challenging assessments to private schools and suburban high schools." Its motto is "Quality Assessment for Quality Schools," and its instructions to its youngest test takers include the recommendation that their parents shouldn't coach them, as their coaching will be "detected." Most private schools in the New York City area, for example, require scores from the Independent Schools Admissions Association of Greater New York (ISAAGNY) test, which is administered by ERB. There are also a number of schools around the country with stringent IQ minimums, like the Mirman School for the Gifted in Los Angeles, whose admissions director is a former Aveda model. Tuition at Mirman for the 2006 school year was $17,300; the required uniforms are, of course, extra. Mirman's IQ minimum of 145, which its founder has described as the "severely gifted," makes it the most desirable destination for Hollywood dwellers (even those who otherwise tend to quantify their achievements with box office numbers rather than brains). Some private schools, like Da Vinci Academy in Elgin, Illinois, require an IQ test score of 125 for admission into the first grade. Others, like Mackintosh Academy in Littleton, Colorado, and Arrowrock Classical School for the Gifted in Boise, Idaho, base admission in part on the IQ score of the applicant. A frequent IQ minimum for gifted schools is 130.

In the land of gifted education, the basis for admission is often pitched as achievement plus aptitude: an assessment includes the evaluator's observation of a child's classroom performance and work, and achievement tests providing working "data points." This is all well and good. But such subtle and thorough testing can be expensive. Linda Silverman's office gives a two-day assortment of tests, at the cost of $250 per hour. Barbara Louis, a psychologist who specialized in gifted assessment at the Institute for the Study of Child Development at the Robert Wood Johnson Medical School in New Jersey, charges $1,500 for three meetings. "I get upper-middle-class families [as clients]," says Louis. "These are parents that spontaneously take their child to the Liberty Science Center nine times a year." Louis encourages parents to wait until their children are six to be tested–unless they have a really good reason for doing so earlier, such as trying to get their three-year-old into an academically oriented preschool.

Neuropsychologist Nadia Webb, who runs a private practice assessing gifted children in Harrisonburg, Virginia, charges $1,000 per evaluation. Her evaluations consist of conversations with the parents and the child, four hours of testing, and an hour of scoring and writing up results. Webb is quite a popular tester, and when I met her, I could see why. Clad in a suit and glasses, she nevertheless could not hide her occasional Gen X mannerisms, including a proclivity for rolling her eyes and a surprising use of the word *like.* The forty-year-old Webb seemed twenty-five, with her winning quirks, what she calls her "round hamster face," and her candor–she told me bluntly that those who can afford private testing are in a much better position than those who cannot. Psychologists charge about $150 an hour, and she herself charges $215 an hour. Medical insurance doesn't tend to cover assessment tests fully, if at all, and a parent must be a "pill," Webb says, to get a child's tests covered. For instance, a parent can lobby hard for an independent medical evaluation for a child, and sometimes get an assessment as part of that evaluation. But for the most part, says Webb, if her office does the testing, "We have to have people who are willing to pay out of pocket. Anyone who can't pay $1,000 can't come to us." The least expensive option for a private assessment is usually an evaluation at a university, supervised by a psychologist. This kind of low-end evaluation, even with some insurance coverage, is still $600 or so.

Alternatives to private testing, Webb believes, are often inadequate, and sometimes completely unavailable. "It's gotten to a point that if a child is assessed in the public schools, there's one school psychologist who doesn't have time to build rapport with the child," she says. "The psychologist may have a thousand other children to see. She probably hasn't talked to the parents. She doesn't know the child. So teachers are picking out who is the smartest in the class–the blond boy with glasses, the one that everybody spots. As a psychologist, I can look for multiple intelligences, talk to the child, to the parent. I have that luxury."

According to Carolyn Callahan, a professor of education at the University of Virginia, former president of the Association for the Gifted and the National Association for Gifted Children, conductor of school gifted program evaluations, and coeditor of the book *Gifted Program Standards,* many public schools can afford only a limited assessment process. They tend simply not to have enough psychologists to perform individual intelligence assessments on gifted children. To cull kids for gifted programs, schools sometimes depend on means like teacher rating scales, not an intelligence test or any of the other data points like a child's written work. In the course of her studies of intelligence assessment, Callahan has found only one state,

Florida, where intelligence testing to locate gifted children was fairly routine. This has meant that numerous private evaluators have sprung up–among them, says Callahan, some evaluators who, if "you pay the right amount of money, get the right score."

In addition, in public schools, screening for students tends to occur later than it does in private evaluation–in second or third grade for placement in third or fourth grades. Children like Justin Chapman and others in the gifted community who visit private evaluators may have their testing done two years earlier, at ages five or six. The desire for a score that leads to school admission has also led companies like Bright Minds to sell books and software that purport to "help children improve their performance on the Stanford-Binet or Otis-Lennon [tests]." Bright Minds employs the home sales model, recruiting "hostesses" to hold parties for friends and neighbors where Bright Minds products–and their promise of "Better Grades & Higher Test Scores–Guaranteed!"–are sold in place of Mary Kay cosmetics or Tupperware.

The belief that it is possible to use intelligence tests to scientifically determine a child's human potential began to spread in the 1920s in the public school system. Intelligence tests were also used in the army. Like those who promoted gifted education, many advocates of mental testing envisioned it as a progressive instrument–a tool for promoting individual merit over racial or economic privilege. Standardized intelligence tests, used to select out children for gifted education, would create a group in which fathers and mothers, accents and names, would not matter. Only ability would be important.

The variety of ability tests has proliferated in the last hundred years. This battery of tests to sort out young minds is a veritable alphabet soup. There's the WISC-IV preschool intelligence test (the Wechsler Intelligence Scale for Children, fourth edition); the WPPSI-III (Wechsler Preschool and Primary Scale of Intelligence, third edition); the WPPSI-R (Wechsler Preschool and Primary Scale of Intelligence, revised edition; Silverman warned that this one sometimes results in false positives); the Stanford-Binet 4 and 5; the DAS (Differential Ability Scale); the WJ-III (the Woodcock-Johnson III Test); the Raven's Progressive Matrices; the K-TEA (Kaufman Test of Educational Achievement); the Rasch Ratio; the Qualitative Assessment; and the Stanford-Binet L-M. The current use of the last-named test is the most surprising, as it was written in 1937, revised in 1960, and last normed in 1972. Norming means that a child's test score will be be assessed by comparing scores to others in the current population–in the case of the L-M, a child's test scores are being compared to a more-than-thirty-year-old test group's scores. Because the L-M has not been renormed for so many years, its scores are even more susceptible to the Flynn effect than the scores obtained by the Stanford-Binet 4. Indeed, some testers call the L-M a "fetish object" because it lets kids get jaw-droppingly high scores: the brightest young things can score 240 and higher. On the flip side, the L-M is, in places, laughably antiquated: it still pins a mental age on its takers, a practice that was seen as offensive to the mentally handicapped and has been abolished by other tests, which have replaced mental age with standard deviations. The L-M still contains vocabulary words like *milksop,* ripped from 1930s conversation but rarely heard today.

The L-M has plenty of enemies. Jerome Sattler, one of the authors of the Stanford-Binet 5, rails against what he feels to be an antiquated IQ test. "Norms change, children change, the population changes," says Sattler. "That's why if you want a scientific psychometric instrument, you can't use a scientifically standardized instrument that's fifty years old." The L-M is most striking for the passion for and rage against it that it provokes, but the other tests have advocates and detractors, each test being critiqued or applauded for different reasons.

The big issue in ability testing, though, is how to make these tests more "culture-fair"–to correct race or social class biases associated with the tests. Nonverbal tests are sometimes championed as a response to the perceived bias in many language-heavy tests. The culture-fair test used by the Iles School, for example, is the Cognitive Assessment Test (CAT) designed by Jack Naglieri, a psychology professor at George Mason University. Naglieri told me that he had created the test because he found the existing ones, such as the WISC and the Stanford-Binet, "inappropriate" tools, given the different results obtained by African-Americans, whites, and Hispanics. Naglieri is part of a growing group of psychometricians who have designed newer tests that aim to correct biases. "We need an expanded definition of giftedness that is still a meaningful definition of giftedness," Naglieri told me. "We all know people who are not knowledgeable but are really smart. The problem is that people confuse achievement and ability."

But even Naglieri's correction of bias has received its correction: its critics, including University of Iowa professor David Lohman, write that tests like the CAT, as well-meaning as they may be politically, are not good assessment tools. While a nonverbal gift may mean a child excels in nonverbal domains, the academic work of school demands high verbal skills. Lohman writes that a nonverbal test is a helpful adjunct to other tests but is not useful unto itself. Academic giftedness should be defined primarily by measures of academic accomplishment, and the best predictor of future academic accomplishment is an ability to reason in what Lohman calls "symbol systems," or verbal, quantitative, and spatial systems.

With their limited resources, public schools often have difficulty doing comprehensive assessment. One element that adds to this confusion is the incidence of evaluators who may not apply as many different kinds of tests, or read them as robustly, as the private testers can, given the luxury of adequate time and funding. There are few hard figures on how many evaluators there are in the public schools nationally; each state is different. States where gifted education comes under the aegis of special education are much more likely to have access to psychologists, for example, than states where gifted education floats alone.

When public-school children receive an individual IQ test, chances are they will get the third edition of the Wechsler Intelligence Scale for Children (WISC-III) and the Stanford-Binet 5. These consist of verbal subtests that are oral, and others that are visual or spatial. The whole thing takes up to an hour. The evaluator arrives at a full or composite score based on most of the subtests. The visual or spatial test may have a block design task, where the blocks are red and white and the child must quickly make their 3-D blocks look like the picture. On the verbal test, the evaluator will ask the child to define words and their connotations. Vocabulary will be graded on how nuanced a child's understanding of a word is, starting out with words like *fork* and *mug* in describing likeness and working up to the high end, where a child will have to define a word like *harangue.* In order to get full credit, a child will have to be able to define *harangue* both as a speech act and also as angry speech, to get both the word's negative valence and its full meaning. A child taking the Wechsler will be asked, "What's missing in this picture?"–an example would be a picture where a little boy is missing a nose, or where there are no laces on the left side of a shoe and a belt has no buckle. This helps the tester to assess the child's attentiveness to detail. There are also problems where a child is asked to define visual similarities, such as how two things are alike, given an array of symbols like a garden hose, a beach ball, and a dog.

A little less than a century ago, intelligence testers had to make their own materials, even compose their own questions. But these IQ tests, in their premise and basic design, were setting out to measure many of the same attributes as they do today. As Stephen Jay Gould writes in his superb classic about intelligence testing, *The Mismeasure of Man,* the aptitudes the early IQ tester sought to measure were "memory, language comprehension, size of vocabulary, orientation in space and time, eye-hand coordination, knowledge of familiar things, judgment, likeness, and difference, arithmetical reasoning," among others. The first iteration of the IQ in the United States was the Stanford-Binet as developed by Lewis Terman, a professor at Stanford who had adapted the French IQ test formulated in 1905 by Alfred Binet. From the earliest days of his career, Terman embraced the dissemination of gifted education, as well as a "hereditarian" perspective about intelligence: he saw gifted programs as sorters of excellence, which would create "the right education" for "superior children." This was a man who gave his book the insensitive title of *Genius and Stupidity.* Terman was very much a nature-over-nurture kind of guy. "[Terman] asked whether the 'so-called lower classes' suffered from that unfortunate position because nature had cheated them or because a poor home environment and bad schools kept them there," writes Joel Shurkin in *Terman's Kids.* "Even without statistical evidence he firmly believed that [the former] was true." In Terman's own words, the "dullness" he perceived in children of color "seems to be racial, or at the least inherent in the family stocks from which they come." As Gould writes of Terman, he took the "hereditarian line on race and class and proclaimed its validation as the primary aim of his work."

The glory of Terman's career was a study of 1,528 California schoolchildren with IQs of 135 or higher. Terman located them by way of teacher recommendations–a practice that, given the teachers' biases, led to retrospective questioning of the results. The kids were called the "Termites," and the study of their lives evolved into the model for future longitudinal psychological studies of all stripes. It remains the longest ongoing psychological study in history. Terman's study started in 1921, setting out to measure the effects of early intellectual gifts over ten years. The last data collection was in 1992, but the study of the remaining Terman sample is ongoing.

Terman intended his study as a proof of the usefulness of specialized education and tracking for gifted children–the idea that, given educational resources and familial support, gifted children will become gifted adults. Terman endlessly defended the gifted population against the popular assumption of the time that these kids were effete freaks. He believed they had great potential for so-called normal lives, but normal plus. Terman and others like him seem driven by an almost metaphysical wish: an aspiration not merely to sort children's minds, but to become seers by way of the scientific method, to peer into the essence of individual minds.

From relatively early on, IQ tests were seen as biased against minorities. Testing's checkered history revolves around three things. The first is the whole proposition that intelligence tests alone measure "true" intellectual capacity. The second is the way the tests were developed, designed with a bias against minorities. The third is how they are administered: they have been administered with bias at certain points in history, and as a result IQ scores have fueled a good deal of racist-tinged argumentation about intelligence through the years.

In 1983 the influential scholar Howard Gardner critiqued the IQ and SAT tests' limited notion of intelligence in the book *Multiple Intelligences.* Gardner argued that while some children are what we have come to understand as conventionally gifted, linguistically or logically, there are those who are gifted in other domains–gifted physically or gifted socially, to name two. Ten years after "multiple intelligences," there was a return to the most Jurassic notion of intelligence in the form of Richard J. Herrnstein and Charles Murray's incendiary 1994 book *The Bell Curve.* The book quickly made its way out of the scientific community and into public debate and popular culture, as well as onto the best-seller lists. *The Bell Curve* purported to describe what Murray called a "cognitive elite"–and its opposite, a kind of cognitive underclass–who lay at either end of a bell curve of intelligence. Herrnstein and Murray analyzed more than a decade's worth of findings of the National Longitudinal Survey of Labor Market Experience of Youth, which looked at 12,500 teens and young adults from 1979 onward. In their book, they described the way the population had cleaved in two: a high-IQ population with access to plum employment, and swelling congeries of the low-IQ unemployed. Within the book's claims lie a few points that are hard to swallow. The first is that one and only one fixed number represents "cognitive ability"–that intelligence can be captured by a single number, ranking people unshakably. The second is the implication Herrnstein and Murray drew from the fact that the gap between the IQ of the average African-American and the IQ of the average white American is 15 points. Dismissing historical explanations, they looked to genetics. The authors did not mention the fact that in Ireland, where Protestants have historically had access to better education and a higher social class than Catholics, the same 15 points separate the average Protestant from the average Catholic–both groups being, of course, quite white. The dubious achievement of the late Herrnstein, a Harvard psychology professor who had studied pigeon behavior with B. F. Skinner, and Murray, a fellow at the conservative American Enterprise Institute, was to bring back into vogue the original use of IQ: to enforce racial distinctions.

An unsigned introduction to the 1995 book *The Bell Curve Debate,* edited by Russell Jacoby and Naomi Glauberman, defines the original book's troublesome nature with deft acidity: "*The Bell Curve* gives a sophisticated voice to a repressed and illiberal sentiment: a belief that ruinous divisions in society are sanctioned by nature itself."

The Bell Curve tended to convince only those who already believed in its political implications (among them, that affirmative action was misguided, and that increased funding for minority education was probably a waste of time). And ten years later, plenty of antitest advocates remain. Monty Neill, the co-executive director of the Boston-based advocacy group FairTest, tells me that no matter its form, the intelligence test has never been able to overcome its racist–or, as Neill puts it, "eugenicist"–background: "Our take is that instead of measuring innate capacity, IQs measure things that one has learned." As a measure of intelligence, says Neill, the test is skewed–it depends upon the obviously false presumption that all children have had the opportunity, and the equal opportunity, to learn.

But what critics of the IQ test are missing, say some psychologists and gifted advocates, is that, flawed as it may be, the Stanford-Binet remains one of the best instruments out there for locating the brightest, poorest children. They say it is superior to the teacher recommendations that are used today to "discover" gifted and talented children in the public schools whose parents cannot pay for individual assessments and cannot advocate for their child's right to gifted education. And to some extent, they convinced me that gimlet-eyed psychologists can get beyond intelligence test limitations: if a psychologist is worried that a foreign-born child's weak grasp of English is lowering his verbal score, she can modify the test for him; and if she sees that a child has a slower processing speed, a sophisticated psychologist will know to give that child more time. Few public schools have psychologists for individual testing at all. As a result, it tends to be the children whose parents are motivated or well-off who get tested by the corps of private evaluators. As one private evaluator put it, "Parents want to know what the IQ test number is as ammunition. If their child has a 155 IQ, they can go back to the school with that as a kind of evidence: '*Here's* the kind of intelligence I am talking about.'"

The futures of those who lack parents with the money and knowledge to advocate for them are left, to a far greater extent, to chance.

After hearing so much about gifted brains and high achievement test scores in the hotel ballrooms of the World Gifted Conference, I found myself wondering less about the terrifyingly gifted and more about those kids who had no gurus, who had never even heard of the L-M, but who had buried promise. Who uncovered and developed their potential if they were overlooked?

I was interested in initiatives around North America attempting to improve the chances of those kids who weren't making their way to gifted and talented classes. I spoke to the man behind JUMP, or Junior Undiscovered Math Prodigies–a Canadian numeracy program founded in 1998. In JUMP's eight years of existence, John Mighton has sought to demonstrate that even children failing at math or labeled as slow learners can go on to learn calculus. He started the program in his apartment, and now thousands of Canadian students are enrolled in JUMP classes, while others are using JUMP workbooks for teachers and parents–16,000 copies of their workbooks were sold in 2005.

The program was inspired by Mighton's own lackluster experience with mathematics as a child and adolescent, and by his own thwarted relationship to giftedness. Now forty-eight-years old, Mighton had read about gifted kids when he was young. "I thought you had to be born with a certain set of qualities to be gifted," says Mighton. "I internalized that. I decided there was a threshold of what I could do."

With JUMP, he took students who couldn't count by twos even though they were twelve, including students at a juvenile detention center, and patiently deployed his method of learning math in small steps–raising the bar incrementally, problem by problem. He was astonished at first when three years later, these remedial students were performing at grade level and even skipping a year in math.

"I am convinced math is the easiest subject and that problems learning it are mostly behavioral and have to do with confidence," says Mighton, who is also the author of a book on the subject, *The Myth of Ability.* "They want to show off to a caring adult and to exercise their minds. I've seen that myself–I've had classes with high-end students and low-end students, and within two weeks couldn't tell who was going to finish the worksheets first."

Part of the success of Mighton's method, he thinks, is due to the fact that he doesn't think math learning should always go from the concrete to the abstract, because some children think abstractly before they think concretely. He also thinks if children are verbally intelligent, using language helps them organize information far better than memorizing numbers.

JUMP is only one of many programs of its kind that have shown remarkable results with children conventionally written off as underachievers. There's the Washington State organization One World Now, which teaches Mandarin and Arabic to underprivileged kids. There are programs that help match talented poor and minority kids with private and preparatory schools, like Prep-for-Prep and the Oliver Program. In 2004, I made several visits to the latter, a privately funded program that brings minority children from public schools to private schools. As of that year, 650 kids had gone through the program, 94 percent of them attending boarding schools. And 36 percent of Oliver Program students from both boarding schools and day schools were going on to the Ivy League. I attended an Oliver open house with the parents of would-be program enrollees, where facilitators reassured parents. The parents, mostly mothers, had not-so-misguided fears about sending their children to the foreign grounds of a prep school. One mother asked an Oliver Program facilitator if she would ever be allowed to visit the boarding school her child might attend. Another mother at the open house, who described herself to me as a single administrative assistant "living on credit cards," told me that she saw the Oliver Program as her daughter's small providence. I wondered, listening to these mothers, whether their children, who might soon be filtering into private and prep schools, would also be defined as "gifted." When I asked Oliver Program's director, Johan Johnson, and his colleagues about whether the students they selected were "gifted," Johnson shrugged and said he didn't think much of the term. And indeed, while visiting the Oliver Program offices and talking to those who worked for or had gone through this program and others like it, I rarely heard the term *gifted* or encountered much mention of students' intelligence or achievement test scores. Instead, these programs' admission criteria tend to emphasize whether the children are hardworking, whether they display what Joseph Renzulli, director of the University of Connecticut's Neag Center for Gifted Education and Talent Development and an eminent figure in gifted education, terms "gifted behaviors." Renzulli's version of giftedness involves task commitment, resilience, and even a moral sense, and it is a definition that makes the most sense to me: giftedness is as giftedness does. Still, "gifted behaviors" can be as murky as giftedness plain. Are we any better at finding children or teenagers with "gifted behaviors" than we are at finding gifted children per se?

Not always. But when you witness the "development" of gifted behaviors with your own eyes–development that, as Renzulli argues, can require numerous educational opportunities and services only very erratically available in regular school programs–it can be a most satisfying vision.

I saw this in New Orleans, but not at the World Gifted Conference. I had to leave the air-conditioned confines of the New Orleans Hyatt Hotel and attend a "book party" for two teenage authors, held at their house on the corner of Lotus and Gladiolus Streets. The event was also a party for the Neighborhood Story Project, a nonprofit started by two public school teachers, Abram Himelstein and Rachel Breunlin. In 2004, kids applied to the project. Six teenagers were told to collect stories about their neighborhoods and families and personal history. The stories were then written up, edited, and turned into bound and published books in 2005, and the teenagers were each given $1,000. All of the teen authors involved in creating the books were African-American, and none had been defined as traditionally gifted before they became authors. One had nearly dropped out of John McDonogh Senior High School, one of the worst public schools in the state. At the event I attended, eighteen-year-old Sam Wylie and his coauthor sister Arlet Wylie were getting the food ready–giant tubs of shrimp and cod covered with a spicy breading. Even in its normal state, their family's front yard looked like it was half set up for a party. The Wylies grew up in the Ninth Ward, a rough area where signs reading "Thou Shalt Not Kill" were posted to neighbors' windows (the Ninth Ward would become known around the world after Hurricane Katrina as the area whose residents faced the very worst devastation and abandonment), and their nonfiction book was about these people. "See, the whole system is like a big net, and the Ninth Ward is where they do a lot of fishing," Sam Wylie writes in the book, entitled *Between Piety and Desire,* a depiction of his family's life in the ward. "I feel like I'm in a river, trying to swim upstream." His girlfriend, Roulette, he wrote, was "swimming in the same sea. . . . Being with her is exactly what her name is: 'Roulette,' a game of chance. . . . All of this is part of the sea I am swimming in, and it's rough, dangerous and deep." Sam also gives a strong account of his father, an amateur magician: "He makes boxes that he uses to make people disappear or cut them in half. One time, when he was test running the disappearing box, he asked me to be his assistant. . . . I heard my siblings say, 'Where Sam at? Where Sam at?' I didn't know either. I thought when I stepped out of the box, I might be on another planet. He seemed to have that kind of power." According to Himelstein, the book's sales in New Orleans ranked just behind those of the Harry Potter books.

I couldn't help but think how unlikely it would be for these teenagers to be singled out for an enrichment program based on an achievement test or a teacher recommendation. One specialist in the gifted education field, Benjamin Bloom, has written that the gifted require unusual levels of support for their talent to develop. And indeed parents of relatively well-off kids work hard to make sure their kids are identified as gifted and given special educational opportunities. But what of kids from the lower-income range, who are left to attend inferior schools and get only the most basic testing? Many such kids, even those with great potential, won't be identified as such. As it happened, these teenagers had been "discovered" by teachers, but they were not teachers looking for students who were glaringly competent at school. In fact, they were looking for just the opposite. Nevertheless, these kids had revealed remarkable talents that were hidden until their book's publication. "You can have large expectations, you can have off-site education that is also a family literacy program," Neighborhood Story Project cofounder Breunlin told me. "This program is open to anyone." One of its benefits for Breunlin and Himelstein was that the project was not just a class–it was people in the neighborhood as well, an "expandable classroom." This is the opposite of the slicing and dicing of giftedness into smaller and smaller slivers that Silverman has been doing at the World Gifted Conference. The fact that the Neighborhood Story Project provided this needed mentoring to these particular children was a matter of luck.

A few weeks later, that luck would turn again: after the intelligence testers and gifted experts had flown back to their universities, special schools, and private practices, the corner where the Wylies lived would be underwater.

Safe back in their homes, watching the consequences of poverty and powerlessness as well as of nature, the parents of the gifted and the gifted gurus would be all the more assured that, given the vicissitudes of existence, they must advocate for their "gifted" children–instruct them, get them into enriching private schools, or move their families to suburbs with well-funded public schools. They could not depend on luck.

JUMP's Mighton thinks that if only educators were intent upon establishing extremely high standards–*and* committed to the idea that all kids can meet them–there would be no need for all of the assessments and the special programs. "I believe in 'emergent intelligence,' the ability of the brain to re-harness itself," says Mighton of his students, some of whom have gone from remedial learning to graduate study in mathematics.

Another question took shape as I talked to children, parents, and professionals in the giftedness community. Is it, in fact, lucky to have a parent who believes her children's gifts must be measured, and measured by the best? Not always, according to gifted specialist and neuropsychologist Nadia Webb. Some of the parents who come to her practice are, as she puts it, "amazingly overinvested" in their children. They subscribe to loads of listservs for the gifted and are constantly on the Web; whenever one has a complaint or a compliment about Webb's work, this sentiment travels swiftly around the Internet-abiding gifted parent community. It has gotten so bad that her staff is trained to protect her from "parent nightmares" who call to ask questions. "I'll get four messages in a row from one mom," she says. "The parents rage. They think that if they are a truly special person with a truly special child, they can only be understood by a truly special specialist." They want a "special" specialist so intently that they will come to see her in rural Virginia. They voyage from other states and sometimes even from other continents, "because there's no one in Europe, no one in Massachusetts, who understands their child. It's a subculture, with all of these parents pushing their kids to the same four testers, starting with Linda Silverman."

The desire for high intelligence test scores and favorable assessments from "top" psychologists for the gifted seems to me to center on an American desire for specialness. As Richard Madsen, Robert Bellah, and others write in *Habits of the Heart: Individualism and Commitment in American Life,* American competitive individualism in the past was "balanced and humanized by the restraining influence" of community responsibility–care for their neighbors, for example. But this "restraining influence" has worn thin, as the extreme levels of desire for children to be special among the most intense members of the giftedness industry seems to show.

The exclusiveness of this cognitive elite is part of the desire for giftedness, of course. Being gifted is being "special" by definition, as exemplified by the ideas of scholars like David Henry Feldman and Ellen Winner. According to Feldman in *Nature's Gambit: Child Prodigies and the Development of*

Human Potential, both the prodigious and gifted are a rare and rather small group. In fact, children capable of composing a symphony or beating a chess master are so uncommon, Feldman writes, they "seem to violate the natural order of things," serving as an unwelcome intrusion into our "perception of stability, continuity and predictability of experience." In her book *Gifted Children*, Winner is also concerned with distinguishing between the child who has merely been sent to a chess class or violin lessons, as she puts it, and the true precocity of the highly gifted. Winner writes that the truly gifted take the first steps in the mastery of some domain at an earlier-than-average age and "make more rapid progress in this domain than do ordinary children, because learning in the domain comes easily to them." They also tend to exhibit an intense and obsessive interest in subjects or activities.

Perhaps in rebellion against the pressures to obtain the "gifted" sobriquet, and exposure to the kinds of parents Webb describes, some parents who can afford to send their children to educational testers and private schooling are now opting out. Adrianne, thirty-six, a parent in New York City who asked that her last name not be used, says of her two young daughters, "We want them to go to Harvard, but it's not what we are trying to do now. The whole New York City kindergarten thing is so competitive. You have four-year-olds interviewing for kindergarten, and it's a status thing, with baby showers where products that make kids 'smarter' are the presents to give. We looked into private schools, and they were so competitive, based on my impression of the other parents on the tours. We decided to send our daughter to public school because with the tests and the interviews for private schools, it's cutthroat, and it's horrible for the whole family. We decided we didn't want to put our family through it. I mean, the children who are tutored at three to get into the right kindergarten–are they happier? Are they more successful?"

Adriane's choice is one supported by Rebecca Eckert, the National Association of Gifted Children's gifted resource specialist. "The question we typically ask parents considering getting their children's intelligence tested is: What is the purpose of the test?" says Eckert. "What will change because of the test? Will it change how you interact with your child? If a student desperately needs some more challenges, taking the IQ test seems reasonable."

"The competition for having the kids identified as gifted is very intense, really overstated–kindergarten teachers tell me that parents are trying to get them to call their children gifted," James Borland, a professor of education at Columbia University Teacher's College, tells me. "They exaggerate the importance in terms of the children's future. I am a parent; I understand the anxiety. But I wish they'd be more relaxed."

Indeed, the only real reason for doing an assessment is education modification, argues University of Virginia professor of education Carolyn Callahan. "The label 'gifted' does nothing–it maybe makes you feel good if you are a parent," she says. "It's a terrible experience for a child to be tested. It's high stress. A child keeps answering questions until they fail. They are sitting one-on-one with an adult in a chair for two and half hours–until they fail! Personally, I'd rather be outside playing."

Silverman and her camp have a mission to look for the terrifyingly gifted. She and some parents of exceptional learners would most likely disagree with the notion that testing is traumatic, seeing it rather as a boon and an educational aid. But Adrianne is right to at the very least wonder about the actual value of intelligence and achievement tests for the very young. By opting out of the early testing sweepstakes, she has put off her child's encounter with the label "gifted," and perhaps with a doyenne of giftedness–at least, for another few years.

SEVEN

Extreme Parenting: Mothers and Fathers as the Ultimate Instructors

Luzhin senior, the Luzhin who wrote books, often thought of how his son would turn out. . . . he more than once, in a pleasant dream resembling a lithograph, descended with a candle at night to the drawing room where a Wunderkind, *dressed in a white nightshirt that came down to his heels, would be playing an enormous piano.*

VLADIMIR NABOKOV, *The Defense*

The Bess children are standing at attention at ballet class. Twelve-year-old Phoenix, the youngest, extends her tremendously long right leg behind her at the bar. The two boys, Austin, seventeen, and Blake, fifteen, plié to Chopin's "Prelude." Their mother, Beth Bess, looks on. Afterward, she tells me that she has raised them to be "supreme humans," ballet just one of their many skills. "I wanted them to be mavericks. The whole point is for them to be superior beings, for their actualization."

The Bess kids look the part of a superior tribe–they are very tall, very thin, and terrifically poised, with alert dark shiny eyes, thick black hair, almond colored skin, and startlingly erect carriages. Their mother, a former dancer, has taught them herself at home in many subjects, but has also taken them to classes or to carefully chosen teachers for private instruction. By thirteen, Austin was not only attending college classes but knew Latin, was learning Japanese on the side, and had taken up jousting. All three have already been extras in a Hollywood film; all play piano and sing; and all know about polynomials. Austin reads Aristotle for his own enjoyment. Blake takes clocks and radios apart and puts them back together just for fun.

"It's taken fifteen years for me to get what Beth wanted to do with the kids," Beth's husband, Earnest Bess, tells me. He is very handsome: tall and bald, he looks like a black Yul Brynner. He's a fireman and a self-proclaimed traditionalist. He admits he was not at all keen on Beth's homeschooling-the-gifted plan at first, although now that he's seen the results, he says he can see its values.

At the Bess home in Matthews, Virginia, the entire family and I sit together for hours on end, drinking iced tea sweetened with the metallic-tasting organic sugar substitute stevia, which Beth, who runs a strictly sugar-free home, drinks incessantly. The family is gathered in a living room piled high with library books and copies of *National Geographic*, all circled around a potbellied stove. Phoenix is silent. Occasionally she stands up and stretches.

Blake, fifteen, an aspiring actor, talks about his plan to move to L.A. just as soon as his agent gets him the right auditions–all three children played bit parts as beautiful Native Americans in Terrence Malick's *The New World*. Austin, seventeen, says he is considering "getting incorporated." Neither boy sounds like a typical teenager. Their innocence and gentleness, though, remind me that they are still young–younger acting, in fact, than many teenagers nowadays, who put a premium on ridding themselves of soft, childlike qualities.

"Right now, my mom has to sign everything when I try to do a land deal," Austin tells me. He thinks it's absurd that those under eighteen are not given the rights of American adults, many of whom are far less competent than a talented, driven adolescent. Austin spends most of his time with his brother. The boys describe themselves as "very selective" about their friends. "I have had not one close friend," says Austin. "I never had any interest in one."

They also have pronounced views about the concept of "giftedness" itself.

"We don't fit into the PG [profoundly gifted] group," Austin says. "No man is an island, though. We need to go beyond superiority and also not be limited by community, you know? I don't think we need IQ tests."

As for the future, Austin is still not sure about college. He took college classes at twelve, but he didn't really mingle, and his memories of college are negative. "Their lifestyle, I couldn't relate to it," says Austin. He has a sweet austerity to his look. "The students were smoking weed and partying. I don't want to go to college. College is just a lottery ticket." He adds, "I agree with Plato's *Republic,* which views a minority as enlightened and the society as a very controlled system of workers."

"What do you think?" Beth then asks eagerly, referring to Plato and also Austin's college prospects. Beth is a bohemian Steel Magnolia, as tall as her children and as lovely: lanky, astral, and fervent, a part-time herbalist with a rather quirky and perhaps quixotic sideline business selling knitting needles with leopard patterns on them. When she asks me what I think of Austin's remarks, I realize I have been cast as a bridge to the world for this appealing family. These kinds of conversations, about the family's individual and shared life philosophy and how much one must participate in conventional forms, transpire endlessly among the Besses, in between dancing on the lawn and doing brain teasers. But all of the conversations transpire in a closed loop. Today, I represent the outside world's ambitious, credentialed clatter.

Phoenix, who has been sitting in utter silence, takes out her knitting. A pink scarf emerges from the clicking needles.

Beth Bess is very thin and pale, with shining eyes: there's the whiff of the late 1960s about her, of a time when even southern belles from Republican families could make a countercultural turn, as Beth has done. "The kids take brush painting classes," she continues. "We take trips to the library. I do think we live in an insulated world, though."

The family goes into the kitchen for supper, and Earnest settles down at the kitchen table. He points at a rust-colored ring within one of the bowls. He and Beth have a routine, wherein he mocks her housekeeping hygiene and she teases him back: the Bad Housekeeping Seal of Approval appears to be their favorite joke. And indeed, the kitchen, like the rest of their house, is far from neat. It's homespun, rickety–even eccentric: on the table, for instance, stand two puce jugs of the stevia-sweetened iced tea that will be ladled out into jam jars to accompany a dinner that is almost entirely meat or eggs. (Vegetarian guests eat rice and beans.)

Austin is on his own diet, the Paleo diet. "It's like how the Indians lived off of the fat of the land," says Austin. He then shows me a big dish of fat.

Beth has created a surrogate system of education, says Earnest, and he admits that paying for specialized instructors in Roman civilization and classical guitar weighs on the family financially. "I take three jobs so I can finance my children's education," he says. "We have had to make do with old cars. I am away from home a lot. We have done without privilege–we have our first new car in eighteen years. We have made huge sacrifices."

Remarking that he has experienced institutional racism in the fire department, Earnest says he believes that his wife's hand-tooled educational system may have helped his sons and daughter escape the inequities he encountered. "My children's independence is phenomenal," he says. "They've learned about Egyptian culture. Austin has founded a corporation and wants to buy land and get into property. He has paid a lawyer with his own money to set it up properly." Earnest is also impressed that his son Austin reads what Earnest calls "adult materials": a college chemistry textbook. At nine and a half, Austin read *A Brief History of Time,"* the Stephen Hawking astrophysics best seller. The one thing Earnest keeps wondering about, though, is what he considers the "elitism" of the gifted community.

Beth and Earnest argue this point constantly and, at least when I was there, playfully. Sometimes their children join in, Earnest taking the part of the "mainstream," as he puts it–those who would have been passed over by the giftedness crowd, whether they deserved to be or not, simply because they didn't speak the right code or answer test questions properly.

Beth knows what he is talking about, as a white woman in a mixed-race couple who has lived for twenty years in a string of Virginia towns. In fact, her experience with her family and her hometown, where she now lives, caused her to distrust institutions to the point that she decided her kids would not go to school. She and her family seem to come from a place markedly different from the eastern Virginia town where they actually live–a town of Wendy's restaurants, hypomanic soccer moms, and family histories that pre-date the Confederacy.

The Bess siblings remind me of Meg and Charles Wallace Murry, the bright, lonesome kids who battle "the Dark Thing" in the children's classic *A Wrinkle in Time.* In the case of the Bess siblings, "the Dark Thing" they battle could well be their own teen rebellion and adolescent dissoluteness. Well-behaved, articulate, they're a little out of sync with their community's teen norms–far from the pop slipstream. The Besses play piano and do math teasers at the kitchen table. The children's voice lessons cost $80 a month each, and $142 a month is spent on piano lessons. Then the family listens to tapes on which a preacher explicates the Hebrew and Greek originals of various biblical passages, and the Besses discuss his conclusions. None of the Bess children date.

"Phoenix has started her own knitwear business, and though she is only twelve, she can do it," says Beth. "None of this would be possible"–she gestures at her kids as they go about piano practice and vocal practice–"in an institution like a public school. I see us like a pioneer family. My kids need education, and they need to help harvest the crops and build the log cabin. Austin attends to his clients. Blake works with his agent. Phoenix has been dancing since she was four, and she could become a professional. I wanted to give them the platform for their own destiny."

For parents who perceive their children as having special talents, taking them out of school and patching together a curricula based on their remarkable interests and talents is part of a larger parenting phenomenon, the world of "extreme parenting." Extreme parenting entails getting involved with children's hobbies and talents and structuring their time from as early an age as possible. These parents pursue their children's gifted status and intensively manage their education, as well as their extensive palette of extracurricular activities. Home education can be a part of extreme parenting. Although the lion's share of home schooling is driven by religious beliefs, the gifted and intensely parented are among the growing number of homeschooled youth–a group that, according to the National Home Education Research Institute, reached 1,700,000 to 2,100,000 children nationwide during the years 2002 to 2003.

This particular group of parents choose to homeschool because they believe that their gifted children's needs will never be met in the public schools–and they may well be right. As giftedness gurus Jan and Bob Davidson, founders of the Davidson Institute for Talented Development, a nonprofit that assists gifted kids and schools, write in their giftedness cri de coeur *Genius Denied,* half of the families they work with homeschool. Why? Because only "a few more than half of the states require school to provide any [gifted and talented] services," and those that do, have "gifted kids doing word puzzles and puppetry, not advanced academic work."

The extreme-parenting crowd includes those parents who attend conferences, from the Beyond IQ Conference to the yearly PG Conference, dealing with the profoundly gifted (those scoring 160 and above on IQ tests). Conference organizers are wary of reporters, citing the need to protect the children–an explanation that sounds convincing until one reflects on how many PG kids have already appeared in newspapers and magazines and on TV. One administrator denied me entry to one of these conferences on the grounds that "families that come to PG Retreat have children who are as different from gifted children as gifted are from normal. These are kids who are 5 and 6 deviations above the norm, so their issues are magnified and intense!" The parents of gifted and profoundly gifted children who attend these conferences say they do so to make contact with a community, but also to keep up with the latest research on giftedness and home educational strategies.

Intense parents also keep up with the giftedness world through the Talented and Gifted and PG listservs on the World Wide Web. They also use a host of other Web sites that act as clearinghouses for "gifted" information. They attend classes and programs designed for parents of the gifted or wannabe gifted (like the How to Multiply Your Baby's Intelligence courses at the Institutes for the Achievement of Human Potential, and their equivalents for older kids). They are constantly educating themselves on how to educate their children.

Many of these parents choose to send their kids to special academically oriented private schools, or specialized institutions like music schools, with plenty of additional enrichment classes after school and on weekends. Others have chosen to take education into their own hands. In terms of social class, the homeschooling of gifted kids tends anecdotally toward the more middle-class and working-class families–those who can't necessarily afford to move to an area with a gifted program or to pay for private education. Both private education and homeschooling are courses of action that make a statement on the perceived value of regular public education for gifted kids. This flight from the public schools represents, in part, a rejection of the philosophy of equality in education that drove the creation of our public school system. It also reflects a number of parental concerns: most obviously, that their kids won't get adequate educations in the public schools, but in addition, that their kids don't, or shouldn't, conform to the norm. Some parents decide upon homeschooling or specialized private schools because they fear their sensitive kids will be ostracized, treated as freaks within the regular public schools. Others take these steps because they want their kids to be free to pursue their own interests at their own pace.

Take Angela Gould, the mother of a brood in Fort Benning, Georgia, where her husband, a career military man, is stationed. Gould decided to homeschool their six-year-old son, Aidan, after he scored 160 on an IQ test. While she says that some in her community imagine she is a slave driver and that it is a "horrible thing to do to your child, to be six but in fourth grade in terms of schoolwork," Gould felt she had no choice. Her son was simply devouring every workbook she gave him.

Then there's Gary Robson, a Largo, Florida, father of an eight-year-old chess champion, who has been "overcome" by his son Ray's "road to success." On competition days, the two get up at six in the morning to embark on a two-hour drive. Local competitions are not challenging for Ray; as Robson puts it, his son needs to play people above him in skill. So they trek long distances in the family's 1985 Mazda to find worthy opponents. "We don't live particularly well-off, as I never put stock in money because of my early love of Thoreau," says Robson. In the course of Ray's short career, the two have traveled to Chicago, Tennessee, Pennsylvania, and New York, to the nationals in Georgia, and to the U.S. Junior Open in Kansas, among other places.

"No adult likes to lose to a little kid," says Robson. "Ray's so skinny, he has to sit up on his knees so he can see the board. To be at eye level, he has to sit on his jacket. I play with him, and I think he's looking into my head. Sometimes I look at Ray, and I feel like he's judging me. He's so scary. To be on the other side of his look . . . when you are playing a kid, you get a little scared. A six-year-old kid who sees combinations better? As an adult you wonder if this kid is smarter than me."

Robson then recites from a Donald Hall poem, "My Son My Executioner," which begins, "My son, my executioner, / I take you in my arms," and ends, "Your cries and hungers document / Our bodily decay. / We twenty-five and twenty-two / Who seemed to live forever, / Observe enduring life in you / And start to die together."

"The theme is the son surpassing his father," says Robson, in case I had missed it. "I am following him. I think about what I could have done. For all chess parents, it's too late. You live through your children."

Extreme parenting can be a very effective strategy for raising gifted and talented children, and in many cases–as in the Bess, Gould, and Robson families–a loving and productive strategy as well. But it can also be problematic. Extreme parenting can become too extreme if parents are so involved that the line between the child's own will and the parent's desires disappears. It can also be too extreme when parents seem to be motivated by a wish less to improve their children than to be part of their lives, as if some of that exceptional sheen might rub off on them.

This intensity of involvement in their children's giftedness can sometimes lead parents to redefine themselves. This was true in the case of Stephanie Tolan, a parent of a gifted child, a gifted education consultant, and a novelist who coined the term "gifted ex children." She came upon the term after attending one of the numerous gifted conferences that attract parents like her. It was there, while watching a film about gifted education pioneer Leta Hollingworth, that Tolan realized, "My son wasn't the only one who was gifted. So was I." Through the experience of discovering she was highly gifted, Tolan says, she "understood a lot of things in my life." She says she realized why she had never had a good relationship with a boss and why she had often felt so isolated. She has decided to turn her awakening experience to the cause of helping others by answering "letters from gifted people who feel they have been victimized by a world that doesn't understand them," as she puts it. This is giftedness as a kind of recovered memory and a saving grace. Sometimes it is giftedness as an explanation for children's negative traits and experiences.

Today, there's a continuum of involved parents, ranging from committed, to extreme committed, to too-extreme.

Too-extreme parenting is likely to be present when parents too avidly apply labels such as "gifted" to their offspring. Joe Kincheloe, a professor of education at the City University of New York's Graduate Center and the coauthor of *The Stigma of Genius: Einstein, Consciousness, and Education,* has some warnings for extreme parents. Kincheloe's studies of giftedness, gifted and talented programs, and assessment tests led him to want parents to understand better "the narrowness of the label 'gifted,'" like the label of "'learning disabled' or simply 'not smart.'" Kincheloe believes that label "can paralyze a child. The child internalizes expectations on both sides of the culture of failure and the culture of success." He concludes that both the gifted and the learning disabled may conclude they are failures.

For instance, praising children for their test scores, for their quasi-professional merits, or for their giftedness, rather than for the earnestness or imaginativeness of their learning process, is not the best parenting strategy, according to Carol Dweck. Dweck is a psychology professor at Stanford University who since the late 1990s has studied the effects of adults' messages to children about their performance. In one study, children were given a nonverbal IQ test. A randomly selected group was told that it was gifted; those children ended up lying about their scores, and stopped enjoying their tasks. Dweck found that praise for ability, which is typically considered to motivate children, didn't do so in the case of the children she studied. The children who were praised for their intelligence went on to be both less persistent in their tasks and less joyful. They performed at a lower level than children in another sample group who had been praised solely for effort. Parents have long been warned of the dangers of being too punitive. Dweck's work shows that it may be nearly as damaging to give the wrong kind of praise. Praise where a parent merely tells a child that she or he is exceptionally gifted and talented can be the wrong kind of praise. When extreme parents become too extreme, they are usually externally naming and bracketing their child's abilities. And this sort of bracketing, according to Dweck, can shadow a child's mental development.

Similarly, child psychologists and educators argue that micromanaging children's time and activities can impair children's ability to manage themselves later in their life. Children who are unaccustomed to making their own choices may fail to develop autonomy or find a social community. This negative quality of some extreme parents has earned them the moniker "helicopter parents" in the popular media. Appearing in the book *Millennials Go to College,* coauthored by William Strauss and Neil Howe, the term was used to describe extreme parents, although not solely those of gifted children. Rather they were described as parents who "hover over the school at all times, waiting to drop in at the least sign of trouble."

A tragic event in March 2005 inspired heated discussions of the possible pitfalls of intense parenting. When Brandenn Bremmer, an exceptionally bright fourteen-year-old, killed himself, the profoundly gifted community–a world of parents, children, and current and former prodigies–struggled to make sense of his act. In death as in life, Brandenn was viewed as a symbol of the community. He had been considered one of the brightest of early achievers. Now he is seen by some as a sign of the hidden depression that may afflict children who have IQs over 160.

Inside the world of the profoundly gifted, Brandenn's death raised the question of whether these children are more sensitive to life's difficulties. For some families in this community, the recent tragedy has stiffened their resolve to create an even more sheltered world in which their children will be nurtured, their abilities actualized.

Beth Bess found Brandenn's suicide disturbing, but his death largely reinforced her conviction that ordinary life is hard for gifted children. The Besses knew Brandenn only in passing, having met him at a gifted conference, but his loss reminded Beth that "the earth is not a happy place for PGs." It also reminded her of a "bad patch" of depression her son Austin went through when he was ten. "I believe my children won't take the shotgun out of our bedroom and kill themselves, because of our faith," Bess says. She described their faith as doctrinal Christianity; their home life includes watching and listening to recorded sermons, as well as Bible study and theological discussion.

Gay McCarter, the mother of a fifteen-year-old college senior in Tennessee, also knew Brandenn remotely from the PG conferences. At age two, Gay's son Alex asked to play the violin, and learned it while working toward his third-degree black belt in karate. He soon became McCarter's full-time occupation; she homeschooled him from "the morning until he went to sleep."

At nine, he took classes at Jackson State Community College and the University of Memphis at Jackson, and when he reached age eleven, he began attending science lectures and classes at the University of Memphis full-time.

McCarter surmises that Brandenn's suicide had something to do with the "hypersensitivity" of PG children to "tastes, sounds, smells, and feelings." Like many parents in the community, McCarter identifies strongly with her son's sensitivity. She believes that all profoundly gifted children are fragile. "I could imagine a profoundly gifted teen could react dramatically to their hormones simply because they are so sensitive," McCarter told me. "We used our resources for Alex. Whatever Alex has needed, we have done. We have geared ourselves around him." After he entered college, he ultimately found "his social niche with the graduate students," in spite of the ten-year age difference.

Was it the delicacy of feeling or the acuteness of the PG or something else entirely that led Brandenn to take his own life? No simple argument can, or should, be made about what drove him to this terrible choice. I interviewed Brandenn Bremmer and his mother, Patti, the year before his suicide. Like many parents in the profoundly gifted community, Patti and Martin Bremmer of Nebraska devoted an inordinate amount of energy to stimulating their son. Only two or three cars took the quiet road by the family house each day, but not long after Brandenn turned six, intermittently one of those cars would be a postal van bringing his high-school-level homework. The homework came compliments of the distance-learning wing of the University of Nebraska–Lincoln (the same institution that served Britney Spears's educational needs.)

Brandenn made national news by entering college at the age of ten. Twice a week, Patti left the Burmese terriers and mountain dogs at the kennel she runs to drive her son 180 miles to a campus of Colorado State University. Brandenn wrote and played music, and Patti funded and then sold CDs that her son recorded; one, *Elements,* resembled the work of his favorite New Age electronic keyboardist, Yanni. Brandenn's CDs were sold on a Web site that he built because, he said, "my mom wanted a Web site for the books she's writing." Patti writes mysteries, with titles like *Tryst with Dolphins: A Party to Die For* and *Victim Wanted: Must Have References,* as part of her Elusive Clue series.

Patti Bremmer was not only a model parent, but also an organizer and agitator for gifted children. A few years ago, she founded a nonprofit organization, the National Gifted Children's Fund, which hands out college scholarships to profoundly gifted kids. "I don't put much stock in the government doing anything for the gifted kid," Patti told me.

Brandenn was thirteen when I talked to him in 2004. "I started high school when I was six," he said. "I would mail back the answers to all the exams. That was very good: we didn't have to move so I could go to a high school nearby. I was different. I am used to being different.

"I am happy with where I am right now," he told me. "I am fortunate that my parents are open and as caring as they are, since I went through high school at such an early age with not many friends. It's quiet out here. I prefer relaxing. I meditate. I clear my mind. I don't think about anything in particular. I try to do schoolwork every day but can't find the time. Lately, I dropped out of university and have been helping around the farm and the kennel."

I asked him what he thought about being seen as gifted. "I think everyone is different, but some people can absorb materials faster than other people, and they are 'gifted,'" he said. "America is a society that demands perfection."

It was interesting that I had asked him about giftedness, but the word *perfection* was foremost in his mind. The gap between giftedness and perfection has trapped many a child who has sought to do well without having to be perfect. The fact that Brandenn had dropped out of university may indicate that he was feeling that pressure. As for homeschooling, he said, "I know my parents are protective of me because they care about me. I would homeschool my children because I don't think public school can fit the individual needs of each child–I am too easily bored for it. I was tested multiple times as a child. I got bored because I could finish them."

The children of the profoundly gifted movement can find themselves at sea in ordinary settings. This was certainly the case for Brandenn. When Brandenn briefly attended a high school class, he found it so slow that "in forty-five minutes, the class accomplished what I could in five minutes." Perhaps even more tellingly, he spoke of the "odd looks" that he would get from the other kids in the class. As a child, he also went though many piano teachers. He would tire of each one. "They were all trying to get me to sight-read," he said, which he didn't enjoy.

Brandenn kept going back to the idea of "difference." "I don't believe people should be treated in a different way though, [just] because they are different," he said.

For Patti Bremmer, ferrying Brandenn to college was not overparenting–it was giving her son the basic stuff of self-betterment and happiness. "Brandenn's a very expensive child to keep," said Patti at the time. But it was clear that for her, the expenses were worth it. "He's got such a good memory he can unsettle you. He memorizes everything. He has total recall. He memorizes classical music."

And Patti also described Brandenn as driven. "We let him take full charge of his education. He tested out of music theory class. He went to public school briefly, where you get teased and laughed at; he never got teased or laughed at at home. He has been taking music classes since he was three. They told us to take the books away from him. He's been reading since he was eighteen months old. I knew he was profoundly gifted when he was concentrating for a long time on the penguin borders of his diaper-changing table."

"Right before he was ten, he decided he wanted to graduate high school the following year. I said, 'Jeez, Brandenn. There's no way you are going to get though your junior and senior year by the time you are ten!'"

Patti identified with what she viewed as her son's iconoclastic spirit. "I think I am like Brandenn," she said. "I like my freedom. I was the same kind of child. I was thirty-nine when he was born, and there are studies showing that older mothers more frequently have kids with higher IQ tests. It's the chemicals in the womb." She followed this chemical claim with a more likely explanation: Older parents spend more time with their kids. She agreed with her son's assessment that he was "different": "He doesn't belong. He doesn't hang out with homeschooled kids in the area. He doesn't have tight-knit friendships."

After his death, an obituary said that "Brandenn felt he could do his best work from the other side" and that his mind was "too powerful for the limitations of the physical world." "It was like he knew the time is here and he couldn't wait," Patti Bremer told a reporter. "He was above religion. The way he taught it to us, most religions are like elementary school and the spiritual level is beyond collegiate level–most people can't grasp it. It shocked us, awed us, and then we had to learn more about it." In another interview, she remarked, "He didn't want to impose on anyone. He was so connected with the spiritual world, we felt he could hear people's needs and desires and their cries. We just felt like something touched him that day, and he knew he had to leave," to get his organs to others–his kidneys went to two people, his liver to an infant, and his heart to a boy.

While no one can know why Brandenn killed himself, I couldn't help wondering in the aftermath. Did Brandenn experience social unease and psychological stresses? Was his suicide symptomatic of the fact that he wasn't socially well adjusted? And which way did the causal chain go–did his parents want to homeschool him because he didn't fit into regular school, or was it vice versa?

Was it significant that Brandenn had expressed his dislike for the idea that gifted kids should be thought of as so "different"–and when he said this, was he obliquely touching on the resentment of the gifted that many former prodigies mention? So many factors can lead to suicide, and in an individual case like Brandenn's, it is impossible to know his reasons. He did not, as far as the public knows, leave an explanatory note. Patti Bremmer, for one, denies that her son was troubled. She refused to talk with me afterward but wrote in an e-mail: "Brandenn NEVER struggled with anything. He was in a different league."

According to a 2001 study by the National Institute of Mental Health, the suicide rate among children Brandenn's age, in the ten-to-fourteen age category, is low, 1.5 out of 100,000. For young people fifteen to twenty-four years of age, however, suicide is the third leading cause of death: 9.9 out of every 100,000 young people take their own lives. While there are no separate studies for the gifted population, some who study the community believe a small correlation between giftedness and depression may be likely. Professors Tracy L. Cross, Karyn Gust-Brey, and P. Bonny Ball wrote that there is "a paucity of research on the suicidal behavior of this group." In their study, Cross and colleagues recount the work of two other researchers, summarizing "current thinking about the characteristics of gifted adolescents often associated with risk of suicide." The troubling traits common to gifted children include perfectionism, isolationism, and unusual sensitivity. Cross, Gust-Brey, and Ball note that other giftedness specialists, including Annemarie Roeper, "have discussed the characteristics and tendencies that they believe put gifted students at risk for suicidal behaviors," listing a "lack of friendships, self-deprecation, sudden shift in school performance, total absorption in school work, and frequent mood shifts." Cross et al. also quoted a 1995 study, in which students at honors colleges scored significantly higher than their peers on an instrument measuring neurotic perfectionism.

Not every homeschooled gifted or profoundly gifted child is isolated from his or her peers. But if they are, such isolation can be a risk factor for depression. As Dona Matthews and Joanne Foster write in *Being Smart about Gifted Children,* "disadvantaged different" children receive more social support than the "over-advantaged gifted child" does. Additionally, the "gifted label" can cause children to question their identity and abilities, to ask why they are different, and even to feel their gifted label was a mistake–a common response that is known as the "impostor syndrome." Their "self-concept" is at risk due to their exceptionality from the norm. They can feel singled out and rejected.

And then there is the question of the sensitivity of the gifted. Many parents in the gifted community, like Gay McCarter, believe that their children have heightened sensitivity because they are gifted, and some experts support this. In the book *Gifted Children,* Ellen Winner writes that some gifted children are more affected by colors and noise, climate and emotion. Gifted education consultant Deborah Ruf writes in *Losing Our Minds: Gifted Children Left Behind* of gifted children's especially high levels of empathy and intensity.

The extreme home education of one's children is not new, of course. Hundreds of years of attention to educational philosophy and child inculcation have led up to today's extreme parenting methods. Jean-Jacques Rousseau's *Emile* is a combination novel and treatise in which a tutor tries to raise the eponymous fictional child. In educating him, the tutor seeks to resolve the age-old conflict between "the natural man" who "lives for himself" and "the citizen that is but the numerator of a fraction, whose value depends on its denominator." This is a quest to create a gifted child who grows up uncontaminated by the larger world, yet is able to lead in the outside world as an adult. Rousseau combines two schools of pedagogy here, arguing for an upbringing that is sheltered enough to hone talent, yet worldly enough to produce a leader.

Extreme parenting in the form of rigorous homeschooling that pushes kids to excel well beyond the learning level of their peers also has a rich history in Victorian England. Today's homeschooled overachieving children and child collegians resemble some the famous British gifted children and prodigies of that era. Like today's children with extreme parents, John Ruskin and John Stuart Mill, among others, were tutored ferociously at home by their fathers. Mill was subjected to a notoriously strict regimen. His father, James, took him out of school early and pressured him mercilessly, and his young world was freighted with fiery adult knowledge. While still a toddler, Mill began studying ancient Greek. By the time he was eight, he had read all of Herodotus, Xenophon's *Cyropaedia,* and the first six dialogues of Plato in the original. He wrote later that it was "totally impossible" for him to understand what he was reading at so young an age. "But my father, in all his teaching, demanded of me not only the utmost that I could do, but much that I could by no possibility have done." Mill had read most of the major economics texts by the time he was twelve. At thirteen, he was editing his father's book *Elements of Political Economy.* But he was kept so far apart from his peers that he had no idea that his scholastic achievements were unusual. Constantly comparing his own youthful achievements to the adult work of his father, he found himself hopelessly inadequate, as Anthony Storr recounts in the 1979 book *The Art of Psychotherapy.* Driven by such feelings, Mill had a nervous breakdown at twenty, and fell into a deep depression, as he described in chapter 5 of his *Autobiography,* entitled "A Crisis in My Mental History: One Stage Onward." As a child, Mary Wollstonecraft Godwin–later Mary Shelley–heard Samuel Coleridge recite *The Rime of the Ancient Mariner* in her father's parlor before bed, and her early education and cultured home life helped her develop as a prodigy. While still a teenager, she would write an enduring masterpiece, *Frankenstein,* which in a sense described the ultimate hothouse child: half genius, half monster, created to meet the needs of his "father."

Other nineteenth-century parents famously alchemized their children, turning them into botanists, Latinists, eschatologists, and political philosophers. The parents behaved like botanists themselves: horticulturalists of childhood. The young Godwin, Mill, and Ruskin were products of an intellectual aristocracy. But they weren't the only ones in their period driven by what critics of Romantic literature have detected as an "idealization of the child" as "other"–innocent and gleeful.

The way that today's extreme parents emphasize family emotions, moral values, and a fortresslike protection of children can seem, well, Victorian. When I think of them, I think of the "angels of the house," the Victorian notion that mothers were angels who exerted moral influence in the home. That morality then was thought to travel through their children and out into the larger world. (Some of today's parents, in fact, see the children themselves as potential angels–beings who will avoid the world's corruption if only they receive the proper training.) Unlike the famous intellectual parents of the Victorian era who hothoused their soon-to-be intellectual children, many of the parents of gifted homeschooled kids that I spoke with don't define themselves as intellectual. Rather, they are ambitious, tenaciously wanting their children to become more exceptional than they themselves.

When we idealize another person, we worship the qualities that person possesses that we only wish we had. We may feel that the idealized person is operating on a different level of refinement. The idealization period in adult friendships and love affairs tends to be blessedly brief. But what of the extreme parent who has slipped into a state of excessive idealization of her own offspring? A parent who elevates her ten-year-old may continue doing so for the rest of that child's life. As the ultimate late Victorian, Sigmund Freud, wrote in *On Narcissism,* "If we look at the most touchy point in the narcissistic system, the immortality of the ego, which is so hard pressed by reality, security is achieved by taking refuge in the child. Parental love, which is so moving and at the bottom so childish, is nothing but the parents' narcissism born again."

Contemporary psychological accounts of parental idealization stress that parental idealization is different from idealization of a lover or a friend. (It is also different from idealization of children per se, an idealization that could well have more to do with a wish to love general humanity than to love oneself through one's offspring.)

To me, an additional peril of extreme parenting and intensive structuring is the threat to a child's sense of independence, as we are dependent on others for recognition of our independence. In the instance of the parent-child situation in particular, the child is in the contradictory position of seeking independence from the very person the child still longs to depend on. (As the psychoanalyst Jessica Benjamin writes, "the self's wish for absolute independence conflicts with the self's need for recognition.") Yet autonomy, or at least relative autonomy, of interests and actions in childhood is a crucial element of a content childhood.

In more pragmatic sociobiological, sociological, and economic analyses, the self-interest within parental idealization is emphasized. Some sociobiological thinkers contend that there's a genetic basis for child-specific love: a parent who raises a child raises half of his own genes.

Parents have a drive to give their children a singular boost, regardless of the sacrifice. One interpretation of such highly involved parenting is that it just represents a somewhat extreme expression of parents' stakes in their children's future in general. This is what some sociologists call "developmental stake." This personal investment in intergenerational relationships differs depending upon whether a person is part of the "child" or "parent" generation. A parent's stake tends to intensify with their growing dependence on the child as the parent ages. I tend to think that the contract between the generations has been tipping lately. A parent's dependence on their successful child starts not when they are seeking caretaking in old age but when the parent is still in middle age.

Julie Matthaei, an economics professor at Wellesley College, also sees a new perception of childhood in America. Increasing numbers of parents, she says, are investing in a notion of "quality" children. She believes this is because there is now more freedom to move up from one's class background, and also because education is so essential in the labor market. In such a fluid environment, investments in a child's education and enrichment are more likely to pay off, in the form of that child's future success and financial security. Matthaei notes that one of the stratagems of today's committed parents of gifted children, homeschooling, "can be very expensive, because the wife can't work," but that now homeschooling's expense "is seen as worth it when it's a competition between children, with only a few positions at the top."

Mitchell L. Stevens, author of *Kingdom of Children: Culture and Controversy in the Homeschooling Movement,* agrees that intensifying parental management reflects a new view of American childhood. An anthropologist at New York University, Stevens tells me he sees the trend of homeschooling as part of a move toward outsourcing and professionalization in all strata of American life. For some homeschooling parents, especially those whose homeschooling is spurred on by the pursuit of giftedness rather than their religious faith, children are clients and parents managers. Stevens writes that these homeschooling mothers may seem to have abandoned liberal feminism, but they haven't: rather, their workplace is their home, where they "are engines of elaborate family projects and the brick and mortar of an impressive social movement infrastructure. While it may look traditional at first blush, homeschooling's dramatically expanded motherhood is also subtly in keeping with liberal feminist demands."

The emotional side of this client-manager relation has been borne out in the research of Missa Murry Eaton, an assistant professor of child development at Pennsylvania State University, who recently studied a large group of parents. The parents were asked to respond to sentences such as, "When my son fails, I feel bad about myself"; "How I feel about myself is often linked to my daughter's accomplishments"; and "My son's failures are a reflection of my own worth."

In this study, the first of its kind, Eaton found that 20 percent of the parents reported that they based their own self-worth on the performance of their children. Describing symptoms of anxiety and depression, these overinvolved moms and dads said they felt nervous and restless about their children. The actual percentage may be higher; presumably, many parents know that a separate sense of self is the "right" answer, and deny such close attachment. "Those parents focused on failure," says Eaton. "As there's always the potential that the child will fail, these parents experienced no joy and a lot more sadness and upset [than other parents]."

Eaton says that basing one's self-worth on one's children can also have a negative effect on the kids. The parents in her study came from upper-income brackets, and their children were all relatively academically talented freshmen. The parents all possessed college degrees, and some had graduate degrees. Eaton found that the parents' own success in life had no relationship to the degree to which they were caught up in their children's academic success. Moreover, the children's scholastic success was hardly correlated at all with the level of parental enmeshment.

Eaton admits that she, herself, has experienced some of the same struggles as the parents she has surveyed. Her daughter was an "excellent musician," Eaton says, who had begun playing the trumpet in fifth grade and then joined band, dedicating a major amount of her nonschool life to it until the eleventh grade. At that point, Eaton's daughter realized that she didn't enjoy band. At the end of her junior year of high school, she decided to quit. Dr. Eaton was devastated: "I was in band," she said. "My mother was in band. We had a tradition of band in our family. . . . She told me that she thought she was doing it all along just for me. That was an eye-opener. Here I am studying these things, and this was unfolding before me."

It was yet another case of parents getting "caught up in their own expectations for their children, and the children will play along to please them," says Eaton. Eaton thinks that her self-awareness helped her keep her sense of self-worth intact: "I am keenly aware that my knowledge of child development and the things that I study helped me in parenting my daughter."

If there are dangers to this kind of idealization, they don't seem to concern Beth Bess, head of the gifted Bess clan, which she calls "smart kids at home." "I see my family as my escape from ordinary life, a sort of immortality," she tells me. She loves being different and "would die if I was normal, if I thought I was like anyone else. I only hope my own children won't be defined by a niche. Did I sacrifice for them? Yes. Did I give my children my drive and focus? Maybe. I have had fifteen incarnations of a career, but every time I get a career I stop, because I could gyp my kids, and this is a finite period for them. When they were born, my whole life ceased to be mine. I tried to give perfection to them. I have chosen excellence. The price of that can be being unusual and alone."

Like most parents, Beth worries for her family. But she says she is secure that her children's exceptional upbringing will be a form of protection. She believes that her approach will insulate them from what she sees as American toxicity–America at its most superficial, and its most ordinary.

EIGHT

Young Competitors: Youth Contests for Good and for Ill

If as it is often said you can't win, it is perhaps because, when you do, you have so much to lose.

DIANE ARBUS

It was the next-to-final round of the National Scrabble Association's Junior Championship, and Stewart Vaughan was nearly crying. The months of preparation at home and school in Tennessee, memorizing word roots rather than playing basketball, had still not led Stewart and his team to the Xanadu of their presumed championship. He was losing, and because he was fourteen, this was his last chance to compete as a junior. To keep everyone from seeing his emotion, he turned his yellow hair and bubblegum lips away from the cameras, the lights, and the man who was conducting interviews.

It was April 2004, and I was at the second tournament the National Scrabble Association had ever held for kids fourteen years old and under. Taking place in Boston, the proceedings were as whimsical as they were ferocious. Some teams were clad in uniforms, but there were also kids in handmade team T-shirts that read "I Eat Racks for Breakfast" and "Expert Rack Management." Some shirts showed higher production values, and were emblazoned with slogans like "Got Scrabble?"; "Scrabble Makes Strong Minds"; and "Real

Men Play Scrabble." There were girls in beige chinos and beige ponytails. A team of pretty Asian-American girls shook hands with their opponents gracefully and simultaneously. A duo of white girls from Bay Shore, New York, both with shiny brown hair, reviewed their tiles and then grabbed simultaneously at the velvet tile bag, producing an image like a Diane Arbus photo. Lost in the crowd, one kid was looking at his letters and his board, running his hand desperately through his hair as if searching for a word among the strands. His shirt spelled out "Jesse" in Scrabble tiles.

On the floor, a team audibly challenged its opposing team's word. An owlish referee, clad in the standard black-and-white-striped ref shirt and a satin sash, raced over to the table. "This play is acceptable," said the ref–meaning that the word existed in *The Official Scrabble Player's Dictionary,* a perversely catholic distillation and augmentation of other standard dictionaries. Words such as *ratteen, quoin,* and *koi* filled the boards of even the lowest-ranked kids.

On the sidelines, parents were abuzz.

"He's biting his nails," fretted a father.

"Can you read your son?" one mother asked another.

"Oh, no," the other replied, proudly. "Mine's got a poker face."

And true to the competitive culture, there was a ballyhooed early winner, envied and feared. The Girl, as her frightened opponents–mostly boys–had dubbed her, was Katie Devanney. She was thirteen, and she spent hours each night playing Scrabble online. Tall, strapping, with lank brown hair divided by an earnest-looking middle part, she had already been profiled in *Philadelphia Magazine.* In its pages, she said she liked to freak out her opponents with an unsettling, immobile expression. Indeed, not a muscle moved in her face as she retrieved her tiles from their velour bag, keeping the bag at regulation eye level. She remained expressionless as she laid down all seven tiles in their wooden holders.

Katie's mother Diane looked on. "I met Katie's father in Mensa–at the local Mensa singles club, to be exact!" Diane said. "Katie's an only child, a child that is always in the company of adults. I think kids like that are *more* gifted. You have to know, this has been a challenge, to be her mother. I am emotionally exhausted. Katie has had her fifteen minutes of fame when she is only thirteen. All I can do is pray for her in church."

Then the word hit that CBS was going to interview Katie. This news passed from mouth to ear down the long rows of cordoned-off seats, which separated the kids on the floor from four rows of anxious onlookers. Diane Devanney rushed off to be at her daughter's side.

The second annual National Scrabble Association Junior Championship was a part of a larger current: the expansion of children's and teenage competitions around the country. Events with long traditions, like the Scripps National Spelling Bee, the Intel Science Talent Search (formerly the Westinghouse), the Math Olympiad, and even music competitions like the one sponsored by the American Society of Composers, Authors and Publishers (ASCAP) have, in recent years, upgraded or intensified. Training has started younger, and the prizes have gotten larger. Meanwhile, the games that were once played for fun at one's grandparents' house (Scrabble) or practiced on the streets (spoken-word poetry) are increasingly being re-created as youth competitions, for better and, at times, for worse. The competitions can have underlying agendas, too: at the ASCAP competition's showcase event, I witnessed dozens of music-prodigy-esque children in bow ties and suits, one playing a giant grand piano that dwarfed him comically, but I also heard an ASCAP muckety-muk loudly compliment a girl prizewinner for her public remarks about the importance of copyrights and music licensing.

Images of these competitions have also exploded in the media, with films like *Mad Hot Ballroom, Bee Season,* and *Spellbound,* and even a Broadway play about spelling bees, drawing audiences. Is it fascination, sentimentality, or schadenfreude that makes adults watch spelling bees as broadcast on ESPN, as well as a range of reality and variety television shows centered around child performers, with titles like *Fame, Showbiz Moms,* and *Sports Moms and Dads?* Perhaps nowhere is the fascination with precocious child performers so transparently on display as at these competitions. (There are exceptions. Participation in certain "classic" children and youth competitive activities–including Little League and debate–has decreased, to be replaced by trendier activities like children's championship soccer.)

Accompanying these images is a lingering taste for dramas about the former child competitors: the three ex-prodigies in *The Royal Tenenbaums,* the louche Brenda Chenoweth on the HBO drama *Six Feet Under,* or Donnie Smith in the 1999 film *Magnolia* (who achieved early stardom on the trivia game show *What Do Kids Know?* in which a team of three children battled adults for money and prestige, and now recalls it from the victimized vantage point of his adult life as an underweight middle-aged barfly hopelessly in love with a hunky bartender).

The explosion of images of child competitors and the proliferation of competitive disciplines and events, alongside the fact that kids are joining them younger and younger, raises the familiar question, Are kids too competitive? The controversy around competition is familiar to parents, teachers, school administrators, and youth counselors. Are children's competitions a breeding ground for adult brutality and ruthlessness, darkly gladiatorial places where one child's coming into being as an individual rests on another child's failure?

On one hand, some coaches and parents and scholars subscribe to the adage that competitions prepare kids for success in later life. They argue that knowledge is gained and skills are acquired through these pursuits. On the other, it is thought that most of those lessons are rote, and if they have any depth, they are better off learned in a climate without flash and rivalry.

Those who question the spread of competition insist that inspiration for pursuing an activity must come from within–be intrinsic–rather than being externally or extrinsically motivated. These critics note that the growing presence of the media at youth events can be an extra hindrance to children's development. Critics of competition also question whether tournaments actually give children from lower-income families a leg up: contest winners, they note, tend to come from families that can afford early and constant training for their children.

As I traveled to a number of these contests for two years in a row, the arguments against competition for kids persistently raced through my mind. Should that kid with the adult mannerisms be affixed to a piano twice his size, performing for an audience of adults, adults high on the whimsy of this child performer? Should that teen poet be reciting her personal angst to a crowd and then getting (or not getting) points for it? The night before the Junior Scrabble Championship, at 9:00 p.m., the Scrabblers couldn't seem to stop playing. They brought to mind the girl in the Hans Christian Andersen fairy tale and classic film *The Red Shoes,* in which a girl couldn't stop dancing. (This being a rather grim fairy tale, the girl danced herself to death.) In the hotel lobby that night, clusters of parents went over "stem words" and homonyms with their children. Ten-year-old Brandon Alford's blond, pearly-toothed mother was reviewing Latin and Greek with him as his father sat quietly by their side.

By the same token, I was also struck by the child competitors' burbling enthusiasm and the teen would-be champions' utter dedication–their "authentic" passion, sometimes verging on obsessive compulsion. This was true for many of the child Scrabble players. It was also true for the debate competitors. I watched some debaters in action at a tournament in New York City in early 2004. At that event, held by the New York Urban Debate League, hundreds of kids from some of the boroughs' poorest districts were debating in small classrooms throughout Hunter College. Many of the teams lacked coaches. Some homeboys wore puffy jackets. A few girls were more formally dressed: dress shirts, dangling earrings.

The college and high school debate topic that year was "Ocean Policy," and a subcategory within it was "Coral Reefs": a debater could argue topics such as "Coral Reefs Face Total Destruction," "Reefs in Trouble," and "Coral Reefs Much Rarer Than Thought." At the NAUDL tournament, one couldn't help wondering how many of the debaters had actually seen a coral reef, or even the glittering aquamarine waves under which a coral reef might be found. One debater, whose patch of dyed red hair exploded like baby fireworks from the rest of his pomaded 'do, asked: "What are the specific regulations and enforcement for the coral reef? Do you plan to limit the exploitation of the corals? If so, how do you limit them? Like, contain them, you know, in the ocean? I am saying how do you, like, enforce it?"

The judge looked at his cell phone and said, "Time, time!" He was timing the round on his Nokia. In a different classroom later that day, the 2003 New York State high school debate champion in the novice division, Christopher Vasquez, was debating an environmental topic limited to coral reefs but spreading outward to include dualism and the Law of the Sea. Christopher and his partner had stickers on their notebooks and plastic files bearing the legends, "A Goal Without a Plan Is Just a Wish" and "We Trust Fox News."

The argument they were using, however, might make the producers at Fox News reach for Xanax. Alluding to the work of the late social historian

Michel Foucault, Christopher began with the claim that Empire is responsible for environmental degradation. "One function of capitalism is that it allows for the devaluation of life," Christopher said, accompanying his speech with hand gestures that were half hip-hop artist, half politician. "We should take away U.S. power. The U.S. leads the world in global violence."

The two girls on the opposing team cobbled together a rebuttal, but it wasn't enough. Christopher and his partner, Caesar, had won.

That same winter, I attended the annual Harvard National High School Invitational Forensics Tournament. These kids sloughed through the same arguments on the environment, the oceans, pollution, and the rights of indigenous people.

Both contests were impressive–the contestants displayed dedication, strong capacity for memorization, and, to a greater or lesser extent, familiarity with the law and American history, at least enough to use facts pertaining to either in arguments. But there were certain differences. At the Harvard debate, many more debaters had clearly been trained and coached from an early age. There was more of an overall perfection to their performances. Many of the participants at the Harvard tournament were dressed like miniature lawyers: black suits, gold-buttoned blue blazers, and ties lined the hallways. Some debaters carried briefcases. (A few of the debaters from affluent suburban communities, it was true, used casualness as a weapon unto itself: one junior took it upon himself to do his whole argument in stocking feet, referring to his opponent as "dude.")

While none of the competitors seemed visibly shaken by their losses, I knew from my conversations with adult former debate champions–whose fear before and sometimes after rounds had been so intense that they experienced nausea–that they might well be covering up their feelings. It was clearly intense: most had spent weeks or months practicing.

At the ASCAP showcase, I asked one of the prizewinning youth composers, a boy who had already won a dozen or so major youth music prizes and was on his way to Juilliard, what he thought of competing. "I mean, I'm competitive but I am suspicious of people who want to make their mark on history," the boy, who has been composing since age five, told me. "You have to be mobile, agile, and hostile. The world isn't what it was when

Mozart and Beethoven walked." To get a better handle on this world, he says, "My dad and I talk for an hour a day about what angle to take in my career."

When I spoke with young competitors like this musician, I thought of the words of the critics of youth competitions, those who find these contests to be far-from-blithe rituals. Rather, youth contests are unsavory, perhaps even pathology-inducing. One family therapist wrote an essay about his parent analysands, whose treatments revolve around their children's sports careers. Books like William Crain's *Reclaiming Childhood: Letting Children Be Children in Our Achievement-Oriented Society* attack bywords like "accountability." Crain writes, "How could anyone oppose 'higher standards' and 'clear goals'? Does anyone question the need for 'accountability' and 'higher test scores' or the need to end 'social promotion'? Actually, a child-centered philosophy does question these aims." Crain sees a child-centered philosophy as one at odds with putting pressure on children to accomplish and win.

Critics of children's competitions see them as of a piece with school bullying (symptomatic of competitive sentiments) and elitism. School district Web sites discuss "Competition vs. Cooperation." These critics believe kids should be taught cooperation over competition. For them, cooperation is aligned with "intrinsic motivation"–skills that are self-defined, driven by the child or teen's own wish to master something. Extrinsic motivation is aligned with competition–activities with the aim of a palpable reward and motivated by external demands. While extrinsic motivation can motivate children–the gold star or trophy of the prize win can certainly rouse children to take part in an activity–experts who critique the ethos of competition say that just being motivated isn't the point. The point is, rather, *how* a child is motivated.

Alfie Kohn, author of *No Contest: The Case against Competition,* supports the arguments made by Crain in *Reclaiming Childhood.* "Competition is our state religion and we mindlessly assume that people must be sorted into categories from their earliest days," Kohn says. "The evidence overwhelmingly suggests that when you have to fail in order for me to succeed at work, at school, at home, at play, the effect is almost uniformly negative in terms of achievement and in terms of psychological health and relationships with others."

Perhaps unsurprisingly, Kohn remembers a childhood of championship misery in Miami Beach in the 1960s. "I was a big-deal debater in high school, and it took me years to unlearn the toxic messages I learned from that activity. I learned that there are exactly two sides to any issue, and that either position can be defended if you are clever enough, that no view is more right than any other, and I developed an adversarial posture. In debate training, you are trained to win, to pummel your opponent, to selectively use evidence to defend a given position. Sure, I acquired good research and speaking skills, but I am still not sure it was worth the cost."

Kohn's book is full of studies decrying competition: one 1981 review of 122 studies on learning, for instance, noted 65 studies that found cooperation to promote higher achievement than did competition. Eight found the reverse, and 42 found no difference.

Scholars who want adults to consider carefully before they promote competition include Scott Scheer, an associate professor at Ohio State University, who coined the term "cooperative imperative"–a wish to work with others. According to Scheer, cooperative learning produces higher achievement, better social skills, and a higher sense of self than competitive programs, especially among children. Children in competitive environments define themselves extrinsically, Scheer argues, creating a weak foundation for their sense of self–and of self-worth. Reading Scheer, I recalled a conversation I had with former child actress Donna Lynne Champlin and her childhood of competitions: "Every time I lost a tap competition as a small child, I went into a shame spiral."

Others have found different grounds on which to question the value of kids' competitions. For one thing, it can take money to participate in them: some of the urban debate teams in the National Forensic League tournaments have trouble attending the invitationals, among them the Harvard tournament, because the costs are simply too prohibitive. And there is also the question of what the children competing in some of these brain sports actually learn, and how "authentic" their knowledge is. Debate is the competition for those who "enjoy talking," as one debate organizer put it to me. Meanwhile, in a verbal competition like Scrabble or the Scripps Spelling Bee, kids or teens are not necessarily approaching mastery in an area of knowledge. Rather, they are learning a skill where they treat words as objects in and of themselves, not as units that contain what philosophers call cognitive significance. The competitions show their participants that language is easily manipulated, that words can be given a numerical value, and that language is a game. In debate, language is a game, but its participants at least are learning both the sense and the reference of language–for them, language operates as a portmanteau for an argument. In Scrabble, as one championship administrator told me of the game, "It's not a literary game, you know. It's a counting game, for kids who are good at math." But what exactly, then, is Scrabble teaching children about math?

A third argument is arrayed not against the competitions themselves, but against what they have become in the media age. Jacques Bailly, an associate professor of classics at the University of Vermont, a "word pronouncer" at the Scripps National Spelling Bee and a spelling bee champion himself in 1980 (he won for spelling the word *elucubrate,* "to read in the dark"), finds the increased media glare a problem, especially with the ESPN concept of spelling bee "favorites," as he puts it: the best returning spellers, on which the cameras zoom in.

The fans of children's competition dismiss such worries. Advocates argue that the esteem these contests build within children and the preparation for the unceasing competition of adult life they afford makes the competitions well worth any risks. According to experts like Gary Alan Fine, a sociology professor at Northwestern University and author of a book on high school debate, *Gifted Tongues,* as well as research into Little League, the competitions don't diminish but enhance participants' confidence, sense of self, and sense of community.

"My oldest son was very talented: he won one of the national debate tournaments, the Tournament of Champions," Fine tells me. He got his kids to "strive to excel, to be able to say they acted to the best of their ability," he says. "My kids learned a lot of skills competing. But it's not just my kids. Kids who compete in spelling bees learn how to stand up onstage.

"Now, parents and school systems have become more cautious and believe it is better to give awards to large groups rather than one victorious individual," Fine says with distaste. "They have leaned too far in that direction, to the point that schools eliminate valedictorians or class rank. Competition is important, for certain."

Fine believes that by creating more winners' places and more valedictorian spots, we have denigrated an American tradition–that of striving for victory in order to rise above one's circumstances. Indeed, some of the pundits advocating competition are particularly worried that the United States, in its move toward relativism and sensitivity training, is forcing too many children, especially male children, to deny their "natural" competitive instincts. Among this lot are those who consider the anticompetitive crowd to be a bunch of "soft" liberals who are emasculating boys–a position espoused in Christina Hoff Sommers's recent book *The War against Boys.* A 1999 article in *City Journal* takes an even more extreme counterintuitive position: its author, Janet Daley, argued that anticompetitive forces were actually rendering British boys *more* hostile.

These proponents of youth competitions and competitiveness are not just saying that contests prepare boys for manhood. They also say such contests prepare children and teens for the competition of life. There is a quiet but evident connection between a view of competition as a key to success and a free-market view of existence. After all, would this be a child-eat-child world if these children could rely on social programs to care for them down the line, and if there wasn't such disdain for those children who grow up to be adult "losers" in the game of life?

But those making the case for kids' competitions are not just a bunch of Ayn Rand fans or people with conservative politics and an essentialist faith in the market-as-metaphor. Will Baker, CEO of the nonprofit urban debate organization known as the Impact Coalition, a member of the National Association of Urban Debate Leagues, which began with an investment from George Soros's Open Society Institute in 1997 and has continued to grow, sees debate as a tool. "There's Riker's Island debate now," says Baker, referring to a program at the New York prison. "It could be a mantra of social change: open debate, one person having a thought and communicating it to another person."

NAUDL, as it is called nationally, claims that it uses "debate as a mechanism for urban education improvement, to promote equal access and opportunity to participate in debate": debate as a classroom activity. For students who may have been "at risk" academically and personally, which is how Baker describes a number of Impact's participants, the debate leagues and the tournaments provide nothing short of an intervention. Debate, after all, evinces none of the stodginess some students associate with traditional academic classes. It is a discipline that rewards the quick and the loud. Competition, in this view, is a tool for the kids' self-betterment: youth competitions often offer kids a way out of a tough environment, or at least another way they can gain some self-esteem and exercise their vitality. As the promotional materials of the National Association of Urban Debate Leagues put it, "Urban Debate is a powerful mechanism for academic improvement and youth empowerment."

According to NAUDL, the debate tournaments are also good vehicles for kids to get scholarships; the association's press materials boast of the "heightened interest that colleges have in debaters." Urban Debate League champion Christopher Vasquez, for example, came from the South Bronx; because of Urban Debate, he says, he went free to debate camp that might have cost $8,000, and he credits the program with getting him into Vanderbilt College on a full scholarship.

Another youth competition that seems to provide some of the same opportunities as the UDL is inspired by the spoken word "slams" first popularized in poetry clubs and other offbeat venues in the 1990s. In the teen version sponsored by Urban World NYC, teen speakers recite poems they have written to an audience, in an emphatic, dramatic style. The teens are then judged on the quality of the content, including rhythm, prosody, and meaning. Presentation counts, too.

Urban Word NYC has been holding an Annual Teen Poetry Slam for just seven years. The way it works is that there is a monthly slam for teens aged thirteen to nineteen, and the top-scoring poets qualify for the semi-final rounds. At these rounds, the poets perform original works of three minutes or less. Each night, five judges determine which poets are good enough to move on to the next level, which culminates in a master match, from which five adolescents are culled for the New York City Teen Poetry Slam Team. That team then goes on to a national slam called Brave New Voices, where it competes with teams from around the country. The 2004 preliminaries drew hundreds of competitors to the Brooklyn Academy of Music. The poems could have been mistaken for unaccompanied rap songs, and the teens, many adorned with bling and clad in giant sports jerseys, looked like aspiring young rappers. But the level of the language play and the expressed feeling had a whole lot more to it than the oeuvre of 50 Cent (or Mr. Cent, as the *New York Times* likes to call him). These teens recounted their brushes with drugs–"rocks the same color as mellow yellow." The boys wrote about girls–one of whom could be mistaken for a "doorbell" due to "all those rings." The rhetoric of promise and survival was also in evidence: "We shall survive" was one poem's refrain.

The strongest poet to emerge that year was Enmanuel Candelario, then seventeen. An excerpt of his masterwork performed at the slams goes as follows:

without blacks the U.S.
probably wouldn't exist so let me assist the observation of the slave
process.
Slaves have changed through the ages
slave chains to slave wages
the change, black is not the only race it encases
Dominicans and Haitians . . .
It's amazing
how slavery never discriminates against us
to tell you the truth I think it loves us
with a passion
cos when I applied for slavery they had no
problem givin' me affirmative action.

What I realized after having attended a few competitive teen slams and then hanging out with the slam team at workshops and on their own was that spoken word was different from the other kids' competitions in a significant way. For starters, spoken word began as a form of expression invented by an urban minority underclass, which was then taken up and developed by bohemian outsiders and aspiring bohemian outsiders. It seemed telling that Brave New Voices did not offer the kind of rewards–scholarships, large cash prizes, mainstream prestige and attention–that the other youth competitions do. What the spoken word teens were looking for was to express themselves in front of a group of peers, and maybe, if they were really lucky, do so on HBO's *Def Poetry*. Maybe the lack of rewards had to do with race and class. It certainly has to do with the hideously lowly role of poetry in America generally–emerging only rarely, and always at weddings and funerals–and also the way that poetry evades audiences, what critic James Longenbach has called "the resistance to poetry." Despite this lack, though, the spoken word poetry contests appeared to have more authentic value to their young participants than other competitions I attended. Not only did they build self-possession and pride, but they provided a release of feeling and thought. For spoken word competitor Emmanuel Arroyo, competing at the spoken word slams afforded him an emotional rescue. "My life was pure chaos," said Arroyo, of the time before he was a spoken word competitor. "I was kicked out of the house. I was on the verge. I lay on the floor, decided to change my life at that moment. There was Old Manny and New Manny. Now, I pour anger onto the pages. God blessed me. When I encounter detractors of poetry, I look at them and tell them poetry is like rap. But it's better."

I heard similar sentiments when I went to visit Enmanuel Candalario at the arts center in a brownstone in Harlem where he wrote and practiced his spoken word pieces, and from the other team members I spoke with in 2004. Generally, there seemed to be less of the downside: none of the hours of rote memorization, for example, involved in spelling competitions. And the audience of 1,500 or so who cumulatively attended the teen Spoken Word Finals, where 500 teens performed over eleven nights, also seemed to have a more communal investment in the competition, clapping and calling out in appreciation of a particularly sharp, witty, or poignant line.

For some other parents of child competitors, competitions can offer a social circle and social life. At the 2004 Scrabble competition, a team from Grain Valley, Missouri, which would not otherwise find itself in an elite-kid achiever zone, saw the competition as a sort of Big Chance. During informal games on the eve of the competition, as dozens of kids ate vanilla ice cream with hot fudge, coconut, and cherries and listened to the championship's event organizer talk about "bagmanship" (a neologism describing good Scrabble sportsmanship–it means, basically, picking tiles without looking at them), two members of the Missouri team, Joseph and Joshua Santoli, and their mother, Jonne, sang the praises of the Scrabble competition.

Santoli, a woman with the booming voice of the local talk radio host she is (KCXL, 1140 AM), her sandy hair shaped into a feathered 'do suitable for a Journey music video, announced her children had been practicing for six months to win $5,000, the grand prize. "That's a lot of money," Santoli said. "But it's not just the money! Last week, my son came to me with the word *hajji.* He's learning things. My son learned the word *quat.* I never learned that. He also learned the word *tranq.*"

Whether Santoli's son knows what the words mean is another question. But maybe he'll learn those things someday, too. "We came all the way here from the Midwest," continued Santoli. "I think these new rules, the use of these new timers in the championships, are ridiculous–these new clock timers, they are just increasing competition. My sons trained with sand timers." Santoli explained that she was used to speaking out against things that she thought were wrong. She and others like her at this year's youth Scrabble competition were full of optimism, however. They felt that because youth Scrabble was a new sport, there was more room for upstarts. The Grain Valley crowd saw it as a chance to get a whiff of life's better things, including Harvard tchotchkes like sweatshirts and mugs. For Santoli, the championship was most exciting because it pitted her kids against kids from private schools in the Northeast, kids who might later attend Ivy League schools, kids who carry cell phones. She reminded me that neither she nor anyone she knows owns a cell phone, just as a kid passed us, talking on one that was a quarter of the size of his head. The boy squinted as he described the championships to the person at the other end of the call.

"These other kids have all been tutored in Scrabble by fancy tutors," Santoli continues. "Their parents spend $25,000 a year on them. These kids practice an hour each day. My son Josh is a big kid, and they keep trying to get him to play football and get a scholarship. In Missouri, the only emphasis is on sports. I prefer Scrabble: it builds vocab. It builds self-esteem."

When it comes to this last article of faith–that training for and competing in events like the Scrabble championship serve to build children's self-esteem–Santoli is not alone. There were the Scrabble "ambassadors," unpaid Scrabble champions who volunteered at the event, walking to and fro during the championships. One ambassador was a woman with coils of gray curly hair under a "Play Scrabble" trucker hat. The curls bounced because of her jerky gait, which combined a limp and a strut. She happily told me that Scrabble was her life. The children started to play games informally at their tables with one another or with their parents. Almost all of the parents were sure to lose to their offspring. In one corner Joel Sherman, the reigning adult national Scrabble champion, with his trademark wiry clown hair and red suspenders, played eight kids simultaneously on four different boards.

Adults involved in the competition may experience more than parental pride or a sense of self-worth attendant on being an "ambassador" or a judge. John Williams, president of the National Scrabble Association, picked up on this eleven years ago as he sought to revitalize the Scrabble brand. Williams decided that Scrabble could fit into the world of tailored school programs and after-school tutoring. He set out to appeal to "new families," as he put it, "where parents don't live with each other, and everyone works and Grandma isn't around and no one is home together playing Scrabble."

Williams quickly realized that the key was to turn Scrabble into a competitive *sport.* Williams, now a patrician silver fox, his sleek face seeming to float above his dark blazer, got his start in advertising, and he still exudes that 1960s "persuaders" aura. A Scrabble master himself, Williams wanted to see Scrabble enter the scholastic curriculum. The National Scrabble Association held Scrabble focus groups at prep schools, where kids quickly racked up triple scores, and then at more rural schools, where, Williams noted, the kids were less confident laying down their double-letter wins. "When we built the program, we saw it as curriculum, as teacher material, as a way to expose the game to people that had no clue, to expose them to it so they learned to understand Scrabble strategically and aesthetically," he says. "Now they have been cultivated. It's unbelievably beautiful. We started the New England Tournament, 1996 through last year. I knew the raw material existed, and these kids were poised to do it."

Williams set out to make Scrabble prodigies a new category of giftedness. However, he prefers to say that the tournaments are "discovering" the prodigies rather than "inventing" them. Getting Scrabble in the classroom would be a great way to create early brand loyalty that might pay dividends down the road. The eureka moment for Williams and his employees came when they realized how nice the Scrabble board design would look on a beach towel.

"Scrabble for kids was a great business opportunity," says Williams. Representatives from Hasbro, the game's manufacturer, attended the championship, as did the Grey Advertising folks who are responsible for the Hasbro account. To his credit, Williams has ensured that the company maintains only what he calls a "whispery presence" here. One can see only hints of marketing–the Scrabble rug, for example, as well as Scrabble dictionaries and baseball caps. (Williams's decision to go subtle is reminiscent of the Scripps National Spelling Bee's alleged refusal to accept the sponsoring presence of Bumble Bee Tuna one year, when the latter company allegedly wanted the Bumble Bee logo to dance onstage next to the young spellers.) Williams benefited from his association with the child competitors. So did Hasbro, and all of the television programs and reporters who, in 2004, captured the momentary downfall of Katie Devanney, "the Girl," who was once considered unbeatable. Katie and her partner made a faulty challenge to her opposing team, after they played EYER/RETAINS/DE for 71 points. In contrast, Katie and her partner laid down KA/ED for 21.

"Katie's losing," one Scrabble guy chimed to another as they surveyed the scene from the back of the room. "Better get the Terman kids on tape. Get the sound bites. Get the whole thing."

It was round five, and Katie and her partner were going head-to-head with a team of boys from Terman Middle School, a public school in the superachiever city of Palo Alto, California. Terman, a school with a gifted and talented program, was named after Lewis Terman, the designer of the Stanford-Binet–the first American IQ test–and the author of the most famous study of gifted children ever conducted. Two Terman students, in their official bright orange-yellow school T-shirts, were competing against the Girl, Katie Devanney, and Katie's partner, whose name was also Katie. Terman Middle then put down SIENITE/EWE for 71 points.

The game indeed went to Terman, 305–415. And the Girl's lost game would exist from then on, on Web sites and in newspaper accounts or on film, missed opportunities frozen in photographic amber.

I left the Scrabble competition and many of the other competitions with an even stronger sense that these contests are as much for their audiences of adults–the parents, teachers, and coaches on the sidelines, those random adults watching their televisions or flicking through their local newspapers or going to their local film theaters and coming across images of the child competitor at the spelling bee–as they are for the children and teens themselves. I thought of the perennial allure of J. D. Salinger's short stories in the middle of the last century: the fey, overweening child-adults Franny, Zooey, and Seymour Glass and their four other chokingly advanced siblings, the stars of a children's quiz radio show, *It's a Wise Child.* In adulthood, these specimens were portrayed as simultaneously miserable and aggressively charming, inhabiting a cloistered world that Mary McCarthy called Salinger's "closed circuit." Nevertheless, to this day, readers can't get enough of them. As I watched children and teens pack up after competitions, the throng of cameras and reporters underlined to me the nation's curious fascination with child performers.

This fixity on the child performer can be more than curious–it can be ghoulish. In fact, we sometimes enjoy depictions of prodigies getting their comeuppance. Even though the wish for a child's downfall, even an arrogant, enviable child, is taboo and bears the whiff of psychic murder, the perpetually mediocre adult audience continues to want to watch the young competitor fail. The published, filmed, and televised former child competitors experiencing the Icarus effect in later life–the real-life child prizewinner who becomes a kleptomaniac, the ex-child actor who flounders in addiction, the former Quiz Kids! star who founders professionally, the fictional ex-prodigy in the film *Magnolia* at age forty, trapped in the dentist's chair, being taunted by the dental assistant ("You were really cute when you were on that show–you can't answer any questions right now though, huh?")–all somehow reflect this. Perhaps it is making good on an unexpressed animus against children with more promise–and therefore more claim on the parental attention all children crave–than the members of the audience. I couldn't help but think that some members of the audience at the competitions I attended, or those watching the spelling bee on film or television, felt some of this dark excitement, taking secret pleasure in the thought that every young winner implies a young loser. Inevitably, the cameras trained on the Scrabblers or the spelling bee kids will capture some child bred to be a champion in his Icarus-falls-to-Earth moment. In 2004, images of the momentary fainting of thirteen-year-old Akshay Buddiga from Colorado during the final round of the Scripps National Spelling Bee circulated across the nation as the light story on the evening news. What made it all the more dramatic was the fact that he stood up just seconds after swooning and spelled a doozy of a word, *alopecoid.* It's compelling as spectacle and as metaphor–transformed in a nanosecond from prodigy, bearer of dreams, to ex-prodigy, carrier of adult failure, he then stands up, a gifted competitor once more. Perhaps it was good television (especially for an embittered late-night audience), but will it be a good memory for Buddiga?

In 2005, Katie Devanney, the Girl, competed again in the National Juniors Scrabble competition, and again first place eluded her. She also participated in about a dozen adult tournaments that year, still studying her word lists for hours per week and playing online with adults every day. Diane thinks Katie's childhood as a denizen of the adult Scrabble world gives her "a huge advantage." And seemingly it has. After all, Katie's losses haven't harmed her–at least, not yet.

NINE

Children of God: The Teen Preaching Tournaments

She had been unforgettable precisely because, at that moment, as a child and as a preacher, she had not belonged to herself.

JAMES BALDWIN, *Just Above My Head*

It's an April morning in Greenville, South Carolina, and seventeen-year-old Joshua Dean is summoning the Lord.

"I know who I am and where I am going," says Josh. "Do you know for certain where *you* are going? Hell is a real place. Sadly, most of the world is going there. Death is absolutely certain. Death is life's most certain experience. It is also the least certain experience: when, how, where, and why? What is most certain is most important."

He stares at the crowd of forty with big, bright blue eyes framed by a long, avian nose, his sandy hair clipped close to his skull. He is wearing a tie with a pattern of the Christian symbol of the fish on it. It's brought him luck during twelve sermons. He holds aloft the object that is both his weapon and his armor: a dented black leather-bound Bible, underlined in red ink.

"A small minority–only a handful–are saved," he says. He cups his hands for emphasis, then narrows them into the shape and size of a grapefruit. His hands then extend out into points, first like semaphores, then like a windmill, then like a God-fearing disco dancer.

"'When gratitude dies on the altar of a man's heart, that man is well-nigh hopeless,'" he says, quoting a common saying.

The crowd responds with *Amens.*

Josh returns to his seat, hands shaking, legs jiggling, eyes darting. His enthusiasm is indeed remarkable. He is sitting in a room lousy with "boy preachers." It's the American Association of Christian Schools' evangelical preaching competition, held at Bob Jones University–a grand or nefarious place, depending on your outlook. Josh's audience are men in their middle years, wearing the clothing of the late 1950s, as well as the fellow preacher boys, all suited up and freshly laundered. The boys are hoping to best Josh with their sermons, although they'd never agree with the concept of besting. Instead, they'd say they were doing the will of God, and God had given them enough talent to win.

At AACS, they tend to say they are gifted by God and inspired by God–even that He has given them their sermons. In fact, they are so leery of being too worldly that some say they feel guilty participating in a competition to see who can best preach the Lord's word. But from the looks of the AACS competitions–contests that include singing, debate, and even Christian youth art–these teens are indeed competitive. You can see the same degree of ruthless drive here as you see in today's secular champions. Take the competition's final Bible Quiz, a tense event. Teen teams, clad in identical suits, are given the first word of a scriptural quotation. The first contestant to press a buzzer and correctly yelp out its source wins the round. The quizzers went at those buzzers with the violent vigor of spelling bee contestants, screaming out "First Corinthians!"

"The Bible Quiz might sound like the NCAA," said a quizmaster, referring to the college-basketball-like din. He then thought better of the unholy metaphor, adding, "But the quiz is more important."

At the evangelical preaching event, no matter how many participants had professed a wish to be selfless, the rivals in the pulpit practically bristled with competitive showmanship. Sixteen-year-old competitor Matt Rivera, for instance, gave his sermon (or "message," as they sometimes call it) as though he were a lawyer making a case for salvation. Diminutive, hair slicked back, clad in a dark and crisp new suit, Matt paced the classroom during his message, logically and calmly drawing the line between faith and eternal life.

When he finished, a murmur went through the crowd of judges and rivals and sundry spiritualist gawkers in recognition of the boy's smooth talent.

Matt has the intensity of one just recently "saved," along with his family, four years earlier. The freshness of his experience might have had something to do with the clear thinking he had put into his sermon. Unlike most of his fellow competitors, Matt was not born "born-again," and was not always a part of this world. A Latino from Denver, Colorado, Matt used to be a Catholic, and describes himself as a typical inner-city kid. Before God blessed him "with talents," he says, he lived with his grandmother and was "a crazy kid, a gangster."

And Matt isn't even the hardest working or the most ambitious of the bunch. James Sumpter III, who is seventeen, spends hours and hours per week watching celebrated evangelists on television and listening to them on his CD player. He copies their moves and even their vocal inflections at home at night.

"Hell is no joking matter," James says, when his time has come to preach. "It's the real expression of God's justice."

Like all of the preacher boys at the AACS (and they're all boys), James provides his listeners with a parable on the importance of true faith and the right behaviors. He tells a fictive tale of two teenagers at church, teens so drunk on love for one another that they ignored the sermon and even had the audacity to exit services early, murmuring to one another, "I'll take my chances" (regarding salvation, that is). James delivers this message with a boomy southern accent. He's tall and athletically thin, with the dark, curly hair, cleft chin, and even features of a matinee idol.

"They laughed, they mocked," James says of the profane couple in his cautionary tale. And they soon died in a car accident. James stands tall at the front of the room, clad in a sand-colored suit, a yellow-and-brown striped tie, and a blue shirt. Regarding the idea of being "almost" faithful to Christ, James shouts, "Almost is not enough!"

In Christianity, there's a long tradition of the charismatic young person drawing a flock, then describing his accomplishment as God's doing rather than the result of his talent or labor. Josh, Matt, and James are part of that tradition. These young religious seers are viewed as exceptionally spiritual beings, as having come to their power as religious messengers by nature and without prodding. Yet these child preachers are often being intensively coached. As in other places where children's giftedness is being built or enriched–or at worst, invented–the question remains whether the kids who are competing are authentic about their interest. Are these boys inspired to pursue their vocation in an "authentic" religious way, and are they becoming more steeped in their religion through the practice of learning how to preach? Or are they just learning mannerisms and memorizing scripture, free of the meaning the teachings entail? There's a certain strangeness in all kid competitions, in the way children are pushed to perform and excel. But it seems stranger still in this particular arena. Religion is supposed to be a "pure" area of human experience. The memorization and discipline required for Christian teen competitions, and their emphasis on mastery, seems to have little to do with guileless fervor. In fact, some of the teen preachers seemed to be working awfully hard to achieve divine inspiration.

James's father, for example, watched his son go over and over his message, for hours and hours per day. "James listens to so many guys preaching," his father says. "God gifts you with a talent, and my son asked the Lord to do whatever He wanted to do with him. But it's not born into him. He works hard. He studies a lot. I see it as a mixture of appetite, behavior, and environment in his study. He listens to CDs incessantly."

In fact, child and teen competitive preaching is such a craft that James's father was concerned that the sermon that his son, along with the other teen preachers, would deliver a number of times (the teen preachers repeat the same sermon over and over again at the competition) had some "redundancies," and "James went too quickly on two or three lines."

One of the competition's judges, Dan Olinger, a Bob Jones theologian, contradicted my overall impression that style and oratorical skill triumph over the "realness" of authentic faith. "We look to see if they are nervous or artificial or if there's too much cognitive dissonance to the sermon," he said. "One kid one year referred to 'a terrible storm at sea' within one's soul, 'like the storm in the television show *Gilligan's Island*.'"

In the Bible Preaching judging forms, the factors Olinger and other judges evaluated in the preacher boy competitors included "vitality," defined as "'life' in the face, body & voice": "eye contact/empathy (direct visual and mental contact with audience)": "Poise/Authority (sense of composure, assurance & authority)": and "Emphasis/Variety (stress on key ideas through appropriate, accurate explanation of Scripture & principles presented)."

"I'd normally judge a sermon given by an adult by its hermeneutics: I'd use literary criticism, evaluating genre, poetry, Bible theology," explained Olinger. "At this level, a high school kid doesn't have much in the way of theological education, so we are judging whether he is real."

But "realness," as anyone familiar with theater or drag knows, can be very much an effect, as constructed as giftedness itself. It can be more about mastery and memorization than belief and knowledge. The 2004 winner in the Scripture Memorization category, Brad Yoder of Macomb, Ohio, admitted that rote memorization has been a key to his success. "Christian schools really have kids memorize verses at an early age," said Yoder. "It was forced on me." Now he believes that the routinized remembrances were a good thing. Brad can learn eight verses by heart in an hour. After all, he won the Scripture Memorization competition by reciting ninety verses. ("It's much like a spelling bee, but instead of asking me to spell *accommodate,* they would ask me to recite Matthew 6:33, 'But seek ye first the kingdom of God, and his righteousness,' or John 3:16.")

Matt Rivera was similarly dedicated to the performance aspect of preaching. He practiced his sermons a couple of times a day and daily, on his own, doing a Bible overview. And one of the 2005 Bible Quiz champions, fifteen-year-old Aaron Wells, a blond boy with wire-rimmed glasses, an expectant smile, a patterned tie, and the overall wholesomeness of a teenager in a 1940s film, says he memorizes a verse a day. It reminded me, as other zones of gifted childhood have reminded me, that the idealization of children's precocity in the nineteenth century by Romantic poets and by Victorian parents and writers alike still echoes through today's hothouse-kid culture. But while a cult of precocity and "earliness" still pervades American culture, today's giftedness takes that idea of some children's uncanny natural ability and tempers it with the axiom "practice makes perfect"–this is specialness that must be cultivated, rather than natural genius. The teen preachers all believe they are gifted by a greater force than training or heredity, but all admit to practicing and memorizing incessantly.

At the AACS, the young students had experienced an almost completely religious curriculum, one highly dependent on the memorization of a religious text, and were bred to become prodigies of God. Notably, the Christian schools that many AACS competitors attend are considerably cheaper than secular private schools, and more coherent than traditional public schools. One cannot help but wonder what the AACS children might discover, invent, or build if they were encouraged to apply their enthusiasm to something other than memorization of the Bible. Does the fact that it is the only means permitted and available to them to express their intelligence and talent pose questions about how "true" a gift their preaching is?

At the AACS competition, parallels between today's evangelical parents with gifted children and the less faithful parents of the gifted were abundant. There were the same grand offspring ambitions. And there was the same tendency to question the ability of public schools to educate their children, though for very different reasons. Evangelical parents tend to demonize public schools nowadays, seeing them as forces of corruption and godlessness. Theirs is the sectarian version of mainstream America's privatization of talent. Visiting the preaching competition led me to wonder about the motives of the teen preachers' parents, the church organizations that sponsor the competitions, and the teens themselves. Do these competitions serve as vehicles for replenishing or building the supply of talented preachers for the churches, or simply to attract young people to religion? Like other competitions for youth, Christian competitions raise the question of how much is too much. Does constant training in scripture memorization from infancy, like the training of child painters and basketball players and Scrabble players, result in damaging early specialization?

One motive for parents training and encouraging their children to partake in Christian competitions is the sense that by doing so, they are setting their children on the path to success. It's in keeping with a shift in evangelical culture, toward affluence, education, power, and even the gifted-kid culture of their liberal opposite numbers. Although they represent an inversion of the latter's values, they paradoxically share many of their aspirations. According to a *New York Times* article about "preaching to an elite," in the spring of 2005, there were 400 evangelically affiliated students at Brown University, out of a student body of 5,700. Also according to the *Times,* in 2005 the Campus Crusade for Christ, an evangelical student group, raised more from private donors than the Public Broadcasting Service. There's even an evangelical organization, the Christian Union, whose mission is, according to its Web site, to advance "the Kingdom of Jesus Christ in the Ivy League: Brown, Columbia, Cornell, Dartmouth, Harvard, Penn, Princeton, Yale."

Like achievements in other areas, from math to football, preaching talent can be a ticket to college and a brighter future. James (Don) Sumpter II, father of teen preacher James, tells me that Pastor Sam Horn has his eye on young James. Horn is on staff at the Northland Baptist Bible College in Dunbar, Wisconsin, and spoke one night at the AACS competition. "Sam Horn knew his name–there's a certain something about James," says Sumpter. "I am getting calls. The National Evangelists [a Missouri-based evangelical organization] wanted to know how he did. Whenever we go to church, my son always wants to sit in the front, not in the back, and introduces himself to the speaker."

This was the culmination, says Sumpter, a pastor of Landmark Baptist in Richmond, Virginia, of a precocious Christian education. James's father began reading the Bible to his son the day he was brought home from hospital, and James was reciting the Bible by three. "Of course, we did Big Bird and Cookie Monster and all of that, too, and the SAT entrance tests," his father adds.

Sumpter says it was a no-brainer that he would accompany his son to the AACS competition. "If my kids go somewhere, I want to be with them," he says. "I want the competition to be something I remember. James picks up on my emotionalism. God gave us them to raise."

Just as the secular extreme parents do, this father's anxiety stems from the demands of the contemporary world. Sumpter speaks with authority about what James will need and what his colleagues now need to be pastors: a professional degree, a knowledge of math or science, and even an advanced degree of some sort, typically in pastoral studies. Sumpter's ambition for his son seemed driven by the same professional and social class anxiety that afflicts parents I have met who are secular, and who are training their kids to compete at spelling, tennis, and debate. He, too, frets about his son's career prospects in a job market teeming with knowledge workers. "Nowadays, far more is offered to make us more competent pastors," Sumpter explains. "I took a psychology class, I took two extended education counseling classes.

"I am forty-one now," Sumpter continues, "but when I was young, so many people could do religion. They would meet under a tree. If they had poor grammar, they could just start a church anyway. Now, in the church, you can't slaughter the English language anymore. Our parishioners expect more of us. You can't stay where you were thirty years ago. Bob Jones is helping to cultivate a Christian elite, and they'll grow up, and so many of them will know each other." I asked him what people wanted from their churches. He said, "Well, everyone wants a church of two thousand people nowadays."

The parents of the competitors tended to be fresh-scrubbed. They exulted in Bob Jones U., seeing it as sign of the evangelical movement's advancement into the seat of political and social power. (George W. Bush's 2000 election-year visit to BJU, an actively homophobic campus that still bans interracial dating, did not come up in our conversations.) They routinely drilled their kids in scripture memorization right after the children were born, spent hours quizzing their children on the Bible, and listened to them as they practiced their sermons.

"He practices two hours on his own, every day," says the mother of fifteen-year-old Bible Quiz champion Aaron Wells. Aaron, who lives in McQuady, Kentucky, led his team to third place in a Bible Quiz. His mother recalled teaching him First and Second Corinthians as a toddler. A round-faced girlish woman, she homeschools both her son and her daughter. "Aaron loves competing," she tells me as she sips tea out of a cup. "He practices quoting, the longest chapter first. He'll memorize fifty-eight verses, or all twenty-eight chapters of Matthew. He is up to 693 of 1006 in the Gospel of John. The Lord gave me the desire to work with them all day. Aaron is a blessing. You give him three words, and he'll finish the verse."

"One of his goals is to memorize the Constitution," says Aaron's father, a minister in a town that installed its first red light five years ago (there were five wrecks immediately thereafter). Like many parents here, Aaron's father is very straightforward about his educational ambitions for his son. "Our plans are for him to go to college in Louisville," says the father. "We've been planning for college for years."

In the course of my conversations with them, just about all of the parents of the young preachers would eventually give the credit to God–as in "God blessed me" with a child's talents. This belief provides an end run around sticky issues like biologically innate talent, or the societal unfairness that some imagine is implicit in a privileged class of gifted children. But despite these declarations of God's will, at the AACS I was struck by the similarities between the new Christian teen elite and the whiz kids I had encountered at secular venues.

Sometimes the two worlds overlap. Even at the junior Scrabble competition in 2004, there were a number of born-again Christian Scrabble teams. "We learn from the Bible to honor the Lord with strength and mind, and I see playing Scrabble as honoring the Lord with mind," said Scrabble coach Ryan Patterson, who had flown up a passel of kids from Christian schools in Tennessee to compete. Coach Patterson was cleft-chinned, tall and muscular, with a thatch of dirty blond hair; he had a buoyant and casually athletic manner. Standing amid his tall-for-their-age players at the precompetition evening, clad in beige Dockers and communicating through swaggering body language, Patterson was very clear in his reasoning. The kids needed to do well in Scrabble to prove that Baptists and other evangelicals are not dumb, but worldly-wise.

According to the AACS president Charles Walker, a sixty-something, unreconstructed fundamentalist (I overheard him complimenting me by telling some contestants' parents that I was "submissive"), there has always been a degree of political ambition behind the training and the competitions. Walker seems to hope that the AACS will function as a hothouse for the evangelical leaders of tomorrow. "Now in the last ten years, you see those kids who won the competition, who came in first, second, and third," he says. "Many have careers in business, and many are still serving the Lord."

For the adults who train students for such contests, championship kids are the evangelical community's young power elite. Many Christian schools now aspire to get their kids into the competitions. Kevin Moody, the principal of Dublin, New Hampshire's Dublin Christian Academy, defined his school as "very aggressive in our preparation of the students. When we go on a national level we usually do fairly well, for a little state. We attribute it to hard work. We are very professional." (A brief visit to Dublin made the number of yearly winners all the more surprising: the school buildings were rundown, the front office stocked with little besides prolife pamphlets for teen mothers.)

The teen preachers themselves have a clear sense of how competing may help them in their religious careers, and of how their talents in turn are thought to help the church. James Sumpter III not only competes but seeks professional guidance from Tom Farrell and Steve Petit, as well as his father. "If you are a basketball player and want to be great, you pattern yourself after Michael Jordan," he says. "Why not use their guidance?" As to why he thinks they are interested in his performance at a competition like AACS, James says, "Young guys draw more youth to a service."

For teen preacher Joshua Dean, preaching and hopefully winning the competitions is part of his larger ambition, to preach to wider audiences and to get a good pastoral job. Like secular kids who are being extreme-parented, Josh struggles with his preacher father's influence. (Along with that birthright comes the problem of how a teen or a child can be born again if they were born into their father or mother's born-again faith.) Josh was memorizing the Bible at two, he says. He learned most of the scriptures at home rather than at church.

"The people in my father's church are uneducated," says Josh, whose father ministers to trailer-park-dwelling, fishing-and-hunting types in Jacksonville, Florida. Josh fishes and hunts with the flock, too, and while pulling in a line or firing a gun, tries to impart "deeper truths" about life and God. "I adapt my testimony to my audience," he admits. "I know them."

Josh is more ambitious than his father, though. Like others in his evangelical generation, he wants to move in the broader secular society and obtain more power and influence than his father ever sought. He has chosen to attend a secular university, University of Florida, and is already planning to get a master's degree and then a doctorate.

"The people in my father's church have rough lives, and I want to relate to more people than just them," Josh tells me in his crackling, woodsy Jacksonville voice, an accent that makes a stark contrast to his gray pin-striped suit. "I've been to a college seminary with my father, and he couldn't relate to the higher educational level. He couldn't relate to how they think. He got mad at a religion professor and flew off the handle at the lady–a fireball, he is. Maybe it was God's plan for him and for me, so I could come up in a small church before I worked in a big church later on." He tells me, "I want to be salt and light in a dark environment."

. . .

The Bob Jones campus is so self-enclosed that it houses its own dry cleaners and film studio (Unusual Films Studios), even an art gallery, and famously, a "chapel" that is really a mega-church. Strolling around the campus is like walking through the town that time forgot, a G-rated *Truman Show.* A teenage barbershop quartet sings, "Christ Is All." There are giant plastic flowers in giant vases in the auditorium, and a stage full of giant black leather chairs that dwarf anyone who sits in them. Wherever you walk, you come across the sentiments people often stitch on pillows–but here they are inscribed on bridges and buildings, and over water fountains. They include Psalm 36:9: "For with thee is the fountain of life, in thy light we will see light"; Proverb 14:27: "The fear of the Lord is the fountain of life"; and the more pedestrian "Life is not divided into the secular and the sacred. For a Christian everything is sacred"; "When in doubt, play safe."

The AACS competitors gathered at the campus coffee shop, which was named, yes, Great Awakenings. The girls were modestly attired, their giggling blond highlighted heads contrasting stylistically with their modest floor-length skirts, although some passed notes of a most earthly nature, and rolled their eyes as a dorky famous pastor spoke during the twice-daily mandatory chapel. The debate events tended to have certain themes: a debate on whether the vouchers for Christian schools conflict with the separation between church and state, for instance. There were frequent exhortations to the children to excel, to do their best. And among the preachers, one felt oneself in the company of a budding religious professional class. In that sense, I saw a continuation of the giftedness complex I knew so well from New York City, Los Angeles, and Seattle, except that on a number of occasions I heard AACS administrators, parents, and teen competitors abhor the noun *tolerance*.

Of course, evangelical teen preachers are not only new symbols of a professional class in the making–they are also symbols of something that is as old as religion itself. Perhaps as long as humans have walked the Earth (a time period that these teen preachers regard as somewhat shorter than do their scientific peers), child prodigies have been viewed as conveyors of God's will. When Tiger Woods's father said that his son was going to be as important as Gandhi, he was drawing on this ingrained prodigy/religious grandee association.

The Bible is full of prodigies, as James reminds me. James particularly favors the Old Testament's David, Jacob, and Joseph. David was still a boy when he single-handedly killed the giant Goliath. Joseph, a young man of seventeen clad in a robe of many colors, was capable of predictive dreams ("prodigies" in the original sense, as in omens). James, a young person, likes biblical accounts of young people: children "who see God's face."

Another child trained to see God's face was Edmund Gosse. In the luminous 1907 memoir *Father and Son,* Gosse recounted his religious hothouse youth, as he was "dedicated" to God by his mother in his cradle and then again at his mother's deathbed. "My Father's religious teaching to me was almost exclusively doctrinal," wrote Gosse. "He was in a tremendous hurry to push on my spiritual growth, and he fed me with theological meat which it was impossible for me to digest."

The boy Edmund developed a remarkable mastery of the Bible while he was groomed to be a young pastor in Britain in the mid-nineteenth century, but he ultimately rebelled. One scene of young Edmund's resistance was remarkably powerful, transpiring in an actual hothouse with his pastor father: "Then came a moment when my self-sufficiency revolted against the police-inspection to which my 'views' were incessantly subjected. There was a morning, in the hothouse at home, among the gorgeous waxed orchids. . . . My father asked was I walking closely with God? Was my sense of the efficacy of the Atonement clear and sound? . . . My replies on this occasion were violent and hysterical."

Twentieth-century America saw the tradition of child and adolescent preachers continue, including writer James Baldwin, who preached in Harlem's storefront churches. (Baldwin wrote that those three years in the pulpit as a child had turned him into a writer–"dealing with all that anguish and that despair and that beauty.") The Reverend Martin Luther King Jr. was ordained as a Baptist minister at the age of eighteen (and enrolled in Morehouse College at fifteen.) More recently, the political field has felt the influence of another former child preacher, the Reverend Al Sharpton. Preaching has long provided a way up–as well as a focus for social activism–for African-Americans, and youth preaching has long been the beginning of that journey.

The child and youth preacher of popular culture can also be a shady figure, like the sidewalk preacher in Flannery O'Connor's novel *Wise Blood,* or Marjoe Gortner, the subject of an Oscar-winning 1972 documentary. Marjoe, whose first name was a contraction of Mary and Joseph, was a child preacher and self-professed charlatan. Marjoe and others like him make up the dark side of the teen preachers. As the film documents, Marjoe was taught to sing "Hallelujah!" in infancy. When he was a toddler, his mother taught him to shout "Glory!" into a mike. "I'm in town to give the devil two black eyes!" Marjoe squealed in a 16mm film when he was six, having preached for three years already and married couples since he was four. "The World's Youngest Ordained Minister," Marjoe first retired from the pulpit at fourteen. "I'm a hype, but I'm not a bad hype," he said at the age of twenty-eight. He goes about what he calls "Jesus business," which is writhing in order to compel an audience of the poor to put their scant dollars on the revival-tent collection plate. Thanks to the film's popularity, the young adult Marjoe, with his snake-hipped sleaze quotient, became an apostolic Mick Jagger. (He did not reply to a request for an interview, but I heard from *Marjoe*'s director, Sarah Kernochan, that he was last seen oh-so-fittingly working as a professional fund-raiser for Hollywood causes.)

As recently as twenty years ago, during the time when religious scholar Randall Balmer was researching his classic book on evangelical culture *Mine Eyes Have Seen the Glory,* parents worried that their children would leave the fold. The "great fear that haunts evangelical parents is that their children will not follow in their footsteps, that they will not sustain the same level of piety as their parents," Balmer wrote. "Will evangelism, then, inevitably suffer from a gradual enervation of religious ardor as the faith passes from one generation to the next?"

Since the mid-1980s, though, Balmer's snapshot of evangelical parental dread has changed. In short, the parents' fears have not come true: the number of freshman entering America's most selective private colleges who call themselves "born again" has doubled. This is not so surprising: a December 2005 Gallup poll had three in ten Americans defining themselves as born again or evaneglical. Perhaps the biggest question Balmer asked was how children who were born "born again" can come into faith anew. The teens I met have never known a time without faith. How strong can faith be if its holder has never experienced faithlessness?

In an interview, Balmer, a professor of American religious history at Barnard College, told me that the teen evangelists are testament to "the strength and insularity of the subculture." The expansion of Christian schools has helped evangelicalism expand, as has been true throughout American history, he notes. Evangelicals have in recent years used "theories" like intelligent design to create a beachhead for their power, just as Christians did in the 1840s, when they taught the King James version of the Bible in public school classrooms. The Roman Catholic response then was to establish a parochial school system: these were the "great school wars." Balmer says that since his book was published, evangelicals have lost their suspicion of affluence. In fact, many now see affluence as a goal. Teen preachers offer the "entertainment factor" but also serve as a vindication, says Balmer. "If they are able to transfer our knowledge to this next generation, it's a vindication." In the past such preaching was more organic, more homegrown, but the spread of Christian schooling has standardized it. "I feel sorry for the kids because it's so programmatic," says Balmer.

Balmer himself was a teen preacher, competing on a regional level in 1970, when he was sixteen. "I was aware of how performative it was at the time," he says. "I shudder to think of it. I imitated the sermons of the time. I felt like an impostor. It's embarrassing, but I also had a sense of being almost invincible, that nothing bad would happen to me because I was supposed to do good things for Jesus. I was going to be a preacher or a leader and redound to Glory of God. Maybe it will happen yet–I am still a person of faith–but looking back I was so immersed and entrenched, with no critical distance." Going off to college, he says, "provided distance and Christian college mentors who shepherded me, gently forced on me self-awareness. It was a crisis. It prompted a new identity. I feel sorry for those kids when they reconsider their faith and with it everything they hold dear. If they get distance on it, their entire value system is up for grabs. And having your entire value system challenged is a wrenching experience."

The boys I spoke to, though, seemed far from Balmer's young adult transformation, from having their sectarian aspirations altered. None of the disillusionment that Balmer expressed about how performative his own experience was seemed to hamper them.

When James Sumpter III lost AACS in previous years, he admits he was disappointed: "When you lose, you don't move on," he says. When I heard the results upon returning home, I was thus relieved that James had come in third, and Matt Rivera had come in first. I was surprised, though, that Josh Dean hadn't even placed. James's father, the pastor James Sumpter II, seemed to feel the same way. "I personally would have scored Josh higher than Ben [the second-place winner]," he wrote in an e-mail, "but again that is just my point of view. As a judge in this category I would give consideration to the 'heart' that is displayed. Preaching must come from your heart. I SAW MORE HEART IN JOSH AND JAMES personally."

Sumpter seemed less than happy with the judging in general. As he put it, one judge "scored [James's] eye contact high while one scored it lower, stating that he seemed to look over the audience. So it really has a large touch of personal appeal."

It certainly did. Matt Rivera, the winner, was the most TV-ready of the preacher boys, the only one who lacked the down-home "religion of the disinherited" quality that the others, including James, emanated. On the face of it, Matt had an air of professionalism rather than the realness that the event judge mentioned, and seemed, to my eyes, more gifted than pious.

After commenting on the competition, Sumpter's e-mail contained a question just for me.

"I wanted to ask you a question before we parted on Thursday," he wrote. "You heard a very clear presentation of the Gospel of Christ. You did not hear what the Baptist, Catholic, Mormons or any other church says–you heard what God said in the Bible. In every conclusion you were given the opportunity to personally respond to God's word. Have you ever placed your faith in Jesus Christ as Savior? Please don't take what you observed as a show of talent or some form of religious promotion. Though this was a competition the message is real and we each must choose for ourselves what we will do with Jesus!"

I didn't respond to his question. I felt irritation–why couldn't they simply stay in their frame as subjects of journalism?–and also mild bewilderment. Another's fervor often makes one wonder what one believes in its stead, and my answer–either nothing or ecumenical enlightenment–sounded like a tinny bell, just a squeak, really. Sumpter's "unseen" has a clear shape, God, and a clear word, the scripture. I realized then that what I had seen at the AACS was a whole different level of pressure than that faced by the teen preachers' secular peers. These boys believed that if they were good enough, if they were gifted enough, they could literally save the soul of a "fallen" adult–even one such as myself. If not, I supposed, then that soul might be lost to hell forever.

James's father was hoping that his son would be that good. And for these genuinely faithful young preachers, it didn't matter how deft their sermons were, or how many lines of scripture they had memorized, if in the end they failed to save souls.

In the secular world, the fall of a gifted child exists for some as a romantic metaphor: for the early bloomer who faded away, the barest hint of moral failing gives the story line extra flair. Among gifted preachers, however, lapsing in adulthood and even failing to be gifted enough to convert *is* a moral failure.

Reading that e-mail, I realized again how hard it would be to escape from entreaties like Reverend Sumpter's. In the case of religious gifted kids, differentiating from one's parents is seen as something far worse than a psychic mutiny. It's an act that might lead to damnation. I recalled the last line of Gosse's memoir, about his rejection of his father and with that the church itself, wondering if any of the teen preachers I had met would ever experience it: "The young man's conscience threw off once for all the yoke of his dedication. . . . he took a human being's privilege to fashion his inner life for himself."

TEN

The Prodigy Hunters: Math Whiz Kids Become Wall Street Recruits

For what is genius, I ask you, but the capacity to be obsessed? Every normal child has that capacity; we have all been geniuses, you and I; but sooner or later it is beaten out of us, the glory fades, and by the age of seven most of us are nothing but wretched little adults.

STEVEN MILLHAUSER, *Edwin Mullhouse: The Life and Death of an American Writer 1943–1954 by Jeffrey Cartwright*

Eric Wepsic used to be the prey. Now he's a hunter. His quarry is neither deer nor bear. Neither is Wepsic a con man or a pickup artist. Rather, he hunts prodigies. His targets, for the most part, aren't officially prodigies, who are extremely rare. Rather, Wepsic seeks the most highly gifted young mathematicians in the nation–kids who can perform feats that an ordinary MBA simply cannot. He does this for an investment firm called D. E. Shaw, where he works as a vice president. To do this work, Wepsic not only attends the American Regional Math League (ARML) each year, but has also written some of ARML's contest questions, graded finished competitions, and mentored the New York City teams. Perhaps most important, he also coordinates D. E. Shaw's sponsorship of this elite high school math competition.

Wepsic is an effective recruiter of math wunderkinder because he is, in his words, an "aging ex-prodigy," a former Math Olympian who has been multiplying and dividing since nursery school. "Their brains are stretched out," he says of the math whizzes he recruits. "They'll be good at algebraic topology, for instance." Met by an uncomprehending look, Wepsic then quickly explains topology, the study of shapes that when altered or stretched are still mathematically equivalent, by comparing a coffee cup to a doughnut–a classic example, and, given the coffee cup before him, more graspable than it might otherwise be. "Both objects have holes in them . . . ," he begins. Such concepts are the everyday thoughts–the mental coffee and doughnuts, if you will–of those high-school students who win or place high in competitions like ARML and the Math Olympiad, and in other motley math and science competitions for high schoolers.

In recent years, verbally gifted children have been the subjects of films where they spell baroque words with uncanny skill and alacrity. Gifted child performers dance in "mad hot ballroom" competitions or play piano sonatas clad in child-size suits and bow ties or sing rock ballads or attend a child's school for rock music on the television or the cinema screen. If they paint in an Art Brut style, the talk shows go for them. All this fanfare obscures the fact that the children most highly prized by adult society–and most regularly rewarded with great jobs and salaries in adulthood–are math and science whizzes. After all, few savants of the child salsa circuit are avidly "trolled" by colleges and companies looking to give them scholarships and employment. The math-and-science-gifted kids are closer to the fairy-tale version of the gifted master narrative, where "natural" gifts and hard work lead a child directly to collect her prize. These kids are metaphors of our contemporary jackpot gestalt: everyone wants, and believes they deserve, precocious talents and a lucrative job. The math and science whizzes who get jobs in finance right out of college exemplify the unblemished dream of precocity–all of the possibility without the fall from grace. Of all of the hothouse kids, they are the ones most likely to make good on their talents, to rise above the fray and escape the employment insecurities many of us face.

This is not to say the competitions in math and science don't have their performative side. One former Westinghouse winner and Math Olympian, Jordan Ellenberg, now a professor of math at the University of Wisconsin–

Madison, says that what he learned from the math competitions was equivalent "to learning to throw a football in a spiral," and that there is a profound difference between the timed tests one tends to get at math competitions and, say, the Riemann hypothesis. But by the same token, those timed tests are akin to some of the time-based corporate work that makes the ex-math-and-science-gifted kids such good hires.

Both colleges and companies, especially investment and finance companies, are now searching for these kids, offering them scholarships, internships, and jobs. The Intel International Science and Engineering Fair serves as a filter for the potential recipients of $100,000 in yearly Department of Homeland Security scholarships and fellowships for Intel winners. The department gave $10 million in 2003 to young math and science whizzes more generally. These students might also attend the gifted math and science high school program in Virginia run by the National Security Agency, America's shadowy electronic surveillance agency. After high school, a former science prodigy or demi-prodigy might be offered a fellowship by Israel's Weitzman Institute, or by the Taiwanese government, as one I know of was. That particular former science wunderkind ultimately received a summer job from the pharmaceutical company Merck. As part of its seduction, the company sent out a black Town Car to pick up the teenager. (He had never been in a company car before, and thought he had to pay someone.) At the time, he was thrilled to be put up in a hotel and be given a sushi dinner, in a bid for his talents that he now describes as simultaneously "clumsy" and "MTV."

Precocious skills at math and science can also win teenagers admission to elite colleges, and huge research scholarship money. After or during college, they may be recruited to work as engineers or as computer analysts, at pharmaceutical companies or in the defense industry. Their early competition wins also can help if the math or science whiz wants to start a company while still in college. One winner of the Westinghouse, the science prize now called Intel, began a health-care start-up business while still in college, a company that created electronic medical records. The backing for his company came together because investors were impressed with his "track record" as a high school competition winner.

Ultimately, the former whizzes may go to work for Amazon, Barra, or D. E. Shaw. The headhunting firm IQ Search Group is one of the institutions that locates them for prospective employers. As IQ Search CEO Paul McCaffrey explains it, former math wunderkinder are 10 to 15 percent of his talent because academic mathematics people "became sexy in the 1990s." Math whizzes are especially desirable on Wall Street, where they are sometimes able to use different models to create a more sophisticated trade: they tend to spot patterns, quickly assimilate them, and apply abstract concepts like cointegration (the statistical term that refers to two processes tending to move together and reverting to the mean). The name for them is quantitative analysts, or quants. Former child math whizzes tend to be faster at pairs trading, making use of the realization that if one stock goes up and a similar stock goes down, then the two are likely to converge in a profitable way. They can create a computational model that can describe large interacting bodies and write computer software that models financial trades to predict effects. They can figure out a standard deviation instantaneously and communicate it. (The latter ability alone makes them golden.) And their very presence can put a halo around a company.

The search for young science and math talent isn't new. After the Soviet Union launched *Sputnik I* in 1957, the winners of the Westinghouse Science Competition were displayed as symbols of American strength. As previously noted, such competitions were part of "the Great Talent Hunt," a response to a fear of Communist excellence that led to a frenzied xenophobic search for "our" gifted children. The American Mathematics Contest 12 (AMC 12), formerly the American High School Mathematics Examination, for high school seniors and below, began in 1950. The more stellar USA Mathematical Olympiad (USAMO) started in 1972, an import of the International Mathematical Olympiad for high school students, first held in 1959 in Romania (American teenagers began participating in 1974). Today, the road to reaching the team of six students who compete in the International Mathematical Olympiad starts with the AMC. The 250 top-scoring students of the AMC get to compete in the USA Mathematical Olympiad, a six-question essay-and-proof examination where the problems can be solved with precalculus methods.

The Westinghouse Science Talent Search had been started before the Cold War, at the dawn of World War II in 1942. It was renamed for its new backer, the Intel Science Talent Search, in 1998. Each year, Intel rewards three hundred entrants with the semifinalist title. That number is then whittled down to forty finalists who attend the Science Talent Institute, and finally ten who win top scholarships, with one winning a scholarship worth $100,000. Its winners may have invented electronic gloves and drugs for cancer and a model for understanding dance.

When I attended the 2004 Intel competition, the forty finalists stood in the National Academy of Sciences Hall in Washington, D.C., beside their highly polished presentations. Amid laminated patterns of El Niño and a study of the cancer drug Tamoxifen, dozens of adult visitors, and nearly as many news cameras and photographers stood Gaurav Subhash Thakur, seventeen, perhaps the least talkative finalist. His brilliant paper on generalized factorial function, in particular the power factorial function, had triumphed, but he barely spoke to curious onlookers. In a brief conversation, Gaurav's father, an urbane International Monetary Fund economist, attempted to translate the remarks of his impassive son, like a diplomat trying to cover for an unruly prince.

"You learned multiplications when you were five, didn't you?" said Gaurav's father. "And you went to Johns Hopkins CTY [the specialized math program for intellectually gifted children] in second grade." Gaurav stared at the floor. The family lives in Rockville, Maryland, and Gaurav didn't like school: he wanted to study advanced math, so he enrolled in a distance-learning program, the Learning Community International.

"Public school was pointless," Gaurav muttered in an uninflected baritone. Clad in a stiff suit and sporting a fine mustache, he shifted from foot to foot. He brightened up for the first time when displaying a thousand-page tome on factorials he was reading for fun. In fact, Gaurav and his father both say Gaurav spends much of his day in his room, reconciling the Riemann hypothesis and string theory and, on the lighter side, designing and constructing Lego models.

Across the hall was Gaurav's opposite, the soon-to-be 2004 Intel first prize winner, a handsome blond boy named Mason Hedberg. Hedberg has a thatch of hair the color of vanilla cake and a smile and build bespeaking Matt Damon on a stretching rack. (Especially Matt Damon as a math prodigy recruited by the defense industry in the film *Good Will Hunting.*)

This super-hothouse kid handed me a business card that read "Brown

University PLME, Class of 2012," referring to a double-degree medical program at the Ivy League university that he would be completing eight years in the future–he had been accepted, but would not even be starting for nearly half a year. Mason had a gift for spinning his own achievements. These achievements were nonetheless genuine–he had isolated the telomerase enzyme found in cancer cells. It may have helped his explorations that his father was the director of a drug-discovery company.

Both these two boys and a number of the other Intel finalists I met had been preparing for the contest and for their adult professional lives for years–almost, it seems, from the time their talent was first recognized. Soon after the competition, they were contacted by Vezen Wu, the former carnivorous-plant prodigy who won the Westinghouse in 1996, and was now hunting prodigies himself, having started the Intel Science Talent Search internship program at Morgan Stanley, where he works as a VP. Wu searches out the three hundred semifinalists identified by the ISTS each year, talks to them, and sometimes interviews them, in the hopes that they will want to work at his firm as interns.

Eric Wepsic may speak to the Intel kids as well, but he is even more interested in the former math champions. "I tell them if they can contribute more to the company, they will get paid more, and that possibly our company is the land of milk and honey," Wepsic says, half jokingly. He looks and acts half young and half old–prematurely receding hairline with boyish face, an incessant amiability with something slightly more jaded. After all, he is merely thirty-four, and has been a very wealthy man since his twenties.

Wepsic describes the work atmosphere as "half cloistered academic," half Wall Street. "You can do a problem involving ten to the negative twelve, and then, somewhat weirdly, a broker comes in yelling at you and it's pure Wall Street again!" he says. And then he adds what must be welcome words to the rough-around-the-edge math teen: "We are interested in talent rather than experience."

Wepsic's pitches get a good reception, and not only due to his personal charm, the example of his own lucrative career, or the very real salaries he promises his gifted candidates. He also benefits from the fact that the math and science whizzes have become accustomed to the blending of "pure" research and commercial interests on a larger scale. This intermingling of the pure and the commercial, a feature of scientific research for at least half a century, has increased over the past couple of decades, as universities form closer and closer partnerships with private companies, and more and more of the money funding research derives from private firms.

Often the math whizzes were not priveleged from birth. Vezen Wu, for instance, was raised by Taiwanese immigrants and grew up in Jacksonville, Florida. Indeed, culling job applicants from the winners of major youth competitions means, more often than not, recruiting the child of an immigrant. Children of immigrants comprised 65 percent of the 2004 U.S. Math Olympiad's top scorers. At the 2004 Intel Science Test Search, 60 percent of the teenage finalists were children of immigrants, and 46 percent of U.S. Physics Team members are the children of immigrants. The 1996 Westinghouse High School Science Prize winner and National Math Olympian Gregory Budunov, whose family emigrated from Moscow to Smithville, Texas, four year before he won these competitions, offers one angle on this phenomenon: "I am talented but not gifted by Russian standards. In Moscow, I was a top student, and I was good in mathematics, but I was not the best."

Budunov's statement echoes the claims of pundits: America has fallen behind other countries, and needs to do a better job of cultivating math and science abilities. Spurring children's interest in careers in these areas is crucial if we are to remain competitive in the global economy. Singaporean eighth-grade students score first in the world in math, according to the Trends in International Mathematics and Science Study, or TIMSS; South Korea placed second, and eighth graders from Hong Kong ranked third in math. It's hard not to notice that three of these four countries are places where jobs that might have once gone to Americans are now alighting. In 2003, the United States ranked twelfth on the TIMSS scale, two countries behind Latvia. In addition, it can seem that American students delude themselves into a cocksure casualness. According to a 2002 study conducted by University of Pennsylvania professor of education Erling Boe and colleagues, students in other countries tend to perform better on their math and science exams, but believe that they have done worse until they actually see their test results;

American students, in contrast, tend to have weaker math and science test performance but think that they're doing just great. (Students from Germany and Switzerland also tend to think they are doing well while students in Singapore and Japan tend to not.) In a 2003 article called "The Democratization of Mathematics," Anthony P. Carnevale and Donna M. Desrochers of the Educational Testing Service wrote that a math achievement gap not only undermines America's high-tech global success but also shows the inequity endemic to our math education. The authors noted that almost 40 percent of the workforce "does not have sufficient quantitative literacy for jobs that pay more than $26,900, on average." The answer to this problem, they say, lies in "making mathematics more accessible and responsive to the needs of all students, citizens, and workers," and not necessarily in rewarding or honing the best and the brightest.

Carnevale and Derochers's arguments for "democratization" of math and science training–the idea that future success depends upon adequately educating millions of average kids, rather than a handful of geniuses–seem eminently sound. But they don't appeal to the popular imagination the way prodigies and gifted math kids do. Concerns about U.S. schoolkids' innumeracy play out against a broader background of insecurity in the American economy and the American mind. We have come to fear the growing economic power of China and, to a lesser degree, India–and not without good reason. In this context, it's easy to see why top-of-the-line math and science whizzes are a sign of hope. Indeed, 2004 Intel Awards emphasized the economic value of science and math prodigies. In an elaborate ceremony in a neon-bedecked room at Portland's Ronald Reagan Building and International Trade Center, Intel's CEO Craig Barrett described the young winners as symbols of America's commitment to staunching overseas job loss. They were, Barrett said, a "weapon" in the war for American economic dominion. This is all part of why high performers in math and science have such perceived value to colleges and companies–they are seen as a needed form of intellectual artillery. On that day, Barrett was indulging in ceremonial cant but was also pointing to a guiding truth of those companies who seek to employ math and science whizzes–that they are objectively useful.

After listening to Barrett's speech, I couldn't help but wonder if the math-and-science-gifted kids might be somehow more absolutely "gifted" (in the sense that they are born, not made) than, say, child artists or ice skaters. But are they? According to Brian Butterworth, professor of cognitive neuropsychology at University College London and author of *What Counts: Why Every Brain is Hardwired for Math,* when it comes to special math intelligence, nature and nurture cooperate. Butterworth terms this "a brain category for numbers." The left parietal lobe processes number information independently from other information, and that specialized circuit, called the number module, enables aptitude. The module allows a very young child to quickly understand small numbers and match or compare groups of numbers. Apart from 5 or 6 percent that are "discalculic" and thus do not possess a number module, all children have the potential to become gifted at math. "Some people who are not good with language are very good with maths and vice versa. Then again, there's no evidence Shakespeare was a great mathematician," he jokes, then mutters that he should check that.

That some children become gifted at math while others do not has something to do with nonmathematical skills, says Butterworth, like an ability to understand the conventions of math problems. But it also has a lot to do with practice. In a forthcoming review of mathematical expertise, Butterworth has concluded that the only common factor among those gifted at math is that they have all spent a lot of time doing math. He cites Florida State University professor of psychology Anders Ericsson's theory that for a child to be highly skilled in any domain, she generally needs to have practiced for 10,000 hours, and Butterworth applies this to math kids.

"The real question is: Why are some kids willing to spend that amount of time doing maths? Do they get intrinsic rewards from churning through it?" says Butterworth. "What some people get from maths is the orderliness of mathematical domain–they get to see that they are doing it right. For some people that is extremely rewarding, as we know getting it right in other areas of life and learning can be a nebulous thing."

I ask Butterworth if early math skills and precocious learning are necessary for children to achieve in this domain. Not really, he says, although such achievement "wires up the brain in the same way that getting a child to be good at anything does. It raises that child's profile. It improves their self-esteem. It doesn't matter what it is."

Ericsson, who has studied "mental calculators"–individuals with a gift for memorizing numbers–says these kids may well conform to the solitary mathlete stereotype, their incessant calculations a form of social and intellectual protection in lonely childhoods. And in this sense, mathematics can be kinder to its experts than other disciplines: child painters with the same singularity of focus that the math and science whizzes display may well founder in later life, says Ericsson, although this has not been scientifically proven. After all, the recognition conferred upon artists is often dependent on their ability to "sell" their work and themselves. Former math and science child stars can, in some contexts, succeed on the basis of their ability alone.

"If you are the top of the maths, you can walk into any job anywhere" in certain countries, says Butterworth. In fact, traits that would be a barrier to employment in other fields–shyness, geekiness, even paltry social skills–are accepted or even expected among math and science whizzes, the cockeyed quirks that come with the territory. For Eric Wepsic and his colleagues, early success at math and science competitions is a great indicator of how well young recruits will do at Shaw. The Shaw folks comb through the records of those who won the Math Olympiad in high school. They look at the winners of other national math championships and contact Ivy League colleges. They sift through the names of national chess champions; chess success is sometimes an indication of mathematical ability. Shaw even ran a recruitment ad in the alumni magazine of New York City's prestigious Hunter College High School. And the company spreads the word that its own staff is thick with prodigies. Its employment ads let you know that Shaw already contains "a considerable number" of employees who have "competed successfully in the United States and International Math Olympiads as well as the Putnam Competition." D. E. Shaw execs brag that one of their own published a book at twenty-three. Another is a national chess champion. A third attended the University of California, Berkeley at age thirteen–UC's youngest student ever. Another won a national classics prize. (The company considered, but decided not to hire, the former horseshoe-throwing champion of the world.)

Charles Ardai, Shaw's managing director, a lightning-fast kid first paid for his writing (a trade magazine review of the old video-arcade game Kangaroo) when he was just thirteen, describes his company as vigilant in its search for exceptional test records–although he is secretive about Shaw's search techniques for attaining "brilliant" workers.

"Our specific methods for talent identification are not widely known," he says coyly. In his mid-thirties, he is skinny and lantern-jawed. Displaying the full-on nervous energy he must also have had as a teenager, he sits in a coolly *moderne* D. E. Shaw conference room. The room is a Manhattan realtor's dreamscape, replete with expansive views of garishly gentrified Times Square. The physical space of the Shaw offices, where even the receptionists, according to Ardai, are likely to have wunderkind pedigrees, recalls high-flying Web industry days. There's the vigilantly minimalist decor–glass everywhere, white-lit hallways that resemble giant iMacs–and, walking through it all, hordes of informally dressed young people earning huge salaries. The company was cofounded in 1988 by David Shaw, a former professor of computer science at Columbia University, and John Overdeck, who came in with an educational background in statistics. Overdeck has since left the company in order to create Two Sigma. (Like Shaw, Overdeck's new company advises job applicants to include their SAT scores, promising them coworkers who are "high achievers" with "Ph.D.s from top universities" as well as the Japanese national backgammon champion, an MIT-trained artificial intelligence expert, and a concert-level pianist.)

As Ardai hinted, D. E. Shaw & Co. has long been famous for its secretiveness, which some critics find gratuitous. Ardai is careful to deemphasize the mystery, so that Shaw sounds less like a Michael Crichtonesque corporation than a capitalist Brook Farm or Blithedale, a high-minded intellectual hive. Ardai says that his dream of Shaw was that it would resemble an adult version of his alma mater, New York's premiere public academy for the gifted, Hunter College High School–with any employee able to discuss calculus or philosophy in the halls. Shaw indeed seems a nest of superperforming workers. "If you wonder whether these top-end quants are worth the investment," says Ardai, "the answer is yes. The normal applicant will be no smarter in six months. I don't think people enhance their intelligence."

Ardai holds an unfashionable belief in fixed abilities–an opinion that stands in stark contrast to the claims of the enrichment zones we visited earlier, where everything is held to be teachable, if only a parent or coach starts early enough. Ardai forwards his own theory of how nurture can complement nature: he believes that it is best to recruit these natural talents young, when it will be easier to cultivate them in the firm's image. "We need to catch these people and get them to work here before they have decided what they *are,*" says Ardai. "We have to find people who weren't considering finance, and convert some resources." In order to do so, he says, they "go through the Mensa mailing list. We collect SATs. Someone we would hire could well have gotten 1600. These are useful data points."

And indeed, after meeting the former math and science whizzes, I came to see that for many of them, early training, talents, and competition wins paved the way for later upward-bound career trajectories. The experience seemed enviable: their minds' excellence made their careers smoother. They didn't have to rely on facile charm or luck.

But I was left wondering about the shadowlands of the science-and-math-gifted kid. Was it ever too competitive? Were those who succeeded as math and science teen whizzes not just "gifted," but also in possession of personality types better suited to competition?

And I did discover darker facets of the math and science wonder kids. Some were ultimately stymied not by a lack of talent but by a temperament or psychology that made the competitive aspect of the field a hardship. As professors Mihaly Csikszentmihalyi, Kevin Rathunde, and Samuel Whalen write in *Talented Teenagers: The Roots of Success and Failure,* the sadness and anxiety of working alone for great stretches of time, as math-and-science-gifted kids tend to do in adolescence, can dissuade gifted young people from continuing their study. These kids drop out, the authors write, not because they lack the cognitive capacity but because it quite simply makes them too lonesome. And while competitive math tournaments mitigate the loneliness, "the cut-throat pressure of math teams tends to alienate those young men and women who prefer a more supportive environment, unable to bear the supercharged atmosphere of math clubs." For those children who were early experts in math and science, choosing not to compete can be the end of not only their youthful but ultimately their adult careers: "Unfortunately, when a student drops out of *the field* of mathematics in high school, he or she is also likely to drop out of the *domain* altogether."

So it was with Eric Minton. Minton, now thirty-three, learned to read at age one, before he could talk. His childhood memories are lustrous and tortured. At five he drew complex maps of invented places. In first grade he corrected the teacher, explaining that what she had written as *Artic* should be spelled A-r-c-t-i-c. The teacher blushed in irritation and hated him for the rest of the year, he says, but that didn't slow his passion for correcting adults. Hostility from teachers didn't affect his progress, either: Minton didn't count on adults to teach him. He taught himself physics from a textbook he discovered at home. Because his mother taught school, his home held many such books.

Minton describes his childhood as a repository for factoids about math and science. Minton was celebrated for his gifts, yet he knew even then that he was being celebrated because he was a child with gifts, and as such had a limited shelf life: he was the escape valve in a family fraught with fighting, the parent-pleasing antidote for his angry mom and the dad he calls "Teflon." He felt he knew a lot of facts, and was thus considered a prodigy, but he could not put them in context. He knew the right answers but "didn't understand them, as I have an easily distractible mind." (He also says that he suffered then from undiagnosed attention deficit disorder and depression; he has since treated both with therapy.) He felt he did well enough on tests to fool those around him into believing that he was actually learning. "I could do the bite-size problem, and then I zoned out," he says. At fourteen, his then-curly red hair stuck up from his head, forming a halo. He idolized kids who were socially adept, and tried to escape into fantasy games like Dungeons and Dragons, as prevalent in high schools in the 1980s as drugs.

Eighteen years later, Minton has the look of a character actor. He has pale skin, a thin sprinkling of red hair, and a taste for the color closest to caramel–one day when we meet, he is clad in a plaid caramel shirt, a wool caramel sweater, and caramel-colored pants. He uses piquant images to describe his childhood unhappiness: the jam jar his father threw at the wall that wound up marking it, the "toxic dump" that was half a mile from his family's house. In fact, he uses the phrase "toxic dump" as a life metaphor, returning to it again and again.

Ultimately, Minton's knack for standardized tests failed him, he thinks, because they only meant he performed well on tests, indicating "only a veneer of education." He ended up relinquishing math and science, and did not compete in these areas in either high school or college. Unlike the Olympians and the Intel kids, Minton thus did not have a ready-made shiny future at Goldman Sachs, a defense firm, or even a university: he worked in various jobs that have little to do with math or science. He eventually found his place playing games set in alternative worlds–worlds peopled with characters named Oberon, inhabiting countries named Amber. Minton and his boyfriend, who has silky flowing hair and an adopted Norse Reconstructionist faith (imagine Norse Orthodox!), travel hundreds of miles to attend role-playing conventions. Minton is in the thrall of this unpaid hobby. He plays every role but the hero: wizards, clerics, the weather, the sheriff, the sun, and the princess. Minton is happy, he says and amazed that he has now stuck with a job for four years.

In short, it takes more than simply early talent and training in math and science to become a "prodigy" job recruit. Minton and others like him, math and science whizzes who grew up with disorientating home lives, attention deficit disorders, or even simply a lack of the required competitive attitude, tend not to feel comfortable joining math teams or entering competitions, let alone becoming the sort of kid who wins them. They may never transform their childhood giftedness into adult capital.

Even for the math and science whizzes who do manage to become and remain fierce competitors, there can be other stumbling blocks. For instance, some scholars have detected gender inequality in this prodigy daydream. Rena Subotnik, coeditor of *Beyond Terman* and a specialist at the American Psychological Association's Center for Gifted Education Policy Center, working at the APA's Pinnacle Model, which sponsors extraordinarily talented high school students, discovered that many female winners dropped out of the sciences soon after they won. Some students of both sexes ended up leaving the sciences during the first two years of college, but women do so in larger numbers. By the end of their second year in university, in fact, two-thirds of female Westinghouse winners had ditched their mathematics or science majors. Subotnik followed a hundred winners of the Westinghouse Science Talent Search (STS) for thirteen years. During that time, twice as many female as male students dropped out of science programs. The women told Subotnik one of the prime reasons for this falloff: they received little support or mentoring from their professors. In other words, among math and science whizzes, the complicating factor of gender inequity can still hinder the career of former kid competitors.

In addition to personality and gender biases, other ethical issues may be involved in turning gifted math and science students into quants. Could siphoning math whizzes off into business be considered a "brain drain"? I thought about those kids and young adults, who might instead have chosen to work on more imaginative and more socially valuable research. Might that work, in fact, be even more vital to keeping the country competitive in the longer term?

Van Molino, now twenty-two, is a math whiz struggling with this particular adult dilemma. In high school, he competed in the U.S. Math, Chemistry, and Physics Olympiads and took college courses. When I spoke with him, he was on the cusp of starting a Ph.D. program at New York University. He has also already been recruited by the defense industry, and was working a summer job at the Center for Computating Sciences, a nonprofit government subcontractor. The office where he works contains between ten and fifteen similarly employed young math whizzes, who are either nearly finished with college or just beginning graduate school. He was contacted for the job via e-mail as a result of a personal recommendation: the note simply told Molino that the Center for Computating Sciences would like him to come in. (Molino also got letters from prodigy hunters for financial companies, including one from D. E. Shaw.) He tells me proudly of his secret clearances and how his girlfriend thinks he's James Bond. He has obtained a fellowship from the Department of Homeland Security that covers his first three years of graduate study at $35,000 a year, with an additional $2,300-a-month stipend. In return, Molino has agreed to complete an internship with a related agency.

But ultimately, Molino faces the same career dilemmas that confront most of today's former child math whizzes. While he is proud to be working for national defense, he also knows the research he does right now belongs to the government. (As Molino puts it, "You have to be careful that your Ph.D. doesn't become classified.") He is considering a career in finance, where the rewards in terms of salary and other perks are clear, but he sees the limits of original thinking when most of what you are doing is applied math. Of course, Molino and whizzes like him use applied math to serve the public interests–although revelations of NSA's domestic spying cast a more doubtful light on this truism. But there is a third way–a pursuit of pure science and math, such as employment in the professoriate. Jordan Ellenberg took this route. This former Math Olympian and teen contestant on a trivia bowl television show, now a professor of math at the University of Wisconsin, has been a professor since he was twenty-six, with a specialty in arithmetic algebraic geometry. He has also published a novel called *The Grasshopper King.* Now thirty-three, he could pass for twenty-three. He wears the sneakerish Camper shoes, big jeans, and goatee of a college student. Speech bursts from his mouth like air from a balloon when he explains what he does: research and teach the concepts of enumeration of number fields and other arithmetic objects, non-abelian Iwasawa theory, curves of low genus, and more.

But whatever choices the math and science whizzes make–whether they answer the siren song of one of the prodigy hunters, hew to the typically more obscure and less remunerative academic line, or drop out of math altogether–somehow they have to negotiate viable lives for themselves, and accept certain trade-offs. Even Eric Wepsic, the former math prodigy, D. E. Shaw VP, and erstwhile prodigy recruiter, expresses some of these conflicts. He runs through the pros and cons of his current line of work out loud–breaking them down, like the ex-Math Olympian he is, into percentages of positive and negative. He compares his job at Shaw to running a restaurant, and extends the metaphor: in his line of work, he says, he may be feeding people to the point of happy satiety–not a profound enterprise, but one that gives pleasure–at least, to his affluent clients. As he puts it, he knows he is good at finding profit opportunities, making the market more efficient, helping to value assets appropriately.

Math whiz dropout Minton was the most ruminative about his life choice. This makes sense, as he stopped studying math long before his talents could be converted into professional value. He now believes he is better off having "gotten knocked down and drifted." If he had wound up a high-paid professional, he thinks, he "would have been a lopsided human being if things fell apart. Now that's not a risk."

While you can see Minton as a squanderer of great talents, he seems to have shrugged off the cloak of precocious failure. Doing so may have enabled him to claim his true gift: the knowledge that he is more than his accomplishments, more even than his failures. When he no longer needed to be gifted, he could simply be.

• • •

Of all of the former math and science competitors I spoke with, prodigy recruiter and ex-prodigy Vezen Wu best exemplified the peculiar dilemma of the gifted math and science child: his abilities earned him a top-flight career in finance, where he then had to put his "pure" research interests aside. At first Wu seemed destined to be a biologist or medical researcher; ultimately, he left his medical research behind for a career in finance. In his years at Morgan Stanley, Wu has had to negotiate a few hurdles. The first were some of his personal eccentricities. He has put a lot of energy into gaining the social polish he knew he needed to work with clients in finance. This meant he did not spend his hours pursuing knowledge for its own sake, as he did as a child and an adolescent. The voyage toward conventional social acceptability took a few years: at eighteen, Wu says, he did not know how to comb his hair, how to dress, or how to conduct himself at a meeting. "From backwoods Florida," as he puts it, he had not attended the proverbial charm schools of the overclass.

Now, Wu's black hair is slick with expensive hair pomade. He is clad in a designer suit ("Hugo Boss!" he says triumphantly), one of many *au courant* costumes that he has learned to don in the last few years. And behaviorally, Wu also tries hard to "pass" in the postprodigy world he now lives in, where social norms often trump talent, even astounding math and science abilities like his own. The second element that he has had to negotiate is his race. His coworkers call him Dr. Wu, an allusion to the Steely Dan song of the same name and a nickname given him by white kids in Florida when he was growing up, which he has always loathed. Wu told me this anecdote lightly, but it reminded me that for whizzes like Wu, entry into the arenas of conventional power can also bring them face-to-face with certain racialized expectations. Asian-Americans are smart, the common wisdom holds, but they will need to remake themselves to conform and succeed in the still white-dominated seats of power and wealth.

All of these acts of self-recreation sprang, says Wu, from his success in the Westinghouse competition. The award, the platform for his later success, also taught him that America is driven by money: through the competition he met moneyed and preeminent people, and he saw what really mattered in his family's adopted culture. "This is why I am not with the plants anymore," he says, half joking. "I was corrupted."

Might Wu not have discovered important cures, a new vaccine, or perhaps a nonaddicting pain reliever had he not been "corrupted"? The Wall Street occupation of quant, the ne plus ultra happy ending for former gifted children, provokes big questions. What is value? What is productivity? Are math-and-science-gifted kids more important or useful to the world than their Scrabble-playing peers? And are they ending up where they have the potential to be the *most* useful?

For math-and-science-gifted kids, competitions may well put them on a career track at a young age and give them a platform for the future. But that career track is increasingly in the private sector.

It makes sense that the explicit success of work in the financial sector would be especially appealing to today's math and science whizzes: they, like so many Americans, avoid the whiff of failure at all cost. After all, failure attaches not to a single event in a person's life but to his or her very essence: failure as something that you *are*, a character trait that will taint every new step you take. If one is not careful, one can overstate one's failures, using the harsh halogen light of quantified achievement to compare oneself to those who are better known. As historian Scott A. Sandage writes in his history of American failure, *Born Losers*, "Today we speak an adolescent language of exclusion: contemporary synonyms for failure include nerd, dork, dweeeb, geek, wimp, freak, jerk, slacker, weirdo. . . . Loser, however, remains the epithet of choice." Sandage notes that "failure" once meant simply "business failure," and carried no moral weight. Today, one can do reasonably well and still see oneself as a failure, simply because one is not rich and famous.

Are these lucrative and powerful jobs, in fact, paving the way to long-term happiness? After all, as the cliché goes, high salaries do not necessarily imply "meaningful" productivity, much less personal and professional satisfaction. Giving children the tools to become self-actualized later in life is not necessarily a matter of training them to be professionals from their earliest days. According to some studies of subjective well-being, income is important but only up to a point. The massive increase in wealth in the United States since World War II has not led to an increase in subjective well-being–

in fact, Americans show a higher rate of serious depression than many industrialized countries. Sure, the math wunderkind's numerical skills tend to have more practical payoffs than the talents of a child tap dancer or poet. But using high-level math skills at competitions and in the workplace are not necessarily related to the sort of self-directed pursuit of knowledge so often aligned with happiness.

What if Wu had become a medical researcher, a botanist, or the scientific equivalent of an outsider artist–an Audubon of the swamps, given to spindly, loving drawings of his beloved carnivorous plants? What if he eschewed elite specialization and professionalization for a pure mathematician's life of the mind, laboring on number theory or the study of symmetry? And what if Wu did what he says he *really* wants to do–study the positive effects of surfing on depression, which he ascribes to ions? Would that not count as success, too?

Perhaps. But prodigy hunters aren't paid to answer such questions.

CONCLUSION

Rethinking Giftedness: Against Perfection

Peter Bogdanovich: I read . . . that you never wanted to be a child, that you wanted to escape childhood.
Orson Welles: That's true.
PB: Have you ever wanted to return?
OW: To childhood? I've been back there ever since I left.

INTERVIEW, *This Is Orson Welles*

Teaching kids to read in infancy, to kick a soccer ball when they're two, or to compete fiercely in spelling bees doesn't, it turns out, mean that children's "gifts" will ultimately be enhanced. I found this out in my encounters with adults who as children were trained as musicians or learned math early or competed in chess and were ultimately disappointed in adulthood and resentful of their early training. A former child Broadway actor who has grown up to teach her craft to the newest generation of child actors told me she did not want her own children to act; similarly, a prodigy musician whom I interviewed wound up suffering nervous breakdowns. They were among the many who convinced me that we should tone down our demand for exceptional childhood performance. We should stop wanting children to have IQs over 150 and testing them at such young ages, and, most important, resist the desire for children to demonstrate abilities ahead of their age group. Learning to read faster, to memorize words earlier, or to play the piano with facility at an early age are not Rosetta stones for accomplished adult life.

One of the things that my research clarified for me was that there are actually very few deeply "gifted" kids with transcendent cognitive or artistic abilities; therefore kids are being incorrectly labeled as exceptionally gifted. The peril is that some children who have been led to believe they are highly gifted will suffer, like Icarus, in their later lives. In my numerous conversations with "formerly gifted" kids, the emotional debits of the Icarus effect were widespread. Their reports of feeling that they were forced to contort themselves to fit the shape of adult life, and their regrets about how intensively they were made to devote themselves to their training, and even about being labeled with the identity at all, should be loud cautionary tales regarding how the pressure that is applied to kids so early these days may be affecting them. Conveying to children that they are so "special" and putting them on public display can lead them to feel that any talent they have is bigger than they are and that, in a sense, they are a mere employee of their talent, that they work for the gift and must manage their endowment. It's as if they were employees of Prodigy Inc. If they can't maintain exceptional performance into adulthood, they may well end up feeling that they have little direction and perhaps their lives have little meaning.

The excesses of "programming" children with too many classes and demanding their precocity should not, however, taint the value of the legitimate style of gifted education to be found in some of our public and private schools. Indeed, there are children who are especially strong learners and who benefit substantially from–and may even need–accelerated schoolwork. Kids who don't have access to the specialized learning they need may tune out and ultimately drop out of school. Access to enriched classes in our schools should be expanded, and funding should be increased. The kind of enriched education that has been shown to have real value for these learners should first be classes where children are permitted to work at different paces. In addition, the children's schoolwork should be different in quality rather than simply higher in quantity: problems and readings can be more abstract, more sophisticated, and less teacher-defined. Another hallmark of high-utility enrichment classes is that teachers insist that the failure-averse yet scholastically able child not just strive for A's but also take greater academic chances, albeit with adequate emotional support for such risks. Finally, good enrichment programs and classes should understand that strong learners may be intellectually uneven–exceptional in one area and weak in another.

Rather than focusing so much attention on rote performance, whether in the arts, sports, or academic competitions, we should be increasing the resources we allocate to school programs for students with good learning skills, and training more teachers in how to teach students with a range of special learning capabilities. At the time of this writing, there is only limited training for teachers in gifted-education techniques and assessment, if teachers receive such training at all. We should also allocate more funding for the hiring of school psychologists who are trained in a wide range of diagnostic techniques, so we are better able to spot children who might otherwise fall through the cracks. Yet, rather than increasing the availability of these enriched classes and resources for our strongest learners, under the No Child Left Behind Act we have actually been gutting these programs.

In particular, it is vital that we make sure enriched classes are available to kids in all income ranges. More and more, enrichment education is available only to the economically privileged, and that is a great injustice. Gifted children come from all social strata and all of them should have access to an enriched education in their neighborhood schools.

As for the experts who argue against the whole notion of giftedness, they have a good point. However, I think the biggest problem in this discussion is not the practice of offering special classes to strong learners, but rather is in the way we reflexively define giftedness in limited terms, and the unpleasant associations of snobbery or elitism that can come with that label. I would argue that we need a more holistic definition of giftedness, one that appreciates the fuller range of abilities that support success in life. We are currently defining giftedness much too narrowly. By emphasizing the electric wow of children's precocious abilities, and by placing so much stress on their being "special" and expert in certain domains early, we have overlooked a set of additional abilities that are highly valuable in leading complete lives. When we use the "gifted" appellation we tend to mean skills in math, reading comprehension, and music, in particular, but these are only some of the skills that can lead to success in adulthood. Paradoxically, by obliging children to be talented in a certain fashion, we fail to appreciate how talented they may be in other ways.

This is, in fact, not a new notion: a broader definition of giftedness has had currency for several decades. In 1971, a federal study, the Marland Report, recommended that "gifted and talented children" be defined by our schools as those with "outstanding abilities," who are "capable of high performance," ranging from kids with "general intellectual ability" to those with leadership and psychomotor abilities–physical endurance, flexibility, balance, and coordination–and gifts in visual arts.

In the late 1970s, the education scholar Joseph Renzulli, now the director of the National Research Center on the Gifted and Talented at the University of Connecticut, came up with a notion of giftedness that could be measured through not only a child's above-average scholastic ability but also through her capacity for task commitment and, more amorphously, creativity. Part of Renzulli's aim was to emphasize that giftedness can be developed in some children, that giftedness wasn't inborn but could be gifted–that is, learned–behaviors. He called those learned qualities "gifted behaviors": Detecting motivation, rather than natural gifts, in children is part of his approach to gifted education, which emphasizes perseverance, endurance, and practice.

In the 1980s, psychological and education expert Howard Gardner pioneered the concept that human beings have multiple intelligences. In addition to the types of cognitive skills we have traditionally included under the rubric of intelligence, such as mathematical ability, logical reasoning, and verbal abilities, he argued that there are a number of other important types of intelligence. These included spatial intelligence, which is the ability to detect and utilize spatial patterns in both wide and narrow areas, bodily-kinesthetic intelligence, along the lines of the psychomotor abilities outlined in the Marland study, musical intelligence and leadership gifts, such as interpersonal and intrapersonal intelligence (meaning special gifts for relating to others and for understanding oneself). These were the original seven multiple intelligences; Gardner ultimately coined an eighth, naturalist intelligence, describing a child who shows an ability to observe and classify elements in the natural environment.

Since Gardner's influential notion of multiple intelligences, there has been further research in the field of gifted education that seeks to expand the definition of talent and ability. In recent years, for instance, Renzulli created something he calls Operation Houndstooth that aims to seek out and develop ethical giftedness, finding children with "sensitivity to human concerns." This is an expansion of Renzulli's belief that we can develop giftedness to include our ability to develop a sort of societal intelligence in children. He describes this educational mandate as the discovery and cultivation of "social capital."

What's curious is that despite the many years of scholarly recommendations for an expanded understanding of giftedness and innovative teaching techniques, a limited focus on precocious math, reading, and musical skills still prevails. Children who can integrate information will be best prepared to be life learners with flexible minds. This sort of flexibility depends, in part, on children not tying learning to obligation–rather, learning how to learn with a certain lightness and adaptability.

In fact, the emphasis on precocity in that narrow a range of skills has only gotten worse. Instead of working on a better appreciation for the range of abilities that constitute intelligence and life skills, our schools are generally focusing on more and more rote learning aimed at improving scores on standardized tests. As educator Deborah Meier has highlighted in her book *In Schools We Trust,* children are being pressed earlier and earlier into formal literacy activities in order to improve their test scores. As Meier has written, learning, even for the youngest children, is now geared toward the standardized tests they must now take. In short, our children are in scholastic environments that neglect intelligences that are not easily measured by tests.

In addition to expanding our definition of giftedness, I think it's important that we also become less frenzied about trying to *make* our kids gifted, even with giftedness defined more broadly. Adults need to refrain from urging and impelling and managing children's lives so that kids don't have the chance to develop their own fascinations and find their own capabilities. An expansive, complex, and even–dare we hope for it?–a happy adulthood doesn't necessarily derive from precocity or from having a whole retinue of "gifts." Rather, it usually stems from having found our strengths and developed them ourselves. This was the case for some "former gifted kids" I spoke with, like Jennifer Koh, the violinist who against her parents' wishes followed up on her early musical talents, ultimately benefiting professionally and personally from blazing her own path.

Indeed, two forms of childhood independence–self-directed pursuit of interests and nondirected play–are by far the most important "gifts" that one can give a child. The great childhood psychologist Erik Erikson wrote of the need for both, that in the absence of childhood autonomy or free choice, a child may "turn against himself all his urge to discriminate and to manipulate." My conversations with adults who felt they were raised with little free choice back this up: they had to struggle to exist and create for themselves, rather than for a parent or an audience in later life. Similarly, playing–an endangered activity in American schools–is a necessary component of a pleasing childhood. Playing can also be integral to the cultivation of exceptional abilities. Playing is often how children discover talents like ones for carnivorous plant experimentation or understanding and memorizing weather patterns, as was the case for one meteorologist I spoke with.

Parents who worry that they are projecting their own interests or wishes onto their children, imposing activities or avocations on them rather than bolstering their more spontaneous enthusiasms, can take steps to avoid doing so. They must listen to the response and be willing to admit that their children may just not be interested in some of the activities they are participating in. Parents have asked me how they can elicit from their children whether they feel imposed upon or actually desire to go to the lessons and classes attended, as getting a clear idea of children's wishes can be a fine-grained process. When I spoke to Alan Edmunds, professor of educational psychology and gifted specialist at the University of Western Ontario, he said he tells parents and educators that they must "check over and over again that a given activity is the one a child wishes to do, so that there's no doubt in anyone's mind. A parent or educator should listen to what children talk about frequently. If they talk about it a lot, that's a good indicator that they are enjoying it, and what they made excuses not to do is a good indicator of what they aren't enjoying."

When parents or teachers do detect in a child rare prodigious talent or intense idiosyncratic fascination about a subject, surely they should seek to support the child's pursuit of that interest and development of that talent. A child's genuine interest looks a little like the fascination of Vezen Wu, whose childhood interest in and talent with carnivorous plants guided much of his life. That said, the nurturing of prodigious or exceptionally gifted children involves teaching them to appreciate the talents of other kids, and not making them see themselves as so "different," as superior, seer-like, or outside or beyond childhood. It is important to remind one's gifted child that many children have gifts of some kind.

When discerning children's interests, parents as well as educators would also do well to exercise restraint in regard to their wishes for their children. Restraint may mean not pushing them to excel, and retiring "genius myth" notions that ultimately revolve more around adult fantasies of greatness, anyway. If we as adults were more able to fully appreciate our nostalgia for our own childhoods–if we could imagine or recollect our own earliest years more fully–we might not be so susceptible to perceiving exceptional learning going on in our infants when they watch educational videos, when they take specialized or advanced classes, or when they compete in youth tournaments.

The regrets of so many ex-prodigies and former gifted children may be harbingers: kids who are praised so much for their early giftedness may be pinioned to childhood in ways that will obstruct fulfillment in later life. Perhaps those gifted children who experience sadness later on do so because they believe they must remain children in order to be loved. For such children, specialness derives not only from being talented but also, crucially, from being *talented while young*. Adulthood, their inevitable fate–can only diminish them. With our focus on future outcomes–how good our children will be years from now after all of these enriching activities–we are privileging the future over the present. If we abridge the activities and the workload we expect children to keep up with, and lessen the mania and cant around the "gifted" label, perhaps we will take crucial steps in helping our children avoid the feelings of failure that so many of the once-gifted children speak of, what I think of as nostalgia for the idea of adulthood one had as a child, the time in life when one's future was always depicted as unimaginably glowing. Then maybe childhood as it is classically imagined will come back into style: more play, more messing about, more experience of emotion, more obliviousness to time's passage, more nondirected activity, more living in the present tense.

Acknowledgments

I'd like to thank all my friends and colleagues who have helped to make this a better book, including John Broughton, Charlie Zorn, David Bornstein, Mark Stafford, Steve Burt, Catherine (Katie) Orenstein, Annie Murphy Paul, Deborah Siegal, Gary Bass and Christine Kenneally, Richard Kay, Noga Arikha, Natasha Schull, and Devorah Baum. Thanks to my monthly authors' group whose members for two years have provided consistent intelligence, support, and warmth–they include Pamela Paul, Rebecca Skloot, Paul Raeburn, Elizabeth DeVita-Raeburn, Tom Zoellner, Harriet Washington, Stacy Sullivan, Sheri Fink, and Abby Ellin. Thanks to David Jacobson, who among other things initially suggested this book, and George Minot, for his thoughts on the proposal. Bill Brazell was a sage help as was Jean Casella. My gratitude also goes to Tayt Harlin, Tim Harris, and Polly Shulman. The thoughtful reads of Mike Scharf and Kimberly Cutter were a boon, as was the input of my dear friends Mark Gimein and Eleana Kim. Thanks for the kind favors of Jennifer Dworkin, Kimberly Bradley, Saul Anton, Chris Anderson, Katy Lederer, Barbara Quart, Jim Ledbetter, and Dan Smith at New York Public

Library Research, as well as for the thoughts of Josh Shenk, Teddy Rose, and Rachel Lehmann-Haupt. Additionally, I couldn't have done this without the love, discernment, and welcome amusement of friends like Rachel Urkowitz, Kat McGowan, Jared Hohlt, Ann Peters, Laura Secor, Nathaniel Wice, and Ruti Teitel. Thanks also to the many families and specialists whom I interviewed. I'd like to thank Ann Godoff and the superlative Melanie Jackson. And finally I'd like to thank Peter Maass, whose love is always transformative.

Notes

1. THE ICARUS EFFECT

1 "And time shall force a gift on each": This line is from one of my favorite poems by one of my and everyone else's favorite poets, John Ashbery, "The Picture of Little J.A. in a Prospect of Flowers," as it appears in the poet's *Selected Poems* (New York: Penguin, 1986). The poem is simultaneously bleak and ludic, and I take one of its subjects to not only be "Little J.A." but precocity itself: "Of my small self in that bank of flowers: / My head among the blazing phlox / Seemed a pale and gigantic fungus. / I had a hard stare, accepting / Everything, taking nothing, / As though the rolled-up future might stink." Coming across the poem again reminded me of having read of Ashbery's stint as a young teenager on the wunderkind trivia radio program *Quiz Kids!* in 1941. As recounted in David Lehman's *Last Avant-Garde: The Making of the New York School of Poets* (New York: Anchor, 1999), Ashbery, along with his cocontestants, would be asked who was on various denominations of bills, as well as questions like, "If you wanted somebody to draw you a cartoon, would you choose Fragonard, Corot, or Daumier?" I feel like you can see this high-culture-low-culture knowledge and general trivia-kid sensibility running through a number of his poems.

4 **the relationship between talented adults and their youthful "deliberative practice":** Anders Ericsson uses the term *expertise* for high levels of skill in everything from chess to video-game play. According to Ericsson and some of his colleagues, expertise is thought to require a minimum of ten years of several hours' focused practice daily. See K. A. Ericsson, R. T. Krampe, and C. Tesch-Romer, "The Role of Deliberate Practice in the Acquisition of Expert Performance," *Psychological Review* 100 (1993); and K. A. Ericsson and J. Smith, eds., *Toward a General Theory of Expertise* (Cambridge: Cambridge University Press, 1993).

5 **A classic longitudinal study:** More on this in Joel N. Shurkin, *Terman's Kids* (New York: Little, Brown, 1992) and also in the ongoing Terman studies published as *Genetic Studies of Genius* (Standford, Calif.: Stanford University Press, 1925–). See also Lewis Madison Terman, *Genius and Stupidity,* Classics in Child Development (Salem, N.H.: Ayer, 1975); Lewis M. Terman and Delita H. Oden, *Gifted Child Grows Up: Twenty-Five Years Follow-Up of a Superior Group,* Genetic Studies of Genius (Stanford, Calif: Stanford University Press, 1947); Lewis M. Terman, *The Intelligence of School Children: How Children Differ in Ability, the Use of Mental Tests in School Grading, and the Proper Education of Exceptional Children* (Boston: Riverside Press, 1921); and Lewis Madison Terman, *The Measurement of Intelligence,* Classics in Child Development (Salem, N.H.: Ayer, 1975). See also Paul Davis Chapman, *Schools as Sorters: Lewis M. Terman, Applied Psychology and the Intelligence Testing Movement, 1890–1930* (New York: New York University Press, 1990).

5 **Study of Mathematically Precocious Youth:** David Lubinski, Rose Mary Webb, Martha J. Morelock, and Camilla Persson Benbow, "Top 1 in 10,000: A 10-year Follow Up of the Profoundly Gifted," *Journal of Applied Psychology* 86 (2001).

6 **a longitudinal study of Presidential Scholars:** F. A. Kaufman, "A Follow-up Study of the 1964–1968 Presidential Scholars" (Ph.D. diss., University of Georgia, 1979).

6 a "modestly gifted group": See S. Dauber and C. Benbow, "Aspects of Personality and Peer Relations of Extremely Talented Adolescents," *Gifted Child Quarterly* 34, no. 1 (1999).

7 Icarus: See Ovid, *Metamorphoses: A New Translation by Charles Martin* (New York: W. W. Norton, 2005). Therein Daedalus "exhorts the boy to follow in his path, / instructing him in their transgressive art, / as he employs his wings in flight and watches / his fledgling Icarus attempt his own." My favorite part is when Daedalus "cursed his arts": "And then he saw the feathers on the waves / and cursed his arts; he built his son a tomb / in the land that takes its name from Icarus."

14 an aesthete's answer to Hollywood's Brat Pack: From author's interview with Haimovitz. See also two articles about the young Matt Haimovitz, "Teen-age Cellist in Philharmonic Debut," *New York Times,* February 9, 1986; and "The Lively Arts: The Aspen Festival Tunes Up on Long Island," *New York Times,* March 30, 1986.

14 the prodigy midlife crisis: Jeanne Bamberger, "Growing-up Prodigies: The Mid-life Crisis," in *Developmental Approaches to Giftedness and Creativity,* ed. David Henry Feldman (San Francisco: Jossey-Bass, 1982). As Feldman writes in an endnote to his and Lynn T. Goldsmith's classic book about prodigies, *Nature's Gambit: Child Prodigies and the Development of Human Potential* (New York: Teachers College Press, 1991), "The prodigy is not used to having to deal with the exigencies of motivation, not used to disruptions in the desire to achieve. . . . This is the situation that Jeanne Bamberger has discovered during the teenage years among music prodigies."

18 Dona Matthews: Dona Matthews and Joanne F. Foster, *Being Smart about Gifted Children: A Guidebook for Parents and Educators* (Scottsdale, Ariz.: Great Potential Press, 2004).

19 young schoolchildren grow increasingly distracted the longer recess is delayed: Olga Jarrett, "Recess in Elementary School: What Does the Research Say?" *ERIC Digest,* 2002; and Olga Jarrett and D. M. Maxwell, "What Research Says about the Need for Recess," in *Elementary School Recess: Selected Readings,*

Games, and Activities for Teachers and Parents, ed. R. Clements (New York: American Press, 2000).

2. THE BABY GENIUS EDUTAINMENT COMPLEX: THE NEW SMART BABY PRODUCTS

24 2003 report by the Henry J. Kaiser: Henry J. Kaiser Family Foundation, *Zero to Six: Electronic Media in the Lives of Infants, Toddlers and Preschoolers* (Washington, D.C.: Henry J. Kaiser Family Foundation, 2003).

24 2005 Kaiser report: Henry J. Kaiser Family Foundation, *A Teacher in the Living Room? Educational Media for Babies, Toddlers and Preschoolers* (Washington, D.C.: Henry J. Kaiser Family Foundation, 2005).

24 American Academy of Pediatrics' 1999 recommendation: "American Academy of Pediatrics Media Education Policy Statement," *Pediatrics,* August 2, 1999. For data on the big business of baby edutainment videos, see G. Khermouch, "Brainier? Maybe. Big Sales? Definitely," *BusinessWeek,* January 12, 2004.

25 The phenomenon called the Mozart effect: One original pro–Mozart effect article is by F. H. Rauscher, G. L. Shaw, and K. N. Ky, "Music and Spatial Task Performance," *Nature* 365 (1993).

25 the two Mozarts coexist: The 1982 film *Amadeus* is one of the few vehicles to portray Mozart as the disturbed Enlightenment wreck.

26 failed to reproduce the results: See K. M. Steele, J. D. Brown, and J. A. Stoecker, "Failure to Confirm the Rauscher and Shaw Description of Recovery of the Mozart Effect," *Perceptual and Motor Skills* 88 (1999); and K. M. Steele, K. E. Bass, and M. D. Crook, "The Mystery of the Mozart Effect: Failure to Replicate," *Psychological Science* 10 (1999).

27 Brent Logan, author: Brent Logan, *Learning before Birth: Every Child Deserves Giftedness* (New York: Authorhouse, 2003).

29 Early manufactured toys and games: I have relied on a number of books on toys here. One good reference is Bernard J. Mergen, *Play and Playthings: A Reference Guide* (New York: Greenwood Press, 1982). The truly perspicacious one is by Stephen Kline's, *Out of the Garden: Toys, TV, and Children's Culture in the Age of Marketing* (New York: Verso, 1995). See also Antonia Fraser, *A History of Toys* (London: Spring Books, 1972); and Colin Heywood, *A History of Childhood: Children and Childhood in the West from Medieval to Modern Times* (New York: Polity Press, 2001).

30 The educator Maria Montessori used toys: She was also, however, critical of the toy industry. As Maria Montessorri writes in *The Absorbent Mind* (New York: Owl Books, 1995), "But in those countries where the toy making industry is less advanced, you will find children with quite different tastes. They are also calmer, more sensible and happy."

30 playthings as products of "chemistry not nature": See Roland Barthes, *Mythologies* (New York: Hill and Wang, 1972).

31 Erikson wrote of the earliest and most primitive play: The necessary classic by Erik H. Erikson, *Toys and Reasons: Stages in the Ritualisation of Experience* (London: Marion Boyars, 1978), republished as *Childhood and Society* (New York: W. W. Norton, 1993).

32 the ultimate maturational television program, *Sesame Street:* James Day, *The Vanishing Vision: The Inside Story of Public Television* (Berkeley and Los Angeles: University of California Press, 1995). See also James Ledbetter, *Made Possible By: The Death of Public Broadcasting in the United States* (Verso, 1998); and Heather Hendershot, *Saturday Morning Censors: Television Regulation before the V-Chip (Console-Ing Passions)* (Durham, N.C.: Duke University Press, 1999).

34 child development pioneer Jean Piaget: Some Piaget books I read while writing this included *Psychology of Intelligence* (New York: Routledge, 2001), and *The Child's Conception of the World: A 20th-Century Classic of Child Psychology* (Sturgeon Bay, Wis.: Littlefield Adams, 1976).

35 As John Bruer recounts: John Bruer, *The Myth of the First Three Years: A New Understanding of Early Brain Development and Lifelong Learning* (New York: Free Press, 2002).

35 studies on rats and enrichment: William Greenough et al., "Effects of Rearing Complexity on Dendritic Branching in Frontolateral and Temporal Cortex of the Rat," *Experimental Neurology* 41, no. 2 (1973).

38 Kaiser Family Foundation report: Kaiser Foundation, "*Teacher in the Living Room.*"

38 three-year-olds in Early Head Start: Similarly, the Abecedarian Project, which began in the 1970s, assigned some low-income families in Chapel Hill, North Carolina, to a high-quality child-care setting, while some were not so assigned. At age twenty-one, the participants assigned to a high-quality setting were discovered to have significantly higher mental test scores than the control group.

39 University of Massachusetts researcher: Daniel R. Anderson's study was referenced in Tamar Lewin, "See Baby Touch a Screen, but Does Baby Get It?" *New York Times,* December 15, 2005. I looked at Anderson's earlier work about toddlers as well; see K. L. Schmitt and D. R. Anderson, "Television and Reality: Toddlers' Use of Visual Information from Video to Guide Behavior," *Media Psychology* 4 (2002).

39 mothers said that they themselves played every day outdoors: Rhonda Clements, "An Investigation of the Status of Outdoor Play," *Contemporary Issues in Early Childhood Education* 5, no. 1 (2004).

41 Educational Records Bureau test: The best account of the history of American achievement tests that I have read, and, I believe, the best that exists, is Nicholas Lemann's *The Big Test: The Secret History of the American Meritocracy* (New York: Farrar, Straus and Giroux, 2000).

42 "an experience of anticipation": Adam Phillips, *On Kissing, Tickling, and Being Bored: Psychoanalytic Essays on the Unexamined Life* (Harvard University Press, 1994); this is a remarkably good book from one of the most enjoyable and smart writers on this subject.

43 "The diagnoses . . . of middle class adolescents": Patricia Meyer Spacks, *Boredom: The Literary History of a State of Mind* (Chicago: University of Chicago Press, 1996). This stirringly un-dull book makes one point, among others: that a few great novelists even recommended boredom as a proper antidote to vice.

43 "If sleep is the apogee of physical relaxation": Walter Benjamin, *Illuminations* (New York: Schocken, 1969).

45 So Smart! and the rest are just the beginning of the expenditure: For two extensive accounts of this expenditure, see the passionate *Consuming Kids: Protecting Our Children from the Onslaught of Marketing and Advertising,* by Susan Linn (New York: Anchor, 2005), and Juliet Schor's excellent *Born to Buy: The Commercialized Child and the New Consumer Culture* (New York: Scribner, 2004).

3. THE EDUCATED INFANT: CLASSES FOR AN IMPROVED CHILDHOOD

46 "As I stared awe-struck at the infant": I really enjoyed Claude Kenneson, *Musical Prodigies: Perilous Journeys, Remarkable Lives* (Pompton Plains, N.J.: Amadeus Press, 2003), especially the story of Clara Schumann's prodigy.

50 The movement sprang up around best-selling books by Garcia and others: And sprang is the word for it. W. Joseph Garcia, *Sign with Your Baby: How to Communicate with Infants before They Can Speak,* rev. ed. (New York: Northlight Communications, 2002); and Linda Acredolo, Susan Goodwyn, and Douglas Abrams, *Baby Signs: How to Talk with Your Baby before Your Baby Can Talk* (New York: McGraw-Hill, 2002).

50 study funded by the National Institutes of Health: Susan W. Goodwyn, Linda P. Acredolo, and Catherine A. Brown, "Impact of Symbolic Gesturing on Early Language Development," *Journal of Nonverbal Behavior,* Summer 2000.

52 as understood by Aldous Huxley: Aldous Huxley, *Brave New World* (1932; reprint, New York: Harper Perennial Modern Classics, 1998).

52 Japanese pedant Shinichi Suzuki: Shinichi Suzuki and Waltraud Suzuki, *Nurtured by Love: The Classic Approach to Talent Education,* 2d ed. (Princeton, N.J.: Suzuki Method International, 1986).

52 multimillion-copy-selling book: Originally published in 1964, this book has been reprinted recently as Glenn Doman, and Janet Doman, *How to Teach Your Baby to Read: The Gentle Revolution* (Wyndmoor, Pa.: Gentle Revolution Press, 2005). It is part of a series that includes other Better Baby texts, such as Glenn Doman, Douglas Doman, and Bruce Hagy, *How to Teach Your Baby to Be Physically Superb: From Birth to Age Six* (Garden City, N.Y.: Square One Publishers, 2006).

53 "wire the circuits of the brain": Sharon Begley, "Your Child's Brain," *Newsweek,* February 19, 1996.

57 one of the "myths" of giftedness: Tracy L. Cross, "Competing with Myths about the Social and Emotional Development of Gifted Students," *Gifted Child Today,* Summer 2002.

60 "go against developmental psychology": Kathy Pasek-Hirsh, *Einstein Never Used Flash Cards: How Our Children Really Learn–And Why They Need to Play More and Memorize Less* (New York: Rodale Books, 2003).

4. CHILD'S PLAY OR CHILD LABOR? PREPROFESSIONAL KIDS

65 "strategic childhood": Jonathan Fineberg, *The Innocent Eye* (Princeton, N.J.: Princeton University Press, 1999).

65 Children's art also influenced the post-Symbolist generation: Jonathan Fineberg, ed., *Discovering Child Art: Essays on Childhood, Primitivism, and Modernism* (Princeton, N.J.: Princeton University Press, 2001); and Colin Rhodes, *Outsider Art: Spontaneous Alternatives* (New York: Thames & Hudson, 2000).

66 As early as 1917, the art critic Roger Fry: Roger Fry and Christopher Reed, *A Roger Fry Reader* (Chicago: University of Chicago Press, 1996). Fry was extremely enthusiastic about children's art. In his 1909 "Essay in Aesthetics," he wrote that children's art helped to prove that the graphic arts express the imaginative life rather than copy the actual. His 1917 essay accompanying an exhibit, "Children's Drawings," argues this point rather aggressively: "The fact is that almost all children's drawings have some merit, almost all have more aesthetic merit than all but the best art of the modern adult. I shall try in this article to make out an *a priori* case for accepting this sweeping statement." I especially like when Fry applies a formalist critique to a drawing by Augustus John's young son David, applauding "the snakiness of a snake" in the boy's art.

66 In 1938, critic Robert Goldwater: Robert Goldwater, *Primitivism in Modern Art* (Cambridge: Belknap Press, 2002).

69 In a 2001 article: Sandra L. Hofferth and John F. Sandberg, "Changes in American Children's Times, 1981–1997," *Advances in Life Course Research* 6 (2001).

72 Anthony Pellegrini: See Anthony D. Pellegrini, *School Recess and Playground Behavior: Educational and Developmental Roles* (Albany, N.Y.: SUNY Press, 1995); and Pellegrini, *Recess: Its Role in Education and Development* (New York: Lawrence Erlbaum, 2005).

72 A founder of play studies and its "great man": In an interview, scholar Brian Sutton-Smith also offered me a cultural relativist perspective on the overstructured work-rather-than-play lives of American children. He described collective cultures, like those in many parts of Brazil, as still child-apprenticeship cultures, where making baskets for play turns into making baskets for profit at the age of nine. The idea that child's play should be free play, said Sutton-Smith, is culturally specific. His further insights and delightful literary style can be found in *The Ambiguity of Play* (Cambridge, Mass.: Harvard University Press, 2001) as well as in *Play: An Interdisciplinary Synthesis* (Lanham, Md.: University Press of America, 2005) and many other volumes. Additionally, a collaboration worth looking at is Shlomo Ariel and Brian Sutton-Smith, *Children's Imaginative Play: A Visit to Wonderland (Child Psychology and Mental Health)* (New York: Praeger, 2002).

73 "children were adults in training": Steven Mintz, *Huck's Raft: A History of American Childhood* (Cambridge, Mass.: Belknap Press, 2004).

73 "economically 'worthless' but emotionally 'priceless' child": Viviana Zelizer, *Pricing the Priceless Child: The Changing Social Value of Children* (Princeton, N.J.: Princeton University Press, 1994).

78 Annette Lareau: Annette Lareau, *Unequal Childhoods: Class, Race, and Family Life* (Berkeley and Los Angeles: University of California Press, 2003).

5. GIFTED AND LEFT BEHIND: ENRICHMENT IN THE PUBLIC SCHOOLS

88 Mrs. Bauer's class is at Iles Elementary, a public school: For an incredible portrait of a student who was suffering from not attending Iles a few years before I went there, see Daniel Golden's "Initiative to Leave No Child Behind Leaves Out Gifted: Educators Divert Resources from Classes for Smartest to Focus on Basic Literacy," *Wall Street Journal*, December 29, 2003.

90 "further and further from their publics: Deborah Meier and George Wood, *Many Children Left Behind: How the No Child Left Behind Act Is Damaging Our Children and Our Schools* (Boston: Beacon Press, 2004).

91 Jonathan Kozol: Jonathan Kozol, *The Shame of the Nation: The Restoration of Apartheid Schooling in America* (New York: Crown, 2005).

91 And indeed, privatization is the key word: Alex Molnar, *School Commercialism: From Democratic Ideal to Market Commodity* (New York: Routledge, 2005).

92 James Borland . . . is one of those critics: James H. Borland, ed., *Rethinking Gifted Education* (New York: Teachers College Press, 2003).

93 "advanced as much as a whole year": Jan and Bob Davidson and Laura Vanderkam, *Genius Denied: How to Stop Wasting Our Brightest Young Minds* (New York: Simon & Schuster, 2005).

95 and as with all gifts, a demand for reciprocation: Marcel Mauss, *The Gift: The Form and Reason for Exchange in Archaic Societies* (New York: W. W. Norton, 2000).

96 In 1981, psychoanalyst Alice Miller's book: Alice Miller, *The Drama of the Gifted Child: The Search for the True Self* (New York: Basic Books, 1996).

98 Our school system . . . was modeled on the German one: See David Nasaw, *Schooled to Order: A Social History of Public Schooling in the United States* (Oxford, England: Oxford University Press, 1979); and John Taylor Gatto, *The Underground History of American Education* (Oxford, England: Oxford Village Press, 2000).

98 Early education reformer Horace Mann: Abraham J. Tannenbaum, *Gifted Children: Psychological and Educational Perspectives* (New York: Macmillan, 1983).

99 But the strongest voice for acceleration belongs to Nicholas Colangelo: Nicholas Colangelo, Susan G. Assouline, and Miraca U. M. Gross, eds., *A Nation Deceived: How Schools Hold Back America's Brightest Students, The Templeton National Report on Education.* Vol. 2. Iowa City: Belin-Blank Center, University of Iowa, 2004.

100 confirmed the ambiguities of acceleration: See *Academic Acceleration: Knowing your Options* (Baltimore: Johns Hopkins University Press, 1995). See also Camilla Persson Benbow and Julian C. Stanley, *Academic Precocity: Aspects of its Development* (Baltimore: Johns Hopkins University Press, 1983): "Although acceleration can be appropriate for many gifted students, it is not for all. John F. Feldhusen . . . makes that point quite clearly when he argues that one must be eclectic when setting up programs for gifted students."

101 Leta Hollingworth formed a curriculum: Ann G. Klein, *A Forgotten Voice: A Biography of Leta Stetter Hollingworth* (Scottsdale, Ariz.: Great Potential Press, 2002).

102 "the aptitude tests used to assign children": Tannenbaum, *Gifted Children.*

103 Marland Report: S. P. Marland, *Education of the Gifted and Talented. Volume I: Report to the Congress of the United States by the Commissioner of Education* (Washington, D.C.: U.S. Government Printing Office, 1971).

6. GURUS OF GIFTEDNESS: INTELLIGENCE TESTING AND TALENT BY OTHER MEASURES

112 the tester of a child named Justin Chapman: Julie Poppen, "Boy Genius: Prodigy or Pawn? The Troubled Saga of Justin Chapman," *Rocky Mountain News,* February 13, 2002.

112 Flynn effect, which notes a rise in average IQs: Ulric Neisser, ed., *The Rising Curve: Long-Term Gains in IQs and Related Measures* (Washington, D.C.: American Psychological Association, 1998).

113 the "Indigo Child" hypothesis: Lee Carroll, *Indigo Children* (Carlsbad, Calif.: Hay House, 1999).

113 a number that is thought to predict a child's scholastic performance: Stephen Jay Gould, *The Mismeasure of Man* (New York: Norton, 1981).

113 the field of psychometrics: For an elegant account of psychological testing, see Annie Murphy Paul, *The Cult of Personality: How Personality Tests Are Leading Us to Miseducate Our Children, Mismanage Our Companies, and Misunderstand Ourselves* (New York: Free Press, 2004).

114 They tend to have something of a monopoly: I liked Stephen Metcalf's piece on the testing industry's monopoly and how it relates to NCLB, "Reading between the Lines," *Nation,* January 28, 2002. Metcalf, sees NCLB as a victory for Bush's "corporate allies" in the test and textbook industry.

120 "memory, language comprehension": Gould, *Mismeasure of Man.*

120 as developed by Lewis Terman: Shurkin, *Terman's Kids.*

121 critiqued the IQ and SAT tests' limited notion: Gardner, *Multiple Intelligences.*

121 incendiary 1994 book: Richard J. Herrnstein and Charles Murray, *The Bell Curve: Intelligence and Class Structure in American Life* (New York: Free Press, 1996).

122 "sanctioned by nature itself": Russell Jacoby and Naomi Glauberman, *The Bell Curve Debate* (New York: Three Rivers Press, 1995).

123 for individual testing at all: Giftedness matriarch Annemarie Roeper's Qualitative Adaptation (QA) Scale, for instance, is entirely dependent on a one-on-one testing situation. Roeper is the gentle, snowy-haired eighty-six-year-old inventor of the QA and founder of the Roeper School for the Gifted in Bloomfield Hills, Michigan. Roeper illustrated QA with a film clip of the method: it was of herself speaking to a boy of thirteen. The two sat together for a few minutes on camera, exchanging gnomic remarks about the nature of giftedness and authority. The boy wound up crying. As a life study, the film clip nearly qualified as art. The viewer saw the boy's wish to be known and understood, the elder assessor's wish to know him, and the spoken agreement that such knowledge and understanding may be impossible and imperfect–and that by acknowledging that, these two people came closer to understanding one another. Roeper told her audience that the most remarkable proof of his giftedness was his ability to process ambiguity, that the boy knew already that "there was no total answer to a question."

124 Mighton, who is also the author of a book on the subject: John Mighton, *The Myth of Ability: Nurturing Mathematical Talent in Every Child* (New York: Walker, 2004).

125 terms "gifted behaviors": J. S. Renzulli, "The Three-ring Conception of Giftedness: A Developmental Model for Creative Productivity," *Conceptions of Giftedness,* eds. R. J. Sternberg and J. E. Davidson (Cambridge, England: Cambridge University Press, 1986).

128 "balanced and humanized": Richard Madsen et al., *Habits of the Heart: Individualism and Commitment in American Life* (Berkeley and Los Angeles: University of California Press, 1996).

128 Being gifted is being "special": Feldman and Goldsmith, *Nature's Gambit*; and Ellen Winner, *Gifted Children: Myths and Realities* (New York: Basic Books, 1997).

7. EXTREME PARENTING: MOTHERS AND FATHERS AS THE ULTIMATE INSTRUCTORS

138 "My Son My Executioner": Donald Hall, *Old and New Poems: Donald Hall* (New York: Mariner Books, 1990).

139 Kincheloe's studies of giftedness: Joe L. Kincheloe, Shirley R. Steinberg, Deborah J. Tippins, *The Stigma of Genius: Einstein, Consciousness, and Education* (Peter Lang Publishing, 1999).

139 according to Carol Dweck: Carol Dweck, "Beliefs that Make Smart People Dumb," *Why Smart People Can Be So Stupid,* ed. R. J. Sternberg (New Haven, Conn.: Yale University Press, 2002); Carol Dweck, "Caution–Praise Can Be Dangerous," *American Educator* 23, no. 1 (1999); C. M. Mueller and C. S.

Dweck, "Intelligence Praise Can Undermine Motivation and Performance," *Journal of Personality and Social Psychology* 75 (1998).

139 the moniker "helicopter parents": William Strauss and Neil Howe, *Millennials Go to College: Strategies for a New Generation on Campus* (Washington, D.C.: American Association of Collegiate Registrars, 2003).

144 a 2001 study by the National Institute of Mental Health: National Institute of Mental Health, *In Harm's Way: Suicide in America, a Brief Overview of Suicide Statistics and Prevention* (Washington, D.C.: National Institute of Mental Health, 2003).

144 "a paucity of research": Tracy L. Cross, Karyn Gust-Brey, and P. Bonny Ball, "A Psychological Autopsy of the Suicide of an Academically Gifted Student: Researchers' and Parents' Perspectives," *Gifted Child Quarterly* 46, no. 4 (Fall 2002).

145 "disadvantaged different" children: Matthews and Foster, *Being Smart about Gifted Children.*

145 some gifted children are more affected by colors: Winner, *Gifted Children.*

145 especially high levels of empathy and intensity: Deborah Ruf, *Losing Our Minds: Gifted Children Left Behind* (Scottsdale, Ariz: Great Potential Press, 2005).

145 a combination novel and treatise: Jean-Jacques Rousseau, *Emile* (New York: J. M. Dent & Sons, 1993).

146 John Ruskin and John Stuart Mill: Accounts of the childhoods of Ruskin, Mill, and Shelley that I have relied on are John Ruskin, *Praeterita* (New York: Everyman's Library, 2005); Muriel Spark, *Mary Shelley: A Biography* (New York: New American Library, 1988); Anthony Storr, *The Art of Psychotherapy* (New York: Routledge, 1990); John Stuart Mill, *Autobiography* (New York: Penguin, 1990).

147 the "angels of the house": One of my favorite literary renditions of extreme parents in the nineteenth century appeared toward that century's end, in the febrile 1897 Willa Cather short story "The Prodigies," as it appears in Virginia Faulkner, ed., *Willa Cather's Collected Short Fiction, 1892–1912* (Lincoln: University of Nebraska Press, 1970). It's about two famous and lugubrious child songbirds, trapped in a Belle Epoque social world, retailed by their *salonnière* mother. They are Americans but nevertheless weighted down by their German-style training, made to sing Schubert's compositions until they are unable to feel the natural joys of their youth. The boy prodigy Hermann is "pitifully fragile, with an unusually large head, all forehead, and those same dark, tired eyes. . . . Although he sang so feelingly there was no fervor, rather a yearning, joyless and hopeless. It was a serenade to which no lattice would open, which expected no answer." The siblings perform until Hermann's overworked prodigy sister ruins her vocal cords. At the end of the story, the kindly doctor Mackenzie, a father of two normal children, is deeded with the task of informing the overbearing mother that her gilded daughter is now a washup–that, as he puts it, the child has had the "life drained out of her veins." Cather is said to have based her story on two actual prodigies of the period, the Nebraska Sisters, whose grandmother forced them on a tour. Cather disapproved stringently of the fashion in which these children were taught and raised.

147 the famous intellectual parents of the Victorian era: And it wasn't just the Victorian era. Two of the most famous prodigies of the early twentieth century in America were also the progeny of extreme parents who were also intellectuals: William James Sidis and Norbert Weiner. Sidis, born in 1898, was very much a creation of his father, Boris Sidis. Wiener's father was friendly with Sidis's father, and like Boris Sidis, the elder Wiener monitored his son continuously, openly declaring Norbert an educational experiment. The elder Sidis believed that the brain was most open to knowledge during the first few years, so he allowed his son no time for play, or playmates, from toddler age onward. He taught young William to spell at two and to type at three. William obliged his father. He had created a new set of logarithms by age eight, and presented a lecture on "Four-Dimensional Bodies" to an assembly of Harvard professors at age eleven. He was off to a good start. By adulthood, however, in 1937, the *New Yorker* could present the adult Sidis as a freakish itinerant clerk working a string of low-level soul-crushing jobs, living in a sordid rooming house. To add to the pathos, Sidis had developed a mania for train schedules and nothing else. He died in 1944. An extensive account can be found in *The Prodigy: A Biography of William Sidis, America's Greatest Child Prodigy,* by Amy Wallace (New York: E. P. Dutton, 1986). Norbert Wiener also started college at eleven and got a doctorate from Harvard at eighteen. Ultimately Wiener wrote that his father's domination ruined his childhood in his remarkably good and honest memoir, *Ex-Prodigy: My Childhood and Youth* (Cambridge, Mass.: MIT Press, 1964). When he made a mathematical mistake, wrote Wiener, his "gentle and loving father was replaced by the avenger of the blood." Wiener was ultimately luckier than Sidis: he had a highly successful career as a math professor at Harvard and is remembered as the founder of cybernetics, the study of the effects of feedback mechanisms on communication and control.

148 more pragmatic sociobiological, sociological, and economic analyses: Psychologists Martin Daly and Margo Wilson, in *The Truth about Cinderella: A Darwinian View of Parental Love* (New Haven, Conn.: Yale University Press, 1999), contend that there's a genetic basis for parental love and that stepparents lack this genetic interest.

148 "developmental stake": V. L. Bengston and J. A. Kuypers, "Generational Difference and the 'Developmental Stake,'" *Aging and Human Development* 2, no. 1 (1971).

149 "engines of elaborate family": Mitchell L. Stevens, *Kingdom of Children: Culture and Controversy in the Homeschooling Movement,* Princeton Studies in Cultural Sociology (Princeton, N.J.: Princeton University Press, 2003).

149 "When my son fails": M. M. Eaton and E. M. Pomerantz, "Parental Contingent Self-Worth: Implications for Achievement Motivation and Parent's Use of Control and Mental Health," forthcoming, 2006.

8. YOUNG COMPETITORS: YOUTH CONTESTS FOR GOOD AND FOR ILL

157 "How could anyone oppose": William Crain, *Reclaiming Childhood: Letting Children Be Children in Our Achievement-Oriented Society,* 2d ed. (New York: Owl Books, 2004).

157 "Competition is our state religion": Alfie Kohn, *No Contest: The Case against Competition* (Princeton, N.J.: Princeton University Press, 2001).

158 coined the term "cooperative imperative": Scott Scheer, "Children and Cooperation: Moving beyond Competition," *Human Development and Family Life Bulletin* 3, no. 1 (1997). See also A. Combs, ed., *Cooperation: Beyond the Age of Competition* (New York: Gordon & Breach, 1992).

159 a sociology professor at Northwestern University: Gary Alan Fine, *Gifted Tongues: High School Debate and Adolescent Culture* (Boston: Mariner Books, 1992).

160 "soft" liberals who are emasculating boys: Christina Hoff Sommers, *The War against Boys: How Misguided Feminism Is Harming Our Young Men* (New York: Simon & Schuster, 2001); and Janet Daley, "Progressive Ed's War on Boys," *City Journal,* Winter 1999.

167 the perennial allure of J. D. Salinger's short stories: J. D. Salinger, *Franny and Zooey* (New York: Little, Brown, 1991). Throughout the writing of this book I also read quite a number of contemporary novels about ex-prodigies and gifted children. My favorites were Richard Powers, *A Time of Our Singing* (New York: Picador, 2004), and David Foster Wallace, *Infinite Jest* (Boston: Back Bay Books, 1997), part of a list that includes the novels *The Last Samurai* and *Bee Season.* The sheer number of novels dedicated to "wise" children and former wise children, especially in the young adult world, where Madeleine L'Engle's books as well as the Harry Potter series are dedicated to this theme, struck me after a while. I realized that many writers see themselves as former wise children laden with uncomfortable gifts, or, as David Foster Wallace puts it, a "feral prodigy."

167 Salinger's "closed circuit": Mary McCarthy, "J. D. Salinger's Closed Circuit," *Harper's,* October 1962; reprinted in A. O. Scott, ed., *A Bolt from the Blue and Other Essays by Mary McCarthy* (New York: New York Review of Books, 2002).

167 former *Quiz Kids!* star: The original *Quiz Kids!* trivia radio show starring children downplayed the resentment of ordinary folks for gifted children. It had an incredibly genial and humble emcee who liked to remark on his third-grade education and served as the ideal foil for the young eggheads. In short, it was quite distinct from today's a-star-is-born youth television shows, which remake kids' looks nightly, telling them what to sing and choreographing their future careers. But it also had a not entirely positive aftereffect on its participants. According to an interview with former Quiz Kid Ruth Feldman Duskin, *Quiz Kids!* was rife with both "perils and profits." *Quiz Kids!* may have "groomed her to be an achiever," but it has also made her live in "fear of not living up to my childhood promise."

9. CHILDREN OF GOD: THE TEEN PREACHING TOURNAMENTS

174 parallels between today's evangelical parents with gifted children and the less faithful parents of the gifted: For more on this, see Heather Hendershot, *Shaking the World for Jesus: Media and Conservative Evangelical Culture* (Chicago: University of Chicago Press, 2004).

174 "preaching to an elite": Laurie Goodstein and David D. Kirkpatrick, "On a Christian Mission to the Top," *New York Times,* May 22, 2005; see also Janny Scott and David Leonhardt, "Class in America: Shadowy Lines That Still Divide," *New York Times,* May 15, 2005, who write, "Religious affiliation, too, is no longer the reliable class marker it once was. The growing economic power of the South has helped lift evangelical Christians into the middle and upper middle classes, just as earlier generations of Roman Catholics moved up in the mid-20th century."

180 "My Father's religious teaching": Edmund Gosse, *Father and Son: A Study of Two Temperaments* (New York: Penguin Classics, 1989).

180 James Baldwin, who preached: As James Baldwin writes in the classic *Go Tell It on the Mountain* (New York: Laurel, 1985): "Everyone had always said that John would be a preacher when he grew up, just like his father. It was said so often that John, without ever thinking about it, had come to believe it himself."

181 sidewalk preacher: Flannery O'Connor, *Wise Blood: A Novel* (New York: Farrar, Straus and Giroux, 1962).

181 "great fear that haunts evangelical parents": Randall Balmer, *Mine Eyes Have Seen the Glory: A Journey into the Evangelical Subculture in America* (Oxford, England: Oxford University Press, 2000).

10. THE PRODIGY HUNTERS: MATH WHIZ KIDS BECOME WALL STREET RECRUITS

191 Budunov's statement echoes the claims of pundits: See Thomas L. Friedman, "Still Eating Our Lunch," *New York Times,* September 16, 2005.

191 Singaporean eighth-grade students score first in the world in math: U.S. Department of Education, National Center for Education Statistics, *Highlights from the Trends in International Mathematics and Science Study:TIMSS: 2003* (Washington, D.C.: Government Printing Office, 2003).

191 According to a 2002 study: Erling E. Boe, Henry May, and Robert F. Boruch, *Student Task Persistence in the Third International Mathematics and Science Study: A Major Source of Achievement Difference at the National, Classroom, and Student Levels* (Philadelphia: Center for Research and Evaluation in Social Policy, 1992); and Erling E. Boe et al., *Predictors of National Difference in Mathematics and Science Achievement: Data from TIMSS for Eighth Grade Students* (Philadelphia: Center for Research and Evaluation in Social Policy, 2002).

192 In a 2003 article called "The Democratization of Mathematics": Anthony P. Carnevale and Donna M. Desrochers, *The Democratization of Mathematics,* in *Quantitative Literacy: Why Numeracy Matters for Schools and Colleges* (Princeton, N.J.: National Council on Education and the Disciplines, 2003).

193 "brain category for numbers": Brian Butterworth, *What Counts: How Every Brain Is Hardwired for Math* (New York: Free Press, 1999).

193 needs to have practiced for 10,000 hours: K. A. Ericsson and A. C. Lehmann, "Expert and Exceptional Performance: Evidence of Maximal Adaptation to Task," *Annual Review of Psychology* 47 (1996).

196 "cut-throat pressure": Mihaly Csikszentmihalyi, Kevin Rathunde, and Samuel Whalen, *Talented Teenagers: The Roots of Success and Failure* (Cambridge, England: Cambridge University Press, 1996).

198 many female winners dropped out: Rena F. Subotnik and Karen D. Arnold, *Beyond Terman: Contemporary Longitudinal Studies of Giftedness and Talent* (Westport, Conn.: Ablex, 1994).

202 studies of subjective well-being: Daniel Kahneman, Ed Diener, and Norbert Schwarz, eds., *Well-Being* (New York: Russell Sage Foundation, 2003).

CONCLUSION. RETHINKING GIFTEDNESS: AGAINST PERFECTION

204 Orson Welles: To childhood? I've been back there ever since I left: See Peter Bogdanovich, Jonathan Rosenbaum, *This Is Orson Welles* (New York: Da Capo Press, 1998), and David Thomson, *Rosebud: The Story of Orson Welles* (New York: Vintage, 1997). Orson Welles, the great prodigy of films and drama, is a case in point. In mature adulthood, after the prodigydom of his teens and twenties, Welles couldn't let go of the lost Eden of childhood. His own Rosebud was his father's Midwest home. Before making *Citizen Kane,* he told the *Saturday Evening Post* that as a child, he hated being young, and wanted to grow up as fast as possible. Now, he said, all he wanted was to return to childhood again. Many adults wish they could be kids again, but for cinema's master-builder Welles–who was once believed capable of decades of titanic achievement and who made his first short film in high school and directed *Citizen Kane* in his middle twenties, but was later said to have frittered away his talents–that wish held real pathos.

207 task commitment: Joseph S. Renzulli, "What Makes Giftedness? Re-examining a Definition," *Phi Delta Kappan* 60, no. 3 (1978). Joseph S. Renzulli, *The Enrichment Triad Model: A Guide for Developing Defensible Programs for the Gifted and Talented* (Mansfield Center, Conn.: Creative Learning Press, 1977).

207 the original seven multiple intelligences: Howard Gardner, *Frames of Mind: The Theory of Multiple Intelligences* (New York: Basic Books, 10th anniv. ed., 1993).

208 "social capital": Joseph S. Renzulli, "Expanding the Conception of Giftedness to Include Co-Cognitive Traits and to Promote Social Capital," *Phi Delta Kappan* 84, no. 1 (2002).

208 learning . . . is now geared toward the standardized tests: Deborah Meier, *In Schools We Trust: Creating Communities of Learning in an Era of Testing and Standardization* (Boston: Beacon Press, 2003).

209 "turn against himself . . .": Erik Erikson, *Childhood and Society,* 2nd ed. (New York: W. W. Norton., 1963).

Bibliography

Academic Acceleration: Knowing Your Options. Baltimore: Johns Hopkins University Press, 1995.

Ackroyd, Peter. *Thomas Chatterton.* New York: Grove Press, 1996.

Acredolo, Linda, Susan Goodwyn, and Douglas Abrams. *Baby Signs: How to Talk with Your Baby before Your Baby Can Talk.* New York: McGraw-Hill, 2002.

"American Academy of Pediatrics Media Education Policy Statement," *Pediatrics,* August 2, 1999.

Ashbery, John. *Selected Poems.* New York: Penguin, 1986.

Balmer, Randall. *Mine Eyes Have Seen the Glory: A Journey into the Evangelical Subculture in America.* Oxford, England: Oxford University Press, 2000.

Barthes, Roland. *Mythologies.* New York: Hill and Wang, 1972.

Begley, Sharon. "Your Child's Brain." *Newsweek,* February 19, 1996.

Belgrad, Daniel. *The Culture of Spontaneity: Improvisation and the Arts in Postwar America.* Chicago: University of Chicago Press, 1998.

Bengston, V. L., and J. A. Kuypers. "Generational Difference and the 'Developmental Stake.'" *Aging and Human Development,* 2, no. 1 (1971).

Benjamin, Walter. *Illuminations.* New York: Schocken, 1969.

Boe, Erling E., Henry May, and Robert F. Boruch. *Student Task Persistence in the Third International Mathematics and Science Study: A Major Source of Achievement Difference at the National, Classroom, and Student Levels.* Philadelphia: Center for Research and Evaluation in Social Policy, 1992.

Boe, Erling E., H. May, G. Barkanic, and R. F. Boruch. *Predictors of National Difference in Mathematics and Science Achievement: Data from TIMSS for Eighth Grade Students.* Philadelphia: Center for Research and Evaluation in Social Policy, 2002.

Borland, James H., ed. *Rethinking Gifted Education.* New York: Teachers College Press, 2003.

Bruer, John. *The Myth of the First Three Years: A New Understanding of Early Brain Development and Lifelong Learning.* New York: Free Press, 2002.

Butterworth, Brian. *What Counts: How Every Brain Is Hardwired for Math.* New York: Free Press, 1999.

Carnevale, Anthony P., and Donna M. Desrochers. "The Democratization of Mathematics." In *Quantitative Literacy: Why Numeracy Matters for Schools and Colleges.* Princeton, N.J.: National Council on Education and the Disciplines, 2003.

Carroll, Lee. *Indigo Children.* Carlsbad, Calif.: Hay House, 1999.

Clements, R., ed. *Elementary School Recess: Selected Readings, Games, and Activities for Teachers and Parents.* New York: American Press, 2000.

Clements, Rhonda. "An Investigation of the Status of Outdoor Play." *Contemporary Issues in Early Childhood Education* 5, no. 1 (2004).

Colangelo, Nicholas, Susan G. Assouline, and Miraca U. M. Gross, eds. *A Nation Deceived: How Schools Hold Back America's Brightest Students, The Templeton National Report on Education.* vol. 2. Iowa City: Belin-Blank Center, University of Iowa, 2004.

Combs, A., ed. *Cooperation: Beyond the Age of Competition.* New York: Gordon & Breach, 1992.

Crain, William. *Reclaiming Childhood: Letting Children Be Children in Our Achievement-Oriented Society.* New York: Owl Books, 2004.

Cross, Tracy L. "Competing with Myths about the Social and Emotional Development of Gifted Students." *Gifted Child Today,* Summer 2002.

Cross, Tracy L., Karyn Gust-Brey, and P. Bonny Ball. "A Psychological Autopsy of the Suicide of an Academically Gifted Student: Researchers' and Parents' Perspectives." *Gifted Child Quarterly* 46, no. 4 (2002).

Csikszentmihalyi, Mihaly, Kevin Rathunde, and Samuel Whalen. *Talented Teenagers: The Roots of Success and Failure.* Cambridge, England: Cambridge University Press, 1996.

Daley, Janet. "Progressive Ed's War on Boys." *City Journal,* Winter 1999.

Daly, Martin, and Margo Wilson. *The Truth about Cinderella: A Darwinian View of Parental Love.* New Haven, Conn.: Yale University Press, 1999.

Dauber, S., and C. Benbow. "Aspects of Personality and Peer Relations of Extremely Talented Adolescents." *Gifted Child Quarterly* 34, no. 1. (1999).

Davidson, Jan, Bob Davidson, and Laura Vanderkam. *Genius Denied: How to Stop Wasting Our Brightest Young Minds.* New York: Simon & Schuster, 2005.

Day, James. *The Vanishing Vision: The Inside Story of Public Television.* Berkeley and Los Angeles: University of California Press, 1995.

Dewey, John. *Individualism Old and New.* Amherst, N.Y.: Prometheus Books, 1999.

Doman, Glenn, and Janet Doman. *How to Teach Your Baby to Read: The Gentle Revolution.* Wyndmoor, Pa.: Gentle Revolution Press, 2005.

Dweck, Carol. "Caution–Praise Can Be Dangerous." *American Educator* 23, no. 1 (1999).

Eaton, M. M., and E. M. Pomerantz. "Parental Contingent Self-worth: Implications for Achievement Motivation and Parent's Use of Control and Mental Health." Forthcoming, 2006.

Ericsson, K. A., R. T. Krampe, and C. Tesch-Romer. "The Role of Deliberate Practice in the Acquisition of Expert Performance." *Psychological Review* 100 (1993).

Ericsson, K. A., and J. Smith, eds. *Toward a General Theory of Expertise.* Cambridge, England: Cambridge University Press, 1993.

Ericsson, K. A., and A. C. Lehmann, "Expert and Exceptional Performance: Evidence of Maximal Adaptation to Task," *Annual Review of Psychology* 47 (1996).

Erikson, Erik H. *Toys and Reasons: Stages in the Ritualisation of Experience.* London: Marion Boyars, 1978.

Faulkner, Virginia, ed. *Willa Cather's Collected Short Fiction, 1892–1912.* Lincoln: University of Nebraska Press, 1970.

Feldman, David Henry, and Lynn T. Goldsmith. *Nature's Gambit: Child Prodigies and the Development of Human Potential.* New York: Teachers College Press, 1991.

Feldman, David Henry, ed. *Developmental Approaches to Giftedness and Creativity.* San Francisco: Jossey-Bass, 1982.

Fine, Gary Alan. *Gifted Tongues: High School Debate and Adolescent Culture.* New York: Mariner Books, 1992.

Fineberg, Jonathan. *The Innocent Eye.* Princeton, N.J.: Princeton University Press, 1999.

——, ed. *Discovering Child Art: Essays on Childhood, Primitivism, and Modernism.* Princeton, N.J.: Princeton University Press, 2001.

Fraser, Antonia. *A History of Toys.* London: Spring Books, 1972.

Freud, Sigmund. *Group Psychology and the Analysis of the Ego.* New York: Norton Library, 1975.

Friedman, Thomas L. "Still Eating Our Lunch." *New York Times,* September 16, 2005.

Fry, Roger, and Christopher Reed. *A Roger Fry Reader.* Chicago: University of Chicago Press, 1996.

Garcia, W. Joseph. *Sign with Your Baby: How to Communicate with Infants before They Can Speak.* New York: Northlight Communications, 2002.

Gardner, Howard. *Multiple Intelligences: The Theory in Practice.* New York: Basic Books, 1993.

Gatto, John Taylor. *The Underground History of American Education.* Oxford, England: Oxford Village Press, 2000.

Golden, Daniel. "Initiative to Leave No Child Behind Leaves Out Gifted: Educators Divert Resources from Classes for Smartest to Focus on Basic Literacy." *Wall Street Journal,* December 29, 2003.

Goldwater, Robert. *Primitivism in Modern Art.* Cambridge, Mass.: Belknap Press, 2002.

Goodstein, Laurie, and David D. Kirkpatrick. "On a Christian Mission to the Top." *New York Times,* May 22, 2005.

Gosse, Edmund. *Father and Son: A Study of Two Temperaments.* New York: Penguin Classics, 1989.

Gould, Stephen Jay. *The Mismeasure of Man.* New York: Norton, 1981.

Greenough, William, F. R. Volkmar, and J. R. Juraska. "Effects of Rearing Complexity on Dendritic Ranching in Frontolateral and Temporal Cortex of the Rat." *Experimental Neurology* 41, no. 2 (1973).

Hall, Donald. *Old and New Poems: Donald Hall.* New York: Mariner Books, 1990.

Hendershot, Heather. *Shaking the World for Jesus: Media and Conservative Evangelical Culture.* Chicago: University of Chicago Press, 2004.

Henry J. Kaiser Family Foundation. *A Teacher in the Living Room? Educational Media for Babies, Toddlers and Preschoolers.* Washington, D.C.: Henry J. Kaiser Family Foundation, 2005.

Herrnstein, Richard J., and Charles Murray. *The Bell Curve: Intelligence and Class Structure in American Life.* New York: Free Press, 1996.

Heywood, Colin. *A History of Childhood: Children and Childhood in the West from Medieval to Modern Times.* New York: Polity Press, 2001.

Hofferth, Sandra L., and John F. Sandberg. "Changes in American Children's Times, 1981–1997." *Advances in Life Course Research* 6 (2001).

Huxley, Aldous. *Brave New World.* New York: Harper Perennial, 1998.

Jacoby, Russell, and Naomi Glauberman. *The Bell Curve Debate.* New York: Nation Books, 1995.

Jarrett, Olga. "Recess in Elementary School: What Does the Research Say?" *ERIC Digest* 17, no. 2 (2002).

Kahneman, Daniel, Ed Diener, and Norbert Schwarz, eds. *Well-Being.* New York: Russell Sage Foundation Publications, 2003.

Kaplan, Louise. *Romance of the Impostor-Poet Thomas Chatterton.* Berkeley and Los Angeles: University of California Press, 1989.

Kaufman, F. A. *A Follow-up Study of the 1964–1968 Presidential Scholars.* Ph.D. diss., University of Georgia, 1979.

Kenneson, Claude. *Musical Prodigies: Perilous Journeys, Remarkable Lives.* Pompton Plains, N.J.: Amadeus Press, 2003.

Khermouch, G. "Brainier? Maybe. Big Sales? Definitely." *BusinessWeek,* January 12, 2004.

Kincheloe, Joe L., Shirley R. Steinberg, and Deborah J. Tippins. *The Stigma of Genius: Einstein, Consciousness, and Education.* New York: Peter Lang, 1999.

Klein, Ann G. *A Forgotten Voice: A Biography of Leta Stetter Hollingworth.* Scottsdale, Ariz.: Great Potential Press, 2002.

Kline, Stephen. *Out of the Garden: Toys, TV, and Children's Culture in the Age of Marketing.* New York: Verso, 1995.

Kohn, Alfie. *No Contest: The Case against Competition.* Princeton, N.J.: Princeton University Press, 2001.

Kozol, Jonathan. *The Shame of the Nation: The Restoration of Apartheid Schooling in America.* New York: Crown, 2005.

Lareau, Annette. *Unequal Childhoods: Class, Race, and Family Life.* Berkeley and Los Angeles: University of California Press, 2003.

Leclaire, Serge. *A Child Is Being Killed: On Primary Narcissism and the Death Drive.* Stanford, Calif.: Stanford University Press, 1998.

Lehman, David. *The Last Avant-Garde: The Making of the New York School of Poets.* New York: Anchor, 1999.

Lemann, Nicholas. *The Big Test: The Secret History of the American Meritocracy.* New York: Farrar, Straus and Giroux, 2000.

Lewin, Tamar. "See Baby Touch A Screen, But Does Baby Get It?" *New York Times,* December 15, 2005.

Linn, Susan. *Consuming Kids: Protecting Our Children from the Onslaught of Marketing and Advertising.* New York: Anchor, 2005.

Logan, Brent. *Learning before Birth: Every Child Deserves Giftedness.* New York: Authorhouse, 2003.

Lubinski, David, Rose Mary Webb, Martha J. Morelock, and Camilla Persson Benbow. "Top 1 in 10,000: A 10-year Follow Up of the Profoundly Gifted." *Journal of Applied Psychology* 86 (2001).

Madsen, Richard, William M. Sullivan, Ann Swidler, Steven M. Tipton, and Robert Neelly Bellah. *Habits of the Heart: Individualism and Commitment in American Life.* Berkeley and Los Angeles: University of California Press, 1996.

Matthews, Dona, and Joanne F. Foster. *Being Smart about Gifted Children: A Guidebook for Parents and Educators.* Scottsdale, Ariz.: Great Potential Press, 2004.

Mauss, Marcel. *The Gift: The Form and Reason for Exchange in Archaic Societies.* New York: W. W. Norton, 2000.

Meier, Deborah, and George Wood. *Many Children Left Behind: How the No Child Left Behind Act Is Damaging Our Children and Our Schools.* Boston: Beacon Press, 2004.

Mergen, Bernard J. *Play and Playthings: A Reference Guide.* New York: Greenwood Press, 1982.

Metcalf, Stephen. "Reading between the Lines." *Nation,* January 28, 2002.

Metzner, Paul. *Crescendo of the Virtuoso: Spectacle, Skill, and Self-Promotion in Paris during the Age of Revolution.* Berkeley and Los Angeles: University of California Press, 1998.

Mighton, John. *The Myth of Ability: Nurturing Mathematical Talent in Every Child.* New York: Walker & Company, 2004.

Mill, John Stuart. *Autobiography.* New York: Penguin, 1990.

Miller, Alice. *The Drama of the Gifted Child: The Search for the True Self.* New York: Basic Books, 1996.

Molnar, Alex. *School Commercialism: From Democratic Ideal to Market Commodity.* New York: Routledge, 2005.

Montessorri, Maria. *The Absorbent Mind.* New York: Owl Books, 1995.

Mueller, C. M., and C. S. Dweck. "Intelligence Praise Can Undermine Motivation and Performance." *Journal of Personality and Social Psychology* 75 (1998).

Nasaw, David. *Schooled to Order: A Social History of Public Schooling in the United States.* Oxford, England: Oxford University Press, 1979.

National Institute of Mental Health. *In Harm's Way: Suicide in America, a Brief Overview of Suicide Statistics and Prevention.* Washington, D.C.: National Institute of Mental Health, 2003.

Neisser, Ulric, ed. *The Rising Curve: Long-Term Gains in IQ and Related Measures.* Washington, D.C.: American Psychological Association, 1998.

O'Connor, Flannery. *Wise Blood: A Novel.* New York: Farrar, Straus and Giroux, 1962.

Ovid. *Metamorphoses: A New Translation by Charles Martin.* New York: W. W. Norton, 2005.

Pasek-Hirsh, Kathy. *Einstein Never Used Flash Cards: How Our Children Really Learn—And Why They Need to Play More and Memorize Less.* New York: Rodale Books, 2003.

Paul, Annie Murphy. *The Cult of Personality: How Personality Tests Are Leading Us to Miseducate Our Children, Mismanage Our Companies, and Misunderstand Ourselves.* New York: Free Press, 2004.

Pellegrini, Anthony D. *Recess: Its Role in Education and Development.* New York: Lawrence Erlbaum Associates, 2005.

——. *School Recess and Playground Behavior: Educational and Developmental Roles.* Albany, N.Y.: SUNY Press, 1995.

Phillips, Adam. *On Kissing, Tickling, and Being Bored: Psychoanalytic Essays on the Unexamined Life.* Cambridge, Mass.: Harvard University Press, 1994.

Piaget, Jean. *The Child's Conception of the World: A 20th-Century Classic of Child Psychology.* Sturgeon Bay, Wis.: Littlefield Adams, 1976.

——. *Psychology of Intelligence.* New York: Routledge, 2001.

Poppen, Julie. "Boy Genius: Prodigy or Pawn? The Troubled Saga of Justin Chapman." *Rocky Mountain News,* February 13, 2002.

Rauscher, F. H., G. L. Shaw, and K. N. Ky. "Music and Spatial Task Performance." *Nature* 365 (1993).

Renzulli, Joseph. "Expanding the Conception of Giftedness to Include Co-Cognitive Traits and to Promote Social Capital." *Phi Delta Kappan* 84, no. 1 (2002).

——. "What Makes Giftedness? Re-examining a Definition." *Phi Delta Kappan* 60, no. 3 (1978).

Rhodes, Colin. *Outsider Art: Spontaneous Alternatives.* New York: Thames & Hudson, 2000.

Rousseau, Jean-Jacques. *Emile.* New York: J. M. Dent & Sons, 1993.

Ruf, Deborah. *Losing Our Minds: Gifted Children Left Behind.* Scottsdale, Ariz.: Great Potential Press, 2005.

Ruskin, John. *Praeterita.* New York: Everyman's Library, 2005.

Salinger, J. D. *Franny and Zooey.* New York: Little, Brown, 1991.

Sandage, Scott. *Born Losers: A History of Failure in America.* Cambridge. Mass.: Harvard University Press, 2005.

Sandel, Michael. "The Pursuit of Perfection: A Conversation on the Ethics of Genetic Engineering." Paper presented at the Pew Forum on Religion and Public Life, March 31, 2004.

Scheer, Scott. "Children and Cooperation: Moving beyond Competition." *Human Development and Family Life Bulletin* 3, no. 1 (1997).

Schmitt, K. L., and D. R. Anderson. "Television and Reality: Toddlers' Use of Visual Information from Video to Guide Behavior." *Media Psychology* 4 (2002).

Schor, Juliet. *Born to Buy: The Commercialized Child and the New Consumer Culture.* New York: Scribner, 2004.

Scott, A. O., ed. *A Bolt from the Blue and Other Essays by Mary McCarthy.* New York: New York Review of Books, 2002.

Scott, Janny, and David Leonhardt. "Class in America: Shadowy Lines That Still Divide." *New York Times,* May 15, 2005.

Shurkin, Joel N. *Terman's Kids.* New York: Little, Brown, 1992.

Sommers, Christina Hoff. *The War against Boys: How Misguided Feminism Is Harming Our Young Men.* New York: Simon & Schuster, 2001.

Spacks, Patricia Meyer. *Boredom.* Chicago: University of Chicago Press, 1996.

Spark, Muriel. *Mary Shelley: A Biography.* New York: New American Library, 1988.

Steele, K. M., J. D. Brown, and J. A. Stoecker. "Failure to Confirm the Rauscher and Shaw Description of Recovery of the Mozart Effect." *Perceptual and Motor Skills* 88 (1999).

Steele, K. M., K. E. Bass, and M. D. Crook. "The Mystery of the Mozart Effect: Failure to Replicate." *Psychological Science* 10 (1999).

Sternberg, R. J., ed. *Why Smart People Can Be So Stupid.* New Haven, Conn.: Yale University Press, 2002.

Sternberg, R. J., and E. Davidson, eds. *Conceptions of Giftedness.* Cambridge, England: Cambridge University Press, 1986.

Stevens, Mitchell L. *Kingdom of Children: Culture and Controversy in the Homeschooling Movement.* Princeton, N.J.: Princeton University Press, 2003.

Storr, Anthony. *The Art of Psychotherapy.* New York: Routledge, 1990.

Strauss, William and Neil Howe. *Millennials Go to College: Strategies for a New Generation on Campus.* Washington, D.C.: American Association of Collegiate Registrars, 2003.

Subotnik, Rena F., and Karen D. Arnold. *Beyond Terman: Contemporary Longitudinal Studies of Giftedness and Talent.* Westport, Conn.: Ablex, 1994.

Sutton-Smith, Brian. *The Ambiguity of Play.* Cambridge, Mass.: Harvard University Press, 2001.

Suzuki, Shinichi, and Waltraud Suzuki. *Nurtured by Love: The Classic Approach to Talent Education.* Princeton, N.J.: Suzuki Method International, 1986.

Tannenbaum, Abraham J. *Gifted Children: Psychological and Educational Perspectives.* New York: Macmillan, 1983.

Terman, Lewis. *Genetic Studies of Genius.* Stanford, Calif.: Stanford University Press, 1925.

Thomson, David. *Rosebud: The Story of Orson Welles.* New York: Vintage, 1997.

U.S. Department of Education, National Center for Education Statistics. *Highlights from the Trends in International Mathematics and Science Study: TIMSS 2003.* Washington, D.C.: Government Printing Office, 2003.

Wallace, Amy. *The Prodigy: A Biography of William Sidis, America's Greatest Child Prodigy.* New York: E. P. Dutton, 1986.

Welles, Orson, Peter Bogdanovich, and Jonathan Rosenbaum. *This Is Orson Welles.* New York: Da Capo Press, 1998.

Wiener, Norbert. *Ex-Prodigy: My Childhood and Youth.* Cambridge, Mass.: MIT Press, 1964.

Winner, Ellen. *Gifted Children: Myths and Realities.* New York: Basic Books, 1997.

Zelizer, Viviana. *Pricing the Priceless Child: The Changing Social Value of Children.* Princeton, N.J.: Princeton University Press, 1994.

Index

AACS (American Association of Christian Schools), 169–71, 182–84
ability tests. *See* intelligence assessment
acceleration, scholastic, 98–101
achievement gap, 88, 192
Acredelo, Joan, 50–51
Advocacy for Radical Acceleration, 98–99
Akbari, Suzanne Conklin, 101
Alejandro, Mary Beth, 103–4
Alejandro, Sarah, 104
Alford, Brandon, 155
Ambiguity of Play, The (Sutton-Smith), 72
American Academy of Pediatrics, 24, 32
American Association for the Child's Right to Play, 19, 72
American Association of Christian Schools (AACS), 169–71, 182–84
American Mathematics Contest 12 (AMC 12; formerly American High School Mathematics Examination), 188
American Psychological Association, Center for Gifted Education Policy, 198
American Regional Math League (ARML), 185
American Society of Composers, Authors and Publishers (ASCAP), 153
Anderegg, David, 4, 6
Annual Teen Poetry Slam, 161
Arbus, Diane, 151
Ardai, Charles, 194–96
ARML (American Regional Math League), 185
Arrowrock Classical School for the Gifted, 115
Arroyo, Emmanuel, 163
artists, 64–67, 68, 79–80
Art of Psychotherapy, The (Storr), 146
ASCAP (American Society of Composers, Authors and Publishers), 153
Ashley, Maurice, 20–21

assessment of intelligence. *See* intelligence assessment
Athletic Baby Company, 33
auditory enrichment products, prenatal, 3, 27, 34, 44, 49
Autobiography (Mill), 146
autocosmic play, 31

Baby BumbleBee, 25
BabyCanSign, 51
Baby Einstein videos, 3, 23, 40, 44
baby formulas, mind-enhancing, 26, 33–34, 36
Baby-Genius Art & Languages School, 48
Baby Genius Edutainment Complex
  boredom, fear of, 42–43
  cost of products, 44
  criticism of, 35–39
  as current fad, 22–25
  imagination, development of, 30–32
  versus learning with parents or peers, 36
  marketing and sales of products, 24–25, 40–41, 117
  motivations of parents, 7–8, 19, 28, 31–33, 39–45, 62
  Mozart effect in, 25–26
  outdoor activity, lack of, 33, 39
  precursors of, 28–32
  prenatal auditory enrichment, 3, 27, 34, 38, 44, 49
  second-language study, 37
  timely progress, 27–28
  underlying cultural history, 34–35
  windows of development, critical periods, 33–37
BabyPlus prenatal enrichment system, 3, 27, 34, 44
BabyPlus Womb Songs, 3
Baby Prodigy DVD, 23
Baby Sign Language (Acredelo and Goodwyn), 51
baby sign language (BSL), 3, 50–52
Bailly, Jacques, 159
Baker, Will, 160–61
Baldwin, James, 169, 180
Ball, P. Bonny, 144–45
Balmer, Randall, 181–82
Bamberger, Jeanne, 14
Barrett, Craig, 192
Barthes, Roland, 30–31
Bauer, Mrs. (teacher), 86–88
Being Smart about Gifted Children (Matthews and Foster), 18, 42, 145
Bellah, Robert, 128
Bell Curve, The (Herrnstein and Murray), 121–22
Bell Curve Debate, The (Jacoby and Glauberman), 122
Benjamin, Jessica, 148
Benjamin, Walter, 43, 64
Bennett, Olivia, 70–71
Bess, Austin, 131–34, 140
Bess, Beth, 131–34, 140, 150
Bess, Earnest, 133–34
Bess, Phoenix, 131, 133, 135
Between Piety and Desire (Wylie), 126
Beyond Terman (Subotnik), 198
bias
  in intelligence assessment, 118–19, 121–23
  in math and science domains, 198
Binet, Alfred, 120
Birth of the Mind, The (Marcus), 38
Bloom, Benjamin, 127
Bob Jones University (BJU), 176, 179
Boe, Erling, 191–92
boredom, 42–43
Boredom (Spacks), 43
Borland, James, 92, 93, 130
Born Losers (Sandage), 202
Bothell, Skyler, 75
Bowlby, John, 35
Bowling Alone (Putnam), 62
brain cell death, 34, 37, 40
brain functions, experience-expectant and experience-dependent, 36–37
brain plasticity, 34, 36, 37
Brainy Baby company, 25, 33
Brainy Baby Left and Right Brain DVD, 23, 40
Brantlinger, Ellen, 92
Brave New Babies (Logan), 34

Brave New Voices poetry competition, 161, 162
Brave New World (Huxley), 52
Bremmer, Brandenn, 112, 140–44
Bremmer, Patti, 141–44
Breunlin, Rachel, 126–27
Bright Beginnings baby formula, 26
Bright Minds books and software, 117
Broadway Babies, 46–47, 63
Brown, Karie, 49, 61
Bruer, John, 35, 36–37
Brunelli, Anthony, 65
Brusco, Jennifer, 74–75
Brusco, Mitchie, 67–68, 74–76
BSL (baby sign language), 3, 50–52
Buddiga, Akshay, 167–68
Budunov, Gregory, 191
Bush, George W., 90–91
Butterworth, Brian, 193–94

Callahan, Carolyn, 116–17, 130
Campbell, Don, 26
Campus Crusade for Christ, 175
Candalario, Enmanuel, 163
Carbajal, Ruben, 108
careers
  mathematics contestants, 186, 196, 198–201, 202–3
  preaching contestants, 178
  See also professionalization of children
Carnevale, Anthony P., 192
CAT (Cognitive Assessment Test), 104, 118–19
cell death, brain, 34, 37, 40
Center for Gifted Education Policy, American Psychological Association, 198
Center for Gifted Studies and Education, Hunter College, 18
Center for Talented Youth, Johns Hopkins University, 5, 94, 100
Champlin, Donna Lynne, 60, 158
"Changes in American Children's Time, 1981–1997" (Hofferth and Sandberg), 69–70
Chapman, Justin, 112
Chapman, Elizabeth, 112
Chenoweth, Brenda, 153
child enrichment. *See* Baby Genius Edutainment Complex; *specific issues*
Children's Television Workshop, 32
Christian Union, 175
Clarenbach, Jane, 89
class and elitism. *See* elitism and social class
classes for infants and toddlers
  aim of, 47–48
  baby sign language, 3, 50–52
  Brave New World (Huxley) envisionment of, 52
  cost of, 63
  harm to infant development, 60–61
  Institutes for the Achievement of Human Potential program, 53–56
  internal motivation, importance of, 57–60
  music, 46–47, 49, 52
  parental ambitions and motivations, 56–57, 61–63
  proliferation of, 47
  second and third languages, 48
  tutoring chains offering, 49–50
  See also gifted education
Clements, Rhonda, 39
Cognitive Assessment Test (CAT), 104, 118–19
Colangelo, Nicholas, 99–100
Cold War and Great Talent Hunt, 102, 188
contests and competitions
  benefits of, 159–61
  cost of participation, 158
  criticism of, 154, 156–59
  dedication and passion of contestants, 155–56
  parents of contestants, 163–65
  proliferation and intensification of, 153
  Scrabble Championship, as business opportunity, 165–66
  Scrabble Championship, proceedings at, 151–53
  as spectacle for adult audiences, 166–68

contests and competitions (*cont.*)
  spoken word contests versus other types, 162–63
  See also preaching tournaments
cooperation versus competition, 157–58
courses. *See* classes for infants and toddlers
Crain, William, 157
Crayola, 29
Cross, Tracy L., 57, 144–45
crucial stages, 34–37
Csikszentmihalyi, Mihaly, 196
culture-fair intelligence tests, 118–19, 121–23

D. E. Shaw & Co., 185, 194–95
Daley, Janet, 160
Davidson, Jan and Bob, 93, 135–36
Davidson Institute for Talented Development, 93, 136
Da Vinci Academy, 115
Dean, Joshua, 169, 178, 183
Def Poetry, 162
"Democratization of Mathematics, The" (Carnevale and Desrochers), 192
Department of Homeland Security scholarships and fellowships, 187, 199
depression and giftedness, correlation between, 144–45
Desrochers, Donna M., 192
Devanney, Diane, 152, 168
Devanney, Katie, 152–53, 166, 168
developmental videos and DVDs. *See* Baby Genius Edutainment Complex
DHA-ARA oils, 26–27, 36
Dick, Fred, 37, 42
Diller-Quaile School of Music, 49, 63
directed play, 19, 69–70, 72–73, 209
discovery of gifted children, 123–28
Disney Company, 24
Dividing Classes (Brantlinger), 92
Doman, Glenn, 52–53
Doman, Janet, 53, 55–56
Drama of the Gifted Child, The (Miller), 96, 97
DVDs. *See* Baby Genius Edutainment Complex
Dweck, Carol, 139

early enrichment. *See* Baby Genius Edutainment Complex; classes for infants and toddlers; *specific issues*
Early Head Start and Head Start programs, 34, 36–37, 52
Eaton, Missa Murry, 149
Eckert, Rebecca, 90, 129
Edmunds, Alan, 209
education, gifted. *See* gifted education
educational media. *See* Baby Genius Edutainment Complex
Educational Records Bureau (ERB) test, 41, 114–15
educational toys. *See* toys and games, educational
edutainment DVDs and videos. *See* Baby Genius Edutainment Complex
Einstein Never Used Flashcards (Pasek-Hirsh), 60
Eisner, Will, 81
elitism and social class
  access to enrichment programs, 19
  class mobility, 8
  desire for specialness, 128–29
  edutainment products and, 44
  in gifted education, 92–96, 102
  resentment toward specialized education, 94–97, 107
Ellenberg, Jordan, 186–87, 199–200
Emerson, Ralph Waldo, 98
Emile (Rousseau), 145–46
Enfamil A+, 26
enrichment. *See* classes for infants and toddlers; gifted education
ERB (Educational Records Bureau) test, 41, 114–15
Erector sets, 29
Ericsson, Anders, 4, 57–58, 59–60, 193–94
Erikson, Erik, 31, 209
Evan Thomas Institute, Institutes for the Achievement of Human Potential (IAHP), 53–57, 62–63

experience-dependent and experience-expectant brain functions, 36–37
extreme parenting
  aggressiveness and competitiveness, 61, 128
  conferences and activities, 136
  developmental stake in child's future, 148
  "helicopter parents," 139–40
  homeschooling, 131–37, 145–47, 149
  idealization of children, perception of childhood, 147–49
  negative aspects and dangers of, 138–39, 140–45, 148
  rejection of giftedness competition, 129
  restraint in, 208–10
  and self-perception of parents, 96–97, 138, 149–50
  and sensitivity of gifted children, 140, 141, 145

FairTest, 122
Farrell, Tom, 178
Father and Son (Gosse), 180
Fedoruk, Dennis, 25, 33
Feldman, David Henry, 128–29
Fenton, Michael, 99
Fenton, Susan, 98–99
fetal enrichment
  auditory, 3, 27, 34, 44, 49
  overstimulation risk, 38
  supplements for, 27
Fine, Gary Alan, 159–60
Fineberg, Jonathan, 65
Fisher-Price, 24–25
Flynn effect in intelligence testing, 112, 118
Forensics Tournament, Harvard National High School Invitational, 156, 158
formulas, mind-enhancing, 26, 33–34, 36, 44–45
Foster, Joanne, 145
Foster, Karen, 33
Francis, Clark, 68, 71
Frankenstein (Shelley), 146
Freud, Sigmund, 147
Fry, Roger, 66

games. *See* toys and games, educational
Garcia, W. Joseph, 50
Gardner, Howard, 110, 121, 207
gender bias in math and science domains, 198
Genetic Studies of Genius (Terman), 5
Genius and Stupidity (Terman), 120
Genius Denied (Davidson and Davidson), 93, 136
gifted children
  harmful effects of enrichment for, 1–3, 6–11, 19, 39, 60–61
  Indigo Child hypothesis, 113
  IQ test scores defining, 3, 113–14, 136
  meaning of "gifted," 3–4
  narrow concept of giftedness, 121, 206–8
  sensitivity of, 140, 141, 145
  success and happiness in adulthood, 13–19, 204–5, 210
  See also specific issues
Gifted Children (Winner), 129, 145
gifted education
  acceleration as alternative to, 98–101
  antecedents for, 97–98
  Cold War and, 102
  criticism of, 92–93, 102–3
  desire for specialness, 128–29
  discovery of gifted children, 123–28
  dropout rate, 93–94
  funding and teacher training for, 89–90
  homeschooling, 131–37, 145–47, 149
  initiatives to expand, 103
  IQ score for, 3
  mainstreaming of gifted children, 18, 129
  No Child Left Behind (NCLB) Act and, 90–91, 107, 206
  in public schools, 88, 136
  resentment toward, 94–97, 107
  stress of testing for, 129–30
  support for and value of, 93–94, 108, 205–6

gifted education (*cont.*)
techniques, 86–88, 94
See also classes for infants and toddlers
gifted parent community. *See* extreme parenting
Gifted Program Standards (Callahan, ed.), 116
Gifted Tongues (Fine), 159
Glauberman, Naomi, 122
Goldwater, Robert, 66
Goodwyn, Susan, 50–51
Gortner, Marjoe, 181
Gosse, Edmund, 180, 184
Gould, Angela, 137
Gould, Stephen Jay, 120
Great Potential Press, 111
Great Talent Hunt, 102, 188
Greenough, William, 35–36
Gust-Brey, Karyn, 144–45
Gymboree, 48
gymnastics, 53

Habits of the Heart (Madsen and Bellah), 128
Haimovitz, Matt, 13–16
Hall, Donald, 138
Hanauer, Nancy, 51
Harris, William T., 98
Harvard National High School Invitational Forensics Tournament, 156, 158
Hasbro, 166
Head Start programs, 34, 36–37, 52
Hedberg, Mason, 189–90
"helicopter parents," 139–40
Henry J. Kaiser Family Foundation, 24, 38
Herrnstein, Richard, 121–22
Himelstein, Abram, 126–27
Himmelfarb, Gertrude, 114
Hofferth, Sandra L., 69–70
Hollingworth, Leta, 101–2
homeschools
decision to homeschool, 131–35
historical examples of, 145–47
isolation from peers, 145
numbers of children in, 135
and perception of childhood, 149
reasons for homeschooling, 136–37
HoopScoop Online, 68
Horn, Sam, 175
Howe, Neil, 140
How to Teach Your Baby to Read (Doman and Doman), 52
Huizinga, Johan, 64
Hunter College Center for Gifted Studies and Education, 18
Huxley, Aldous, 52

IAHP (Institutes for the Achievement of Human Potential), 53–57, 62–63, 136
Icarus effect, 7
Iftikhar, Liz, 25
Iles Elementary School, 86–89, 106–7, 118
Illinois schools gifted programs, 86–89, 91, 94–95, 103, 106–7
imagination, stifling of, 30–31
Impact Coalition, 160–61
independence of children, threat to, 139, 148
Independent Schools Admissions Association of Greater New York (ISAAGNY), 115
Indigo Child hypothesis, 113
infant brain cell death, 34, 37, 40
infant edutainment. *See* Baby Genius Edutainment Complex
In Schools We Trust (Meier), 208
Institute for the Study of Advanced Development, 111
Institute for the Study of Child Development, Robert Wood Johnson Medical School, 71, 115
Institutes for the Achievement of Human Potential (IAHP), 53–57, 62–63, 136
intelligence assessment
age of child, 3, 114, 115, 117
bias in, 118–19, 121–23
Cognitive Assessment Test (CAT; Naglieri), 104, 118–19
cost of private testing, 115–16

Educational Records Bureau (ERB) test, 41, 114–15
Flynn effect, 112, 118
general unitary factor, 113
hoax, 112
levels of giftedness, 3, 101–2, 113–14, 136
for private school admission, 115
in public schools, 116–17, 119
skills evaluated, 120
Stanford-Binet, 101, 113, 118–20, 123
stress of, 129–30
variety of tests, 117–18
Wechsler Intelligence Scale for Children (WISC), 51, 118–20
Intel Science Talent Search (ISTS), 18, 187, 188–89, 190, 191, 192
International Mathematical Olympiad, 188
Iowa Acceleration Scale, 99
IQ Search Group, 187–88
IQ tests. *See* intelligence assessment
ISAAGNY (Independent Schools Admissions Association of Greater New York), 115
ISTS (Intel Science Talent Search), 18, 187, 188–89, 190, 191, 192

Jacoby, Russell, 122
Jarrett, Olga, 70
Jefferson, Thomas, 97–98
Jensen, Dylana, 1–2
Johns Hopkins University Center for Talented Youth, 5, 94, 100
Johnson, Johan, 125
Junior Kumon classes, 50, 63
Junior Undiscovered Math Prodigies (JUMP), 123–24

Kaiser Family Foundation, 24, 38
Kant, Immanuel, 98
Kaplan, Inc., 50
Kaufman, Felice, 6
Kennedy, Jay, 81
Kenneson, Claude, 46
Kernochan, Sarah, 181
Kincheloe, Joe, 139
King, Martin Luther, Jr., 180
Kingdom of Children (Stevens), 149
Kitchen, Alexa, Denis, and Stacy, 80–85
Kline, Stephen, 29
Koh, Jennifer, 58–59, 209
Kohn, Alfie, 157–58
Kozol, Jonathan, 91
Kumon, Toru, 50
Kumon North America, 50, 63
Kumpf, Colleen, 54

language study, 37, 48
Lareau, Annette, 78
LeapPad Plus Writing and Microphone System, 44
Leapster Multimedia Learning System, 44
Learning before Birth (Logan), 27
Learning Community International, 189
Lego, 32
L'Engle, Madeleine, 109
Lerman, Alan, 80
Lerman, Jonathan, 79–80
Lil' Kickers, 48
Lincoln Logs, 29
Little Man Tate, 54
L-M intelligence test, 113, 118
Logan, Brent, 27, 34
Lohman, David, 119
Longenbach, James, 163
Losing Our Minds (Ruf), 145
Louis, Barbara, 115
Louisiana, literacy rate in, 126

McCaffrey, Paul, 188
McCarter, Gay, 140–41
Mackintosh Academy, 115
Madsen, Peggy, 28
Madsen, Richard, 128
mainstreaming of gifted children, 18, 129
Mann, Horace, 98
Many Children Left Behind (Meier), 90
Marcus, Gary, 38
marketing
edutainment products, 24–25, 40–41, 117
"smart" baby formulas, 33, 44–45
sponsorship of competitions, 165–66

Marland Report, 103, 207
Martek, 33–34
math and science competitions, 18, 187, 188–89, 190, 191, 192
mathematicians and scientists
  blending of pure and commercial interests, 190–91
  career opportunities, 186, 196
  children of immigrants, 191
  Cold War and Great Talent Hunt, 102, 188
  competitiveness, difficulties with, 196–98
  ethical issues in career choices, 198–201
  gender bias toward, 198
  happiness in careers, 202–3
  natural abilities, 193–96
  recruitment of, 185–88, 192, 194–95
  U.S. rankings, global achievement gap, 191–92
Math Olympiads, 188, 191
Mattel, 24–25, 67
Matthaei, Julie, 148
Matthews, Dona, 18, 42, 145
maturational playthings, 29, 32
media, educational. *See* Baby Genius Edutainment Complex
Meier, Deborah, 90, 208
Menn, Stephen, 101
mental tests. *See* intelligence assessment
Merck, 187
Merzenich, Michael, 37
Metzner, Paul, 25
Michigan schools gifted programs, 89
Midori, 14
Mighton, John, 124, 127–28
Mill, John Stuart, 146
Millennials Go to College (Strauss and Howe), 140
Miller, Alice, 96, 97
Miller, Zell, 25
Millhauser, Steven, 185
Milton Bradley, 29
mind-enhancing baby formulas, 26, 33–34, 36
Mine Eyes Have Seen the Glory (Balmer), 181
Minton, Eric, 196–98, 200
Mintz, Steven, 73
Mirman School for the Gifted, 115
Mismeasure of Man, The (Gould), 120
Molino, Van, 199
Monopoly (game), 29
Montessori, Maria, 30, 32, 56
Moody, Kevin, 177
Mozart effect, 25–26
Mulder, Liesl Smith and Marlie, 105–6
Multiple Intelligences (Gardner), 110, 121, 207
Murray, Charles, 121–22
music
  Mozart effect, 25–26
  prenatal auditory enrichment, 3, 27, 34, 44, 49
  training for children, 46–47, 49, 52
Musical Kids, 48
Music Prodigies (Kenneson), 46
My Gym, 48
"My Son My Executioner" (Hall), 138
Myth of Ability, The (Mighton), 124
Myth of the First Three Years, The (Bruer), 35
Mythologies (Barthes), 30–31

Nabokov, Vladimir, 131
Naglieri, Jack, Cognitive Assessment Test (CAT), 104, 118–19
Nasaw, David, 98
National Association for Gifted Children, 89, 90, 93, 129
National Association of Urban Debate Leagues (NAUDL), 155, 160–61
National Forensic League tournament, 156, 158
National Gifted Children's Fund, 142
National Institute of Mental Health, 144
National Longitudinal Survey of Labor Market Experience of Youth, 122
National Research Center on the Gifted and Talented, University of Connecticut, 207

National Scrabble Association Junior Championship. *See* Scrabble Championship
National Security Agency, 187
Nation Deceived, A (Colangelo), 99
Nature's Gambit (Feldman and Goldsmith), 128–29
NAUDL (National Association of Urban Debate Leagues), 155, 160–61
NCLB (No Child Left Behind) Act, 90–91, 107, 206
Neag Center for Gifted Education and Talent Development, University of Connecticut, 111, 125, 207
Nechita, Alexandra, 70–71
Neighborhood Story Project, 126–27
Neill, Monty, 122–23
Nelson, Charles, 34, 36, 38
Nestle, Marion, 44
Nestle Good Start, 26
New Age views within giftedness community, 113
New York Urban Debate League, 155
No Child Left Behind (NCLB) Act, 90–91, 107, 206
No Contest (Kohn), 157
nutritional formulas and supplements, 26–27, 33–34, 36, 44–45

Okumakpeyi, Monique, 101
Olinger, Dan, 172–73
Oliver Program, 124–25
Olmstead, Laura, 76–77
Olmstead, Mark, 64, 76–77
Olmstead, Marla, 64–67, 76–77
One World Now, 124
On Kissing, Tickling, and Being Bored (Phillips), 42
On Narcissism (Freud), 147
Osborn, Julia, 93
Out of the Garden (Kline), 29
Overdeck, John, 195

parents. *See* extreme parenting
Parker Bros., 29
Pasek-Hirsh, Kathy, 60–61
Pasternak, Boris, 86
Patterson, Ryan, 177
Pellegrini, Anthony, 72
Petit, Steve, 178
PG children. *See* gifted children
PG Conference, 136
Phillips, Adam, 42
physical training, 48
Physics Team, U.S., 191
Piaget, Jean, 34
Plato, 97
play, professionalized, 19, 69–70, 72–73, 209
Playskool, 29
playthings. *See* toys and games, educational
preaching tournaments
  adult trainers, aspirations of, 177
  career ambitions of participants, 178
  and expansion of Christian schooling, 182
  faith, authenticity of, 172–74
  judging criteria, 172–73
  opportunities afforded by, 175
  parents of contestants, 174–77
  pressures faced by teen preachers, 184
  proceedings at, 169–71, 179
  tradition of teen preachers, 179–81
"Prelude or Requiem for the 'Mozart Effect'?" (Steele), 26
prenatal enrichment
  auditory, 3, 27, 34, 44, 49
  overstimulation risk, 38
  supplements for, 27
Prep-for-Prep, 124
preschool tutoring. *See* classes for infants and toddlers
Presidential Scholars, study of, 6
Pricing the Priceless Child (Zelizer), 73
Prisoners of Childhood (Miller), 96
privatization of education, 91
prodigies. *See* gifted children
professionalization of children
  camps, specialized, 69
  compared to child labor, 73–74

professionalization of children (*cont.*)
  decision to pursue, 80–85
  examples, 64–69, 74–77
  exploitation by adults, 70
  guilt, feelings of, 71
  parental attitudes and motivations, 74–78
  passion of child for avocation, work-play flow state, 78–80
  and reduction of child-directed play, 19, 69–70, 72–73, 209
  sports injuries, 71
  sports training and recruitment, 67
professionalized play, 19, 69–70, 72–73, 209
profoundly gifted children. *See* gifted children
psychometrics, 113
public schools
  evangelical opinion of, 174
  gifted education in, 89–90, 136
  Illinois gifted program, 86–89, 91, 94–95, 103, 106–7
  intelligence assessment in, 116–17, 119
  No Child Left Behind (NCLB) Act and, 90–91, 107, 206
  scholastic acceleration in, 98–101
Putnam, Robert, 62

Quart, Alissa, 11–13

Rathunde, Kevin, 196
Rauscher, Frances, 25
recess in school day, free play, 19, 33, 70, 72–73, 209
Recess (Pellegrini), 72
Reclaiming Childhood (Crain), 157
Redinger, Ty, 61, 62
Reiner, Rob, 35
religion. *See* preaching tournaments
Renzulli, Joseph, 111, 125, 207, 208
Republic, The (Plato), 97
Rhodes, Susan, 88–89, 106–7
Rivera, Matt, 170–71, 173, 183
Robert Wood Johnson Medical School, Institute for the Study of Child Development, 71, 115
Robson, Gary, 137–38
Roeper, Annemarie, 145
Rosenblum, Gianine D., 71
Rosenzweig, Mark, 35
Rousseau, Jean-Jacques, 145–46
Ruf, Deborah, 145
Ruskin, John, 146

Sacks, Peter, 93
Salinger, J. D., 22
Sandage, Scott A., 202
Sandberg, John F., 69–70
Santoli, Joseph, Joshua, and Jonne, 163–64
SAT test, 121
Sattler, Jerome, 118
Scheer, Scott, 158
Schlaggar, Bradley, 36
schools. *See* classes for infants and toddlers; gifted education; public schools
Schuss, Kerry, 79
science competitions. *See* math and science competitions
scientists. *See* mathematicians and scientists
Score tutoring chain, 50
Scrabble Championship
  born-again Christian teams, 177
  as business opportunity, 165–66
  competitors and proceedings, 151–53, 154–55
  criticism of, 158–59
  parents of competitors, 163–65
screen media. *See* Baby Genius Edutainment Complex
screen time, 24, 32, 39
Scripps National Spelling Bee, 159, 166
Sesame Street, 32
Shapiro, David, 6
Sharpton, Al, 180
Shaw, David, 195
Shaw, Gordon, 25
Shelley, Mary, 146
Shemtov, Baruch, 74
Sherman, Joel, 165
Shurkin, Joel, 120

sign language for babies, 3, 50–52
Silverman, Linda, 110–11, 112–14, 115, 128
Similac Advance, 26
Simpson, Stuart, 66
skipping of grades, 98–101
slam competitions, 161–63
"smart" baby formulas, 26, 33–34, 36, 44–45
Smith, Donnie, 153–54
SMPY (Study of Mathematically Precocious Youth), 5, 6–7
social class. *See* elitism and social class
solitary play, 29
Sommers, Christina Hoff, 160
So Smart DVD, 23
Spacks, Patricia Meyer, 43
Spaeth, George, 8–11
Spaeth, Sigmund, 9
Spelling Bee, Scripps National, 159, 166
Speyer School, 102
spoken word competitions, 162–63
sports and athletics, 33, 48, 53, 67–68, 71
Standardized Minds (Sacks), 93
Stanford-Binet tests, 101, 113, 118–20, 123
Stanley, Julian, 5, 100–101
Steele, Kenneth, 26
Stephan, Larisa, 1–3
Stevens, Mitchell L., 149
Stigma of Genius, The (Kincheloe), 139
Storr, Anthony, 146
Strauss, William, 140
Study of Mathematically Precocious Youth (SMPY), 5, 6–7
Subotnik, Rena, 198
suicide, giftedness and, 112, 140–45
Sumpter, James, III, 171, 178, 182–83
Sumpter, James (Don), II, 175–76, 183–84
Supreme with DHA and ARA, 26
Sutton-Smith, Brian, 72–73
Suzuki, Shinichi, 52
Suzuki Baby Music, 49
Sylvan tutoring chain, 50
Talented Teenagers (Csikszentmihalyi, Rathunde, and Whalen), 196
Tappe, Nancy Ann, 113
Teacher in the Living Room, A? (Henry J. Kaiser Family Foundation), 24, 38
Teacher's Manual for Use with the Common Sense of Music in Classroom and Assembly and Great Symphonies (Spaeth), 9
teddy bears, 29
Terman, Lewis, 5, 101, 120–21, 166
Terman's Kids (Shurkin), 120
tests for giftedness. *See* intelligence assessment
Thakur, Gaurav Subhash, 189
Time Tracker, 27–28, 44
TIMSS (Trends in International Mathematics and Science Study), 191
toddlers, DVDs and videos for. *See* Baby Genius Edutainment Complex
toddlers, intelligence testing of, 3, 114, 115
Tolan, Stephanie, 138
tournaments. *See* contests and competitions; preaching tournaments
toys and games, educational
  child development and, 30–31
  history of, 28–29
  versus learning with parent or peers, 36
  marketing of, 40–41
  maturational, 29, 32
  nostalgia of parents, 31
  for solitary play, 29
Trends in International Mathematics and Science Study (TIMSS), 191
Tsetsis, Angela, 33–34
tutoring services. *See* classes for infants and toddlers
Two Sigma, 195

undiscovered gifted children, 123–28
Unequal Childhoods (Lareau), 78
University of Connecticut, Neag Center for Gifted Education and Talent Development, 111, 125, 207
Urban Debate League (UDL), 161

Urban Word NYC, 161
U.S. Physics Team, 191
USA Mathematical Olympiad (USAMO), 188, 191

V. Smile DVD, 23
Valenty, Ben, 70–71
Varner, Lynne, 39–40
Vasquez, Christopher, 155–56, 161
Vaughan, Stewart, 151
velocity, educational, 34–35
videos. *See* Baby Genius Edutainment Complex

Walker, Charles, 177
War Against Boys, The (Sommers), 160
Warner Brothers Studios, 24
WCGTC (World Council for Gifted and Talented Children), World Gifted Conference, 110–11
Webb, Nadia, 97, 115–16, 128
Wechsler Intelligence Scale for Children (WISC), 51, 118–20
Weissman, Simone, 41
Weitzman Institute, 187
Welles, Orson, 204
Wells, Aaron, 173, 176
Wepsick, Eric, 185–86, 190, 194, 200
Westinghouse Science Talent Search. *See* Intel Science Talent Search (ISTS)
Whalen, Samuel, 196
What Counts (Butterworth), 193
What Do Kids Know?, 154
White House Conference on Child Development, 35
Williams, John, 165–66
Wilson, Nick, 87
windows of development, critical periods, 33–37
Winner, Ellen, 16, 129, 145
WISC (Wechsler Intelligence Scale for Children), 51, 118–20
womb, child enrichment in
  auditory enrichment, 3, 27, 34, 44, 49
  overstimulation risk, 38
  supplements for, 27
Wordsworth, William, 86
World Council for Gifted and Talented Children (WCGTC), World Gifted Conference, 110–11
Worried All the Time (Anderegg), 4
Wright, John Lloyd, 29
Wright, Judith Anderson, 51–52
Wright, Skelly, 102–3
Wu, Vezen, 16–18, 190, 191, 201–2
Wylie, Arlet and Sam, 126

Yakov-Feldman, Moisha, 62–63
Yoder, Brad, 173
youth competitions. *See* contests and competitions; preaching tournaments

Zelizer, Viviana, 73
Zero to Six (Henry J. Kaiser Family Foundation), 24
zero-to-three enrichment. *See* Baby Genius Edutainment Complex; *specific issues*
Zorn, Charles, 37, 43